Missed Information

Missed Information

Better Information for a Wealthier, Fairer, and More Sustainable World

David Sarokin and Jay Schulkin

The MIT Press
Cambridge, Massachusetts
London, England

Set in Stone Serif and Stone Sans by Toppan Best-set Premedia Limited. Printed and bound in the United States of America.

Cataloging-in-Publication information is available from the Library of Congress.

ISBN: 978-0-262-03492-0

10 9 8 7 6 5 4 3 2 1

Contents

Preface

We'd like to take a page or two to introduce ourselves.

We have been friends since our days as undergraduate roommates back in 1973 at SUNY Purchase, where David majored in environmental science and Jay studied philosophy and neurobiology. Our friendship morphed into a collaboration with our first jointly authored paper, "Environmentalism and the right-to-know: Expanding the practice of democracy," published in *Ecological Economics* in 1991. Even then, our focus was on the importance of information as an instrument of public policy, as a means of fostering participation, and as a tool for identifying and synthesizing the concerns of broad swaths of the general public.

The focus on information is also evident in our other co-authored works on issues ranging from banking to environmental justice. Our conversations have evolved, meandered, stalled, matured, occasionally startled us, and eventually led us to write this book.

We share an optimistic outlook. Optimism that collaborations can lead to interesting ideas, interesting ideas can spur broader conversations, conversations can define worthwhile actions, actions can happen, and, with luck, the world becomes a better place, even if only by the smallest of frail increments. *Missed Information* embraces that outlook. The world runs on information, and by improving the quality of information going into our human-built systems we get better results coming out. Let's flip the old cautionary axiom on its head: Instead of "garbage in, garbage out," we can focus on "quality in, quality out." The trick, of course, lies in figuring out what high-quality information looks like and finding ways to bring it forward, streamline its management, and make it available while keeping it secure. In this book we examine these challenges and present what we hope are a few interesting ideas of our own to get conversations going.

There are several people we want to acknowledge.

Paul Kleindorfer of the Wharton School at the University of Pennsylvania was a wonderful colleague of Jay; the book is partly dedicated to him. He loved the very idea of what we have set out to do here.

Our thanks as well to George Loewenstein from Carnegie Mellon, who has been a wonderful colleague; to Warren Muir, for immediately recognizing the significance of information as a new tool of environmental policy, and championing its use ever since; to Joanna Underwood, for doing the same and for founding a research organization with information in its very title; to Sarah Shaw, for always challenging us and always being on the lookout for new information tools; and to April Oliver, for endless honesty and critical acumen.

Introduction

If one accepts the conventional wisdom that information is power—and there is no reason not to accept it—then our Information Age is really the Age of Power. Even in view of the slipperiness of such terms (both 'information' and 'power' are hard to define), it is abundantly clear that new information tools have multiplied human capabilities many times over. Information spurs participation in new forums and more active engagement in existing ones. It drives commerce, empowers the disenfranchised, promotes participation, creates opportunities (of both noble and crass varieties), and results in new societal arrangements between information haves and information have-nots.

The technology that makes it practicable to collect, store, retrieve, and analyze information advances at an almost unbelievable pace. As it does, so does our collective access to the power that such information brings into being. It seems as if only yesterday megabytes of storage seemed enough for any one person's needs; now gigabytes are barely adequate, and terabytes are creeping into our vocabularies and into the specifications for off-the-shelf hardware.

Information technology routinely leaps ahead, a thousand times as fast and robust as its predecessor technology. Is social power increasing just as rapidly? If so, we face what may be the most important question for our age: Who gets to wield all that power?

Governments get to wield a lot of it, of course. For better or for worse, Edward Snowden made the world aware of how extensive government's cyber-snooping apparatus had become. This is particularly true for the spy agencies of the United States, whose data-collection and eavesdropping capabilities are commensurate with the country's status as a superpower. The reach of the US government's information gathering extends not only to 300+ million Americans, but also to billions of people all over the world. Information gathering isn't limited to the US government, however. Britain has become known (infamous, some might say) for its nationwide surveillance network of closed-circuit television cameras, estimated at one camera for every eleven people in the UK. What mechanisms the Chinese or the Saudis have in place for monitoring people isn't widely known, but one has to suppose that their networks for gathering and controlling information are extensive and even more aggressively intrusive than those of the UK and the US.

And spy agencies aren't the only agencies collecting information on behalf of the US government. The Internal Revenue Service and the Social Security Administration know how much money you make. The Transportation Security Administration, Customs and Border Protection, and the Passport Office all compile information on people's travel habits. Local police departments track their comings and goings through the use of automated license-plate readers. The state of New York monitors traffic patterns through the signals sent by the E-ZPass transponders in many cars, even when they are miles from the nearest toll booth. The Medicare and Medicaid programs have the medical records of hundreds of millions of American patients and doctors, as well as consolidated records for health-care institutions. So does the Department of Veterans Affairs. State health departments know when babies are born and when people die. Courts compile information on bankruptcy filings, lawsuit histories, and criminal records.

Information is collected for legitimate purposes, such as public safety, administrative efficiency, and traffic planning, and information has been collected for hundreds of years. But cumbersome paper files have given way to instant-access computer networks. Bureaucratic isolation has yielded, ever so reluctantly, to data-handling platforms shared by multiple agencies. Transparency has made some information widely available; secrecy has hidden vast networks from public scrutiny. Information puts power in the hands of public officials who ask the population at large to trust them with its wise and proper use.

Businesses also collect and utilize data on a scale that probably rivals even the efforts of the most inquisitive governments. Credit-card records, housing histories, mortgages, car loans, employment status, check-writing habits, and bank transactions are just a few of the data elements that go into crafting commercially prepared credit reports. Children's schooling is increasingly carried out with online tools, and consequently everything that students do online can be tracked. Our website visits, online sales, email traffic, search engine queries, app downloads, and photo uploads are amassed, massaged, and commercialized in huge and sophisticated databases.

A 2012 *New York Times* article headlined "How Companies Learn Your Secrets" described some of the uses that the corporate world makes of the information it collects about consumers. In one particularly striking example, the article detailed how the retail-store chain Target used its analytical data tools to recognize that a particular teenage shopper was pregnant and to begin targeting its personalized outreach accordingly, all before the girl's parents knew of the pregnancy. No single purchase necessarily signals a pregnancy, but a combination of purchases (e.g., of prenatal vitamins and maternity clothes) and changes in buying habits (e.g., switching from scented to unscented soaps) can provide a market signal of one. Other life events, such as an impending graduation or a new job, also are identifiable, to greater and lesser degrees of reliability, from the market signals that emanate from particular combinations of purchases.

Educational companies that prepare online tests and study materials for students in kindergarten through college are routinely capturing tens of millions of data points on each student as he or she reads online study guides, takes interactive tests, writes essays, and uploads assignments—what questions a student answers correctly and what questions incorrectly, and when a student pauses on a question and for how long. Those companies are gaining an understanding of each student's strengths and weaknesses—useful information for custom-tailoring the next set of materials to present. But they also collect information on such things as students' preferences in computers and browsers and how often they upgrade their mobile phones, and use all that information in ways known only to them.

A different sort of business enterprise, criminal activity, also makes widespread use of newfound powers in the Information Age. Whereas thieves used to rob one bank at a time, they can now target worldwide networks of customers' accounts, automated teller machines, wire transfers. and even digital currencies such as Bitcoin. Terrorists recruit, communicate, research, and plan online. Hackers probe the weaknesses of information networks at banks, stores, stock exchanges, government agencies, armies, and schools, attacking targets of opportunity when a back door opens up. Off-brand cell phones arrive on stores' shelves with "Trojan Horse" software that sniffs out usernames and passwords. The terms 'cyber-crime', 'cyber-warfare', 'cyber-terrorism', and 'identity theft' are already well entrenched in our vocabularies.

Governments, businesses, and criminals find power in their information tools. So do ordinary individuals. The ability of technology to facilitate continuous access to our email messages, for example, has multiplied our capacity to stay in touch, whether for work purposes or for the purpose of personal communication. We can write memos, supervise employees, schedule meetings, chat with friends, play games, and watch movies in places and situations where these things weren't possible in the recent past—riding a train, sitting on a toilet, jogging in a gym. The ease of access to information over the Internet can be broadly empowering, whether for a patient getting ready to discuss his or her symptoms with a doctor or for a potential customer getting ready to negotiate the price of a new car.

Crowdsourcing sites such as Kickstarter.com and DonorsChoose.org—essentially tools for rapidly consolidating, disseminating, and tallying information—have enabled people to obtain funding for entrepreneurial and charitable projects that would otherwise never have received a grant from a foundation grant or a check from a venture capitalist. One enterprising fellow sought to raise $10 to make potato salad and ended up with more than $50,000 from donors. At sites such as Fundly.com and Gofundme. com, one can ask for donations with which to care for a sick child, pay an overdue utility bill, or get through some other financial emergency. With other Information Age tools, authors can publish and sell their own books, musicians their own music, and artists their own art, sidestepping traditional middlemen, agents, and galleries.

Information tools create new forms of participation and strengthen existing ones, enabling individuals to exercise leverage with institutions—and with one another—in ways that weren't possible a few years ago. A brief Twitter post from a dissatisfied commenter can draw a swift and meaningful response from a company, a government agency, or a celebrity hoping to nip the complaint in the bud before it has a chance to "go viral." Ask Me Anything forums at Reddit and elsewhere create exchanges between people, from the president of the United States on down, who wouldn't be likely to converse otherwise.

In a sense, then, everyone gets a piece of the pie. The Information Age provides new tools for concentrating, multiplying, and better utilizing our human power. Information expands our base of knowledge, magnifies our capabilities, and opens new, often unexpected channels of participation. Governments, businesses, nonprofit organizations, syndicates, communities, churches, and billions of individuals all share in the empowerment that modern information tools make possible.

What does it really mean to say that information is power? In what ways and by what mechanisms does "information" convey "power"—terms we easily recognize and understand, yet terms that are difficult to articulate? Information provides greater capabilities to do *what*? Creates participation opportunities *where*? Empowers us *how*? When you can answer an email message from your boss at 11 o'clock on a Saturday night, is that empowerment, or is it exploitation? Does the ability to watch *Mission: Impossible* on the subway truly make us more capable, or does it merely numb us into insensitivity? Is spending ten hours on Facebook a form of participation, or a form of isolation? Perhaps it is less in the watching of the movie, the answering of the email message, or the posting to a social network as in the *capacity* to do these things that empowerment really resides.

Consider one example of how the availability of information can lead to a shift in the relationships between individuals and institutions. Companies usually keep their employees' salaries secret; in general, no one knows how much his or her colleagues in the office or on the factory floor get paid. This arrangement may suit employees who want to keep their salaries private, but it also creates a deep imbalance in the availability of information. The company knows who gets paid how much. The employees do not. The information imbalance creates a power imbalance.

A new employee asking for a starting salary or a current employee hoping for a raise is at a disadvantage in negotiations with the company. Neither has a framework for what a typical salary should be, or what other employees in similar positions and with similar experience earn. The company, on the other hand, has complete knowledge of its employees' salaries—a state approaching what economists sometimes call "perfect information." The company also has an enormous economic incentive to "lowball" salary offers. A company that knows that the average salary for a Field Superintendent position is $50,000 would do well, financially, to offer a new Field Superintendent less. A prospective employee, in the dark about how much others in a position are earning, has no context within which to gauge the appropriateness of a salary offer.

If company-wide salary information becomes available, as sometimes happens (owing to discovery during a lawsuit, a leak of confidential information, or a glitch in human resources, or simply as a matter of company policy), the information creates opportunities for employees to participate in dialogues with their employer that simply weren't possible before. Put another way, the balance of power between employees and the company has shifted. The simple provision of information enables an individual to compare his or her economic status in the company with those of all other employees, and also provides a factual basis for comparisons among groups of employees. For example, the availability of information allows anyone with an interest in doing so to compare the salaries of male and female employees. If the situation warrants, it also allows documentation of the fact that women in the company are getting paid much less for the same work in the same positions than men with the same experience.

Take another example of how the simple provision of information can bring about substantial change in the world at large—a hypothetical example, but well within the reach of the imagination. Suppose that the food industry's facilities are open to public tours, news crews can film on any farm, and there are webcams in every warehouse. The public now has a fully transparent, unfiltered view of food production from farm to table: how Thanksgiving turkeys are raised, how potatoes become McDonald's french fries, how pigs are transported, how cattle are slaughtered, and so on. No rules have been changed, no inspectors are involved, no new guidelines have been published. All that has happened is that more information about how food is handled is available—much more information. Does the industry change in the face of this newfound information? Do people's eating habits change? One can imagine that there will be more vegetarians once the slaughterhouse is made visible, or a larger market for organic vegetables once pesticide spraying is viewable. Whether the provision of new information would actually bring about such changes isn't knowable in advance, but that information alone *could* bring about a change of large magnitude seems self-evident.

Information with a Capital I

The title of this book, *Missed Information*, is an obvious (and deliberate) play on the word 'misinformation'. Why not just use that word as the title? 'Misinformation' has a strong connotation of intent; misinformation is the hallmark of spies, propagandists, political hacks, aggressive salesmen, and anyone else with a desire to mislead. *Missed Information* is more subtle. Even if the outcome is the same (that is, faulty decisions based on erroneous information), "missed information" refers to information that is unintentionally (for the most part) overlooked in the decision-making process— overlooked both by those who provide information and by those who use it. It is all too easy to omit important information from our economic, social, and political systems, and the omission of information weakens the capacity and effectiveness of these systems. In this book we examine why this is so and speculate on steps that can be taken to fill in the informational gaps.

We also explore the underappreciated but central role that information has in human endeavors and institutions. We examine how availability or unavailability of information influences the relationships between sectors of society and the wisdom of our decisions in all spheres of human activity. We examine the role of information quality (or the lack of same) as an influence, what questions are truly important, and what information is available (or could be made available) to answer these questions. We also suggest new information mechanisms that, we believe, can result in more robust, more efficient, and more fair decision making in systems as varied as health care, finance, government, and everyday shopping.

It may seem superfluous to make a case that information is central to anything. After all, it is obvious that information is at the heart of everything that we do as human beings. Each day begins with information. You open your eyes, gauge whether it is dark or light, glance at a clock, and use information in your memory to line up the day's events. As you shower, your knowledge of the world enables you to identify the soap, distinguish the hot and cold faucets, and complete the complex process of getting yourself clean. By the time you sit down to breakfast, you probably have accessed information from dozens of external sources and countless internal memories, all without any particular awareness of the role information is playing in making your morning's activities possible.

Only when the usual flow of information is interrupted, as when visiting a country where we don't speak the language, do we begin to appreciate how crucial ordinary information transactions are to our day-to-day operations. And even in such a situation—say, that of an English-speaking visitor to a French city—the language barrier isn't a hard and fast barrier to the flow of information. A tourist still knows how bathrooms function, how pedestrians safely cross a heavily trafficked street, which buildings are residences and which are businesses, and which of the businesses are restaurants and which are hardware stores. One has to travel to a considerably more foreign destination—perhaps the Kalahari or the Amazon rainforest—to really feel at a profound informational disadvantage when it comes to maneuvering through a day's activities.

For most of human history, we have hardly given information much thought. It is— like air to an animal, or water to a fish—simply the environment we occupy, move through, and function in, without any great need to ever bring its existence to the foreground. Information is what we find out about other topics, but rarely has information itself been the topic. Only in the past few decades has it been possible to open the "I" volume of an encyclopedia and find a meaningful entry on information. Circumstances have changed rapidly, however—so much so that we call our age the Information Age. Not only encyclopedias but also textbooks and even popular books in a wide variety of areas include extensive discussions of the role of information in economics, biology, sociology, and physics. Technology dominates our attention, but there is much more going on than just a technological revolution. In chapter 1 we lay out a bit of the history of the use of information tools and the dawning awareness of information with a capital I.

This is not a treatise on information technology. In fact, there is very little technology in it. The fantastic information-technology machines that permeate modern life are conduits for amassing, storing, manipulating, securing, and delivering information with a power and a facility that hadn't been dreamed of a generation ago. But it isn't the conduits that change lives, redesign economies, reinvent governments, and alter social structures; it is the information they deliver. In this book we focus much more on the information than on the delivery mechanisms. Concepts such as "freedom of information," "privacy," and "right to know" are more important to us than computers' processing speeds, systems' storage capacities, or the pixel densities of the latest mobile phones.

We are particularly interested in the importance of information to the smooth functioning of the global economy. In chapter 2, we examine the role of information in the market. The ability of the market to act as an information processor that deftly reads and responds to countless market transactions is at the heart of the global economy. The "invisible hand" of the market is really more of an invisible artificial intelligence, handling input in the form of trillions of daily market signals and producing meaningful output to meet consumers' needs and—not incidentally—propel society forward by meeting the market's demand for shoes, wood screws, short-term loans, and other things. Systems that interfere with this automatic flow of information run the risk of collapsing from their inherent inefficiency, the fate that befell Soviet Communism. Consciously trying to manage the information needed to make the market run, rather than giving the market free rein to manage the information on its own, is (and has shown itself to be) a recipe for economic malaise.

Not all markets have the luxury of freely moving information. Health care is a prime example of an information-constrained market. (When was the last time you shopped for a doctor on the basis of price?) Society tends to place the blame for faults in the health-care system on other institutions: pharmaceutical companies that price life-saving medicines out of the reach of patients, insurance companies that won't let doctors make the medically best decisions, government regulations that overburden health-care professionals. Rarely is the role of information highlighted as a significant obstacle to a well-functioning health-care system. The absence of freely moving information makes for a very inefficient market across almost all aspects of the delivery of health care.

The importance of information to the efficient functioning of the market—or inefficient dysfunctioning, as the case may be—reminds us of an old adage that engineers apply to computer models: garbage in, garbage out. By viewing market sectors as large-scale information processors, the comparison with information technology comes to make more sense. If faulty data are input, the output is not to be trusted, no matter how sophisticated the system. Bad data make for poor weather forecasts and for a fractured, jerky, stubbornly unresponsive health-care system. On any Sunday, consumers can shop for groceries, see a movie, or browse a bookstore. But try finding a doctor! In chapter 3 we elaborate on the connection between inefficient handling of health-care information and broader inefficiencies throughout the health-care system. We present some ideas for making changes in what information should come forward, how to get it to do so, and what benefits might flow from doing so.

In chapter 4 we take a detailed look at the information available in a typical corporation's annual report. How well does it address the questions that an interested reader—a shareholder, a potential investor, a broker, a financial reporter, a regulator—would ask? Not particularly well, it turns out. Some such reports are deliberately designed to be confounding and to reveal as little genuine information as is possible. (No one understood the Enron Corporation's cryptic accounting models.) But even the most straightforward of reports (we use Starbucks' reports as an example) are hamstrung by an excessive amount of missed information. Again, we offer a few suggestions for improving the flow of information.

We are free-marketeers. But even the freest and most robust market loses critical information as products move through the supply chain, particularly information regarding collective societal values. Goods manage to arrive on stores' shelves with certain information intact—brand names, ingredients, country of origin, price—but somehow don't maintain a clear indication of, for example, whether they were produced in sweatshops by child workers. In chapters 5 and 6 we propose a way to bring such information forward, and we argue (convincingly, we hope) that the market can better reflect human values and simultaneously become a more efficient market doing an even better job of creating new wealth.

A key feature of the Information Age is that it is reshaping the ways in which we seek out new information. Humans are information foragers, looking to maximize interesting input with a minimum of effort. Old ways of foraging for information—libraries, the Dewey Decimal System, phone books, 411 service—are being supplanted by Google, Siri, and other new information tools that put a world of access on our desks or even in our pockets. In chapter 7 we take a look at some emerging strategies for information foraging.

Information was in the headlines almost daily as we were writing this book. Many of those headlines concerned the activities of government security agencies that amass information on billions of people around the world, and in ways that few people have been aware of. It is technology that makes such large-scale data collection possible, but our discussion focuses on the uses and the limits of such information more than on the technology. We believe the cat is out of the bag. Governments (not just the US government, by any means) will continue to collect information on virtually every person who ever makes a phone call or sends an email message. Large-scale government snooping may be dialed back a bit and subjected to stricter supervision, but it isn't likely to cease.

Insofar as each person's life is much more of an open book than ever before, isn't it fair to ask the same of governments? If the email messages and the phone records of government agencies were vastly more transparent, might government respond to that openness as significantly as we imagined the food industry might? The idea isn't to annoy bureaucrats (though that may have its satisfactions for many); rather, it is to reconfigure the balance of power between bureaucracies and ordinary citizens and to put the power of information to use in helping our governments to work more effectively. We explore these ideas in chapter 8.

In chapter 9 we turn our attention to the Toxics Release Inventory. TRI is a mechanism for reporting the use of toxic chemicals in industry—something of an environmental report card for facilities that send in their annual forms. It creates interesting motivations for reducing waste generation. It also reshuffles the balance of social power between government, business and the public in ways that can be clearly seen by looking back at the three-decade history of the program.

In chapter 10 we look ahead to what might be in store in the coming decades as information technology creates new opportunities and new challenges and as it continues to alter the landscape of capabilities, participation, and power in which people and institutions find themselves.

Core Concepts

Our discussions are informed by the following concepts, beliefs, and values, which strike us as true and important.

Information is emergent in myriad ways.

The Information Age in which we find ourselves is about much more than information technology. "Information" has emerged as a central tenet in a broad array of disciplines and activities. Biology now is largely an information science, economics has incorporated information as a core concept, and physicists are coming to see information as a fundamental (perhaps *the* fundamental) unit of matter and energy. Information policy has always been central to democracy, even when not labeled as such. Some of the most important pillars of society—free press, mail delivery, public education—are mechanisms for ensuring widespread and unfettered dissemination of information; more recent innovations, including Freedom of Information and Right-to-Know laws, have expanded the importance of information in the policy sphere. We are coming to understand that fundamental questions about information—who has it, who sees it, what is public, what is private—will be at the heart of how society takes shape in the coming decades. Information technologies play an important supporting role in all these areas, but the main concepts don't depend on technology.

Better information leads to better decisions.
Information drives every decision in every sphere of human activity. The better the quality of information underlying those decisions, the greater the likelihood that good decisions will be made. This is true regardless of whether the decision maker is a shopper in a grocery store, serves on a corporation's board of directors, or is the president of a country. As the old programming expression we have already cited goes, "garbage in, garbage out." Working with faulty information as input makes it highly likely that the output too will be faulty. As a corollary, we also hold to the principle that information quality trumps information quantity, even though it is often difficult to precisely state the criteria for distinguishing high-quality information from low-quality information.

Deliberate secrecy comes at a large cost.
Secrets are hard to hold. We know this as human beings, and recognize the psychic cost of carrying secrets. Institutions too bear the cost of secrecy, especially when secrets have no expiration date. The mechanisms necessary to create secrets, to maintain them as secrets, and to hold individuals accountable for the loss of secrets entail large organizational costs in money, time, and inconvenience. We aren't saying that secrets should be banished, but we do believe that secrecy should be relied on with much greater selectively.

Inadvertent secrets are as significant as deliberate secrets.
Some information is hidden after it is stamped "Eyes Only," meaning that it is intended only for a specific set of readers. But a great deal of information becomes secret inadvertently. This is most obvious in the realm of government, where information that is available in principle becomes buried in practice, never to see the light of day. Inadvertent secrets are also prevalent in the marketplace, where a "don't ask, don't tell" style of commerce leads to the loss of important information about products' attributes—a loss that leads to lower-quality information, poor decisions, and economic inefficiencies.

Information is the new social contract.
Individuals the world over are being asked by security-conscious governments to surrender a great deal of information about their day-to-day activities, including (in the electronic realm) making phone calls, sending email messages, and browsing the Web and (in the physical world) walking, driving, or flying. Companies too compile enormous databases detailing people's financial transactions, demographic information, and much of the same electronic information that is of interest to government. Access to information has been far too one-sided. If we are to lose significant privacy in the name of security and commerce, we need to know far more about the institutions collecting the information. Governments and businesses must become more transparent, and large governments and large businesses must become hypertransparent. The only way to establish trust is to greatly strengthen individuals' right to know as a counterbalance to institutions' right to snoop. We see this as an important part of the modern social contract.

Information technology is a cornerstone of greater institutional transparency.
Modern tools of information management and information dissemination can make possible a degree of openness undreamed of in decades past. In addition to creating access to existing information (the current focus of the Internet), information technology can help create new, high-quality information to better inform human decision making across the board.

1 Information: A Brief Modern History

Those of us who grew up with encyclopedias used them as a source of information about thousands of discrete topics. The twenty-or-more-volume sets occupied prime real estate in our bookshelves. We consulted them as an aid in doing our homework, solving a crossword puzzle, settling an argument, or simply when we were curious to know more about almost anything. The breadth of encyclopedias was impressive. In its heyday, the print version of the *Encyclopaedia Britannica* included about half a million entries.

For much of the twentieth century, however, encyclopedias weren't a good source of information about information. The entry on Information in the 1911 *Britannica* (which is freely available online) consists of only two paragraphs—between In Forma Pauperis and Informer—and focuses on an arcane use of the term in English law:

A criminal information is a proceeding in the King's bench by the attorney-general without the intervention of a grand jury.

Compare that to the *Britannica* of a century later. The 2015 edition (no longer in print, now available exclusively online) includes index entries and (often voluminous) articles for the following:

information theory
information economics
information society
information (communications)
information (law)
information asymmetry (economics and insurance)
information bias
Information Bureau of the Communist and Workers' Parties (international
    agency)

information, freedom of (legal right)

Information Management System (computing)

Information, Please! (American radio program)

Information Processing Language (computer language)

Information Processing Techniques Office (United States military department)

information processor (communications technology)

information requirement (intelligence)

information retrieval (computer and information science)

information retrieval system

information science

information society (society)

information storage and retrieval system

information storage system

information system

information system infrastructure

information systems audit (information system)

Information Techniques Program Office (United States military department)

Information Technology Agreement (international trade)

Information, The (album by Beck)

information theory (mathematics)

information-access law

digital information

analog information

imperfect information

algorithmic information theory

geographic information system

data mining

data compression

data encryption

It also includes a host of related articles on topics as diverse as computer technologies, cybernetics, government agencies, business practices, and public policy.

The same holds true in academia. In decades past, among thousands of college course offerings ranging from accounting to zoology, you weren't likely to find a course on information. Nor did any courses include a focused discussion on information as a serious topic; open a college textbook from

UNIVERSITY OF CALIFORNIA

General Catalogue

**Primarily for Students in the
DEPARTMENTS AT LOS ANGELES**

**Fall and Spring Semesters
1950–1951**

112B. The Communication of Information. (3) II.   Mr. Hershberger
    Prerequisite: courses 100A, 112A.
    Delineation of the fundamental problem of communication between
human beings with emphasis on factors common to all systems. The course
includes a study of information theory, signals and their spectra, and the
factors that determine system performance as distortion, element variation,
and band width; noise, and the characteristics of the human voice and sense
organs. Illustrative material is drawn from telephony, radar, television, computers, and automatic control systems.

Figure 1.1
The University of California's only information course in the 1950s (from a catalogue
available at: http://www.registrar.ucla.edu/archive/catalog/50-51catalog.pdf).

1950 or earlier and you are unlikely to find 'information' included as
an entry in the book's index. This is true regardless of the field chosen,
whether mathematics, physics, history, political science, medicine, technology, business, biology, or any of the hard, soft, or social sciences. These
disciplines routinely and specifically address information as a topic today,
but this is a fairly recent development.

It takes a fair amount of scrounging to find any focus on information as
a topic worthy of academic attention. The University of California's 1951
course offerings included a single course on "the communication of information." (See figure 1.1.)

Even after the 1950s, for several decades information was treated
as a discrete topic largely in texts focused on electrical engineering and

communications technology. These fields, with an inherent focus on the transmission and transformation of information, by necessity had to create formal definitions for information and describe the constraints that limited the speed and reliability of the main information technologies of the time—the telegraph, the telephone, radios, televisions—in terms of their ability to faithfully send information from a sender to a recipient, whether across a room or across the Atlantic Ocean.

The transformation from small-i information to capital-I Information is a hallmark of our times. Today 'Information' is capitalized in job titles, in book titles, in journal titles, in policy pronouncements, in legislation, in course catalogs, in organization flowcharts, in international conferences, and for our times themselves. We live in the Information Age, and really, how many periods of human history are so succinctly and appropriately named?

The first highly formalized definition and technical treatment of information is probably that provided by Ralph Hartley in his influential 1928 paper "Transmission of Information." Hartley, an electronics engineer at the Bell Telephone Laboratories, developed "a quantitative measure of 'information'" in order to accurately describe the degradation of information as it is electronically transmitted over a distance, and the ability of communication technologies to distinguish information from system noise.

Hartley's paper treated information as a measurable, almost physical quantity, not very different from length or mass. This notion is simultaneously intuitive and counterintuitive. We readily recognize some resources as containing "more" or "less" information than others. But even in our age of kilobytes and gigabits (terms unknown to Hartley), we are hard pressed to quantify information differences. Put an 8-by-10-inch photograph next to the front page of a daily newspaper and it is trivially easy to know which item is longer or wider or larger or even heavier than the other. But does the photograph contain more information than the newspaper, or less? The answer isn't obvious, and in some respects it depends on the particular observer. For people who don't read English, the front page of the *New York Times* isn't particularly informative, and the photograph "wins" every time.

Hartley, noting that information is a very "elastic" term in ordinary usage, strives to eliminate what he calls the "psychological factors" in communicating and interpreting information. He limits his considerations to

Figure 1.2
Ralph Hartley, 1888–1970.

the ability to successfully communicate a message—a news story, a family photo, or a telegram—from point A to point B. Though Hartley doesn't put it quite this simply, from an electrical engineering point of view, the item requiring the most electrons to transmit is the one containing the most information.

Hartley's work laid the basis for the contributions to information theory by Claude Shannon, whose 1948 paper "A Mathematical Theory of Communication" is widely regarded as the cornerstone of modern information theory, tying the concept of information to the physical concept of entropy and, in essence, defining information as the opposite of uncertainty. Shannon also gets credit for coining the term 'bit' (a contraction of 'binary digit') to mean a unit of measure for information, though a few others may have used 'bit' even earlier.

Information slowly emerged from the confines of the engineering world to play a major role in other disciplines. In 1962, a Nobel Prize was awarded for a discovery that, for the first time, had information as a central theme. Francis Crick, James Watson, and Maurice Wilkins received the Nobel Prize in Physiology or Medicine for "their discoveries concerning the molecular

Figure 1.3
Claude Shannon, 1916–2001.

structure of nucleic acids and its significance for information transfer in living material."

Academic disciplines have become information-centric in ways that were scarcely imaginable a few decades back. Modern biology is practically a subdiscipline of information science. In genetics, some of the largest data development/management/delivery systems in creation focus on managing information on human, animal, plant, and bacterial genomes. Economics has moved information from a minor consideration to a central tenet of modern theory, with one Nobel Prize after another awarded for concepts related to decision making under conditions of incomplete, uncertain, or asymmetric information. Physics is leaning toward defining the most fundamental units of the universe not as matter or energy, but as information-processing objects.

The world of business jumped on the information bandwagon in the 1960s. Recognizing the rapidly changing capabilities of computers to help manage the vast inputs and outputs that business activities

photopticheminforonics

Odd word.

However, it's one way to compound Photography, Optics, Chemistry, Information Science, and Electronics—the basic disciplines that apply to Information Technology—into one word.

A better word is Itek.

The technical charter by which Itek derives its name and on which its business mission is based is the advancement of Information Technology.

What is Information Technology?

Itek defines it as the development, production and marketing of advanced systems and equipment for acquiring, transmitting, storing, reproducing and displaying graphic and textual information. Itek's best known accomplishments and strongest capabilities have thus far related to systems and components used in photo-optical acquisition, photographic and electronic data processing, and the display and dissemination of information.

How is Itek different?

In the course of Itek's development, its strength has increased considerably in a wide range of corollary technologies. This multi-disciple base affords a unique, stimulating environment for the perceptive scientist and engineer. Itek's extensive programs in its selected areas of interest have created professional opportunities over a wide range, with particular emphasis on the positions described below.

Figure 1.4
The term 'information technology' entered the business vocabulary around 1960, as evidenced by this item (the preface of a help-wanted ad) from August 7 of that year.

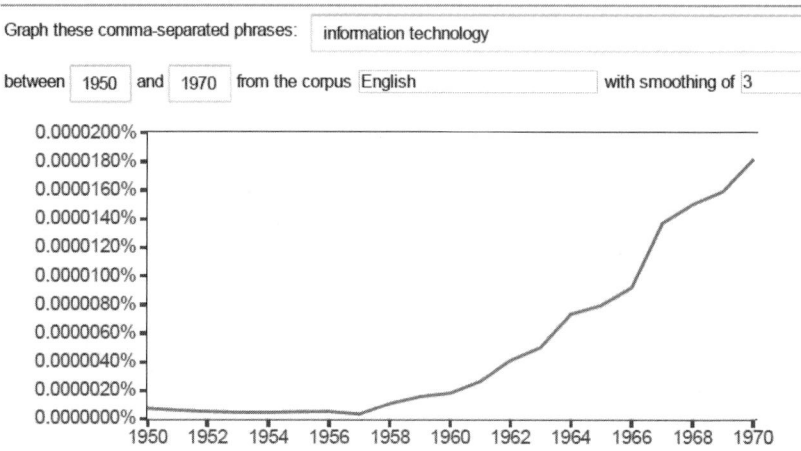

Figure 1.5
Blossoming of the term 'information technology'.

create—customer records, correspondence files, temperature and pressure recordings for industrial processes, payroll records, shipping manifests, transportation schedules, inventories, financial accounts—the corporate world embraced the term 'information technology' and began reorganizing corporate structures to give IT greater prominence. Before long, there emerged a new position: that of the Chief Information Officer, whose job it was to ensure the integrity of corporate information management.

The development of science and technology wasn't the only factor propelling the concept of information to greater prominence. The phrase "freedom of information," seemingly fundamental to the practice of democracy, didn't emerge as a compelling topic until the 1940s, when information (and so much else) was under tyrannical control in Nazi Germany. In no small measure, the phrase was also championed by those with concerns that press freedoms and a free flow of information were also at risk in the world's democracies, particularly during wartime. Franklin Roosevelt's famous 1941 list of Four Freedoms—freedom of speech, freedom of worship, freedom from want, freedom from fear—included freedom of information in earlier incarnations, before the concept was consolidated into the broader notion of free speech and free expression. In the postwar years, Eleanor Roosevelt strongly championed freedom of information at the United Nations, deeming it the "one absolute necessity" to promoting human rights around the world.

President Roosevelt's concerns about open and transparent government were codified in the 1946 Administrative Procedures Act, which, despite a title suggesting a bureaucrats-only interest, is an important document for ensuring the public's involvement in an open process of rulemaking by the federal government. APA was followed by the 1966 Freedom of Information Act, requiring more open access to government documents and data, and the 1976 Government in Sunshine Act, requiring open meetings. American laws are echoed in many other countries; at least seventy countries have some form of a Freedom of Information statute. Other public policy developments explicitly addressed information as well in laws pertaining to the right to know, to information transparency, to intellectual property, and to other areas of law and society.

More than public policy is at stake. Information is now at the forefront of warfare. The Internet is now a battlefield, and "cyber-warfare" is a growing concern. Although primarily limited to nuisance attacks and apparent shots across the bow (such as remotely dismantling Iran's centrifuges for processing nuclear materials), military and security experts are preparing for a day when large-scale cyber-attacks could significantly disable the Internet. Information-related attacks—only the stuff of movies for the moment—could, in the future, cause broad economic disruption and could undermine power grids, transportation hubs, water-delivery systems, and other national infrastructure and security systems that rely on active information management for day-to-day operations. In the first known incident of a cyber-attack causing an actual disruption to a regional power grid, hackers caused a blackout in Ukraine over the 2015 Christmas season.

Closely related concerns about cyber-crime are escalating as well, as unauthorized computer intrusions can put millions of customers' accounts and billions of dollars at risk in a single action. Even government files are at risk, as multiple intrusions into the US Office of Personnel Management's databases in 2015 painfully demonstrated; more than 20 million records were compromised in the OPM attacks, resulting in the loss of Social Security numbers, usernames, passwords, and even fingerprints. Cyber-warfare has a more conventional battlefield aspect as well, as modern soldiers are constantly networked to their compatriots and to central command, with electronics and sensors built into their uniforms to provide communication, establish location, identify friend from foe, and monitor environmental and health conditions.

The Information Age is not just about innovations in technology. Information has conceptually emerged along several paths, driven not only by solid-state electronics but also by developments in biology, physics, medicine, ecology, public policy, economics, business, finance, human rights, and other fields. Collectively these developments have given rise to an Information Age much broader than access to desktop computers, mobile devices, and the World Wide Web.

Information has come forward as a topic for encyclopedias and textbooks, to be sure, but its primary significance is its emergence as a key factor in shaping the modern world. Information is a force for change as fundamental as technology, wealth, natural resources, education, politics, and conflict in defining how the world will look in the decades ahead. The old adage that information is power has never been more true, and has never been valid along so many different pathways.

2 Information and the Market Economy

The Soviet Union's Fourth Five-Year Plan called for the production of 230 million pairs of leather shoes in 1950, or about 2.2 pairs of shoes per person for a population of 103 million. A government bureaucracy devoted almost exclusively to footwear determined not only the number of shoes needed in the coming years but also all the pertinent details of the marketplace: the allocation of shoes vs. boots, how many leather hides would be needed, and color choices, styles, and distribution of sizes appropriate to the demographics of the Soviet Union at the time.

In a centrally planned economy, bureaucracy decides how many millions of pairs of shoes should be produced in the coming years and dictates almost all major decisions regarding their production. Beyond that, though, the central planners must place shoes in the context of the overall economic planning for other consumer goods and industrial goods. Factory capacity is parceled out, some to shoe manufacturing, some to furniture, some to clothing, some to all the other items of commerce; plans for new factories are specified when additional capacity is called for. With apparent mathematical precision, the planners divide up the labor pool, allocating the numbers of laborers needed to produce shoes vs. other consumer goods, and the types of labor—from machinists and leatherworkers to truck drivers and dyers—in each area. The bureaucracy decides what materials to use and where to source them. A specialist computes the necessary distribution of shoes for evening wear and boots for heavy work. And of course, bureaucrats set the prices of all these items. The decisions are based on the predicted needs of the population, the available raw material inputs and production facilities for the manufacture of shoes, and the priorities of the central government in steering production toward the items deemed to be most important.

Here is how the footwear plans in the Soviet Union's 10th Five-Year Plan were described in a 1982 Soviet government report:

[T]he Administration of the Development of the Footwear, Leather and Leather Goods Industry jointly with the ministries of light industry of the union republics need to elaborate versions of the efficient making up of all types of footwear, starting with fashionable and especially elegant footwear and ending with Russian leather work shoes … . It is necessary to compile a material, technical and production passport for each type of footwear, which will make it possible to use with the greatest sensibility the available resources and to decrease the unjustified fluctuations in the material, production and labor expenditures on the production of similar types of footwear at different enterprises. …

[T]he assimilation of four fundamentally new types of footwear: "after skiing," men's half boots in the design of moccasins, women's boots made of a combination of natural and synthetic leather, women's shoes of thong designs on soles made of rigid polyurethane and with heel-instep blocks made of ABS plastic, were outlined by the plan. In the time that has passed more than 7 million pair of women's footwear of thong designs with the use of rigid polyurethane, which was purchased through imports, and about 150,000 pair of women's summer footwear with a heel-instep block made of ABS plastic have been produced. The output of men's footwear, including with the use of elastic leathers of increased thicknesses, has been organized. … However, the work on the development of "after ski" footwear and women's boots made of synthetic leathers is being performed extremely slowly.

Despite the attention to detail, the Soviet system itself acknowledged its difficulties in creating high-quality products:

The percentage of products, which have been returned for repair and have been transferred to lower grades, is the highest in the Georgian SSR Ministry of Light Industry (22.5 percent) and the Azerbaijan SSR Ministry of Light Industry (20.2 percent). At the Baku Factory of Fashionable Footwear the amount of such footwear came to 49.2 percent and at the Tbilisi Isani Footwear Factory—40.9 percent. Trade organizations are lodging many complaints about the quality of the footwear which is being produced by the Kiselevsk Kuzbassobuv, the Odessa and Shakhtinsk Footwear Production Associations, the Rostov Factory of Fashionable Footwear, the Birobidzhan, Kherson, Tbilisi Narikala, Karaganda, Samarkand and Andizhan Footwear Factories.

To put it another way, the central bureaucracy was carefully evaluating the available information on both the supply side (number of animal hides to be made into leather, number of factories that can manufacture shoes, the labor pool) and the demand side (overall population, breakout of men, women, children and associated shoe sizes, types of footwear needed) and was consciously, deliberately making production decisions for the society as a whole. It was a "top-down" approach characteristic of central planning, involving active, conscious, society-scale information management. The leaders of the Soviet Union made basic decisions about marketplace products "with the greatest sensibility," in the belief that doing so allowed, the use of society's resources to match society's needs. Good intentions notwithstanding, they also acknowledged that producing high-quality goods in a Soviet-style system was not without its difficulties.

The capitalist economy operates pretty much in the opposite fashion, from the bottom up. Millions upon millions of individual choices by consumers propel the system forward, with no single organization at the helm. Almost miraculously, enterprises in a capitalist economy appear to produce the right number of shoes, with the right mix of sizes and styles, at the right prices, so that society's footwear needs are met without any conscious, bureaucratic planning. There is no centralized, national-scale footwear database tracking materials, factories, imports, production, shoe types, sales, and all the other details of commerce. Bureaucratic oversight of a sort generally exists, but it aims to rein in the potential dangers of manufacturing (threats to consumers' safety, pollution) and finance (bank panics); the bureaucracy leaves production to the producers.

Herman Daly and John Cobb, in their book *For the Common Good*, use the example of wood screws to compare and contrast how centrally planned and capitalistic markets differ, especially in how the two systems handle information:

How many different kinds are there? Screws differ along the continuum of length, and of diameter, measured in inches or centimeters, or in some other special metric. The helical pitch of the threads can differ. The materials differ: steel, aluminum, brass, Monel. Screws of one metal can be plated with another: chromium, nickel, cadmium, copper, zinc. The heads of screw differ greatly: flat or oval countersunk; round, square, hexagon; slotted, Phillips or Allen heads; pan head. Clearly there are infinitely many types of wood screw, each designed for particular uses.

A market system can handle all the information about these qualitative differences. Central planning cannot. To have only, say, a dozen types of wood screw … is like playing piano with your fists rather than your fingers. For allocating resources among commodity uses, the market is the most efficient institution we have come up with thanks to its ability to use information.

The capitalist marketplace works, according to Daly and Cobb, "thanks to its ability to use information." Daly and Cobb identify the information-processing capabilities of capitalism as the critical quality that makes it more effective and—as history has shown—more successful than central planning. Capitalism relies on an automatic, undirected, non-central sort of information processing, so very different from the clunky, clumsy attempts at consciously managing information in a centralized economy. There is something deeply counterintuitive about capitalism—like taking your hands off the steering wheel in order to find the best route forward—but it manages the tasks of production remarkably well.

The workings of the invisible hand of economics that so marvelously steers production in the right directions ceased to be mysterious long ago. Although not conventionally cast in the now-familiar terms of the Information Age, the role of information in the market is fairly clear, at least in its broad outlines. The marketplace serves as an enormous information processor, relaying signals about supply and demand to all participants and responding in a manner that elegantly provides the numbers and types of shoes or the specialized types of screws needed by the population at large, without any bureaucratic intervention. Repeat the process for millions of products, purchased by billions of people, in trillions of marketplace trans-actions, and it is a marvel that capitalism handles the information with a seeming effortlessness, and it is little wonder that central economies col-lapse under the weight of trying to take on the information-management task themselves.

Adam Smith was of the opinion that "no human wisdom or knowledge could ever be sufficient" for the task of "superintending the industry of pri-vate people, and of directing it towards the employments most suitable to the interest of the society." Why even try to "superintend" the mechanics of the market? Just sit back and let the invisible hand do the job for us. This was Smith's great insight: markets could self-organize without a sovereign or a government ministry providing conscious direction as long as it had unfettered access to the proper signals. Not only was such self-organization possible; it might be the only way the market can work with reasonable efficiency.

That the capitalist market works is obvious. A stroll through the aisles of any store—whether a giant big-box retailer or a corner convenience store—offers up a wide variety of goods at prices that are usually competitive with those of similar goods sold in other shops. Awareness of the cost of an item, or of the price consumers are willing to pay, tends to prevent prices from varying too wildly from one market to another. The price differentials that do exist between products are also driven by information—information that a particular product is somehow superior to its near-equivalent, or that a company offers better service and greater convenience, or that a specific brand carries a cachet not available from a generic product.

Of course, price differences can also be driven by a *lack* of information. For most of human history, a shopper had no quick and convenient way to compare prices for a product between a merchant in Town A and one in Town B. Information filtered through the overall system at a leisurely pace. Over time, one shop might develop a reputation as over-priced, leading would-be shoppers to weigh the costs and benefits of where to take their business. The emergence of newspapers and, more particularly, advertising, facilitated the flow of consumer information and the ability to compare product offerings and prices.

The availability of consumer information and of shopping sites on the Internet has given rise to an even more information-centric form of capitalism by making it easier to "shop around" for the best deals. When a consumer can scan a barcode with her mobile phone and compare products and prices from merchants across town, across country, or anywhere in the world, it isn't difficult to see how easy and instant access to information helps to drive pricing and purchasing decisions.

Of course, a well-informed buyer needs much more information than merely the price of a particular good or service. Buyers want to know the specifics of what they are buying—specifications, quality, reliability, workmanship, guarantees, and much, much more. Sellers too need information, particularly on the trustworthiness of their potential customers.

The Internet magnified the role of information in the marketplace, but it didn't create it. The marketplace has functioned as an information processor for centuries, since long before the advent of electronic computer technology. This point is worth making if for no other reason than to emphasize that the market as an information processor is distinct from our understanding of information processing: the market doesn't need information technology to do its job.

Adam Smith described some of the information-processing attributes of Scottish financial institutions in *The Wealth of Nations*:

The banking companies of Scotland ... were for a long time very careful to require frequent and regular repayments from all their customers, and did not care to deal with any person, whatever might be his fortune or credit, who did not make, what they called, frequent and regular operations with them. By this attention, besides saving almost entirely the extraordinary expence of replenishing their coffers, they gained two other very considerable advantages ... .

"By this attention," Smith says in his eighteenth-century manner, but we can understand this as a means of collecting information on bank customers, with a particular focus on how often and how timely their loan payments are made. Smith continues with an elaboration of the advantages gained by such attentions:

[B]y this attention they were enabled to make some tolerable judgment concerning the thriving or declining circumstances of their debtors, without being obliged to look out for any other evidence besides what their own books afforded them; men being for the most part either regular or irregular in their repayments, according as their circumstances are either thriving or declining. A private man who lends out his money to perhaps half a dozen or a dozen of debtors, may, either by himself or his agents, observe and inquire both constantly and carefully into the conduct and situation of each of them. But a banking company, which lends money to perhaps five hundred different people, and of which the attention is continually occupied by objects of a very different kind, can have no regular information concerning the conduct and circumstances of the greater part of its debtors beyond what its own books afford it ... .

An individual lending money to a few acquaintances, or to only one person, can keep a careful eye on each person's "circumstances" and can stay reasonably well informed about each person's ability to repay the loan. A bank, with hundreds of clients (in Smith's day) or millions of clients (today), uses an information proxy to make a judgment about creditworthiness, and, finding the proxy a reliable guide, is spared the need to pursue "any other evidence" about its clients. The information regarding regular loan repayments helps guide the bank's decisions regarding future transactions, a task that has evolved significantly over the centuries. We can see in Smith's description the nascent steps toward development of a modern-day credit reporting industry, one that collects tremendous amounts of information on consumers to spare the financial industry from the task of having to "inquire both constantly and carefully" into the financial status of its actual or would-be clients.

An additional advantage to the bank's information collection cited by Smith is somewhat unexpected:

Secondly, by this attention they secured themselves from the possibility of issuing more paper money than what the circulation of the country could easily absorb and employ ... .

In the late 1700s, Scotland had only recently adopted a system of relying on paper money for most commercial transactions. The state-sponsored banks operated as both commercial banks and central banks, managing the money supply of the country and ensuring that the issuance of paper money didn't exceed the supply of precious metal to back it up:

[W]hen they observed that within moderate periods of time the repayments of a particular customer were upon most occasions fully equal to the advances which they had made to him, they might be assured that the paper money which they had advanced to him had not at any time exceeded the quantity of gold and silver which he would otherwise have been obliged to keep by him for answering occasional demands; and that, consequently, the paper money, which they had circulated by his means, had not at any time exceeded the quantity of gold and silver which would have circulated in the country had there been no paper money ... .

Smith likens lending and repayments to a pond, with water flowing in and out, that is in danger of running dry if the inflows and outflows aren't well matched. The stream of funds flowing into and out of the banks becomes another source of raw data processed by the marketplace into meaningful information about the money supply, and leading to well-informed decisions about managing the supply of precious metals and paper currency.

Let's step back a moment to examine the market as information processor in a bit more detail with a twenty-first-century frame of mind. As we noted earlier, the term 'information processor' evokes a technological image—a global-scale computerized network that tracks information on each and every transaction. Indeed, this is pretty much what happens in some neatly proscribed markets, such as a stock exchange that operates enormous banks of computers to track activity on the stock market, ties its computer system to other computers in other trading venues, and pumps out information on stock prices and trading volume almost instantaneously. But there is no central equivalent in the market for tracking billions of transactions involving shoes or wood screws. The distinction is important, but it is also increasingly blurry as information technology comes to play an ever-larger role in the world of commerce. Still, it should be abundantly clear that computerized information technology isn't a necessary prerequisite to the information-processing capabilities of the market. As Daly and

Cobb noted, the market works because of its "ability to use information." But that sophisticated ability was manifest long before modern information technology came into being.

How *does* the non-centralized marketplace process its data?

The Market as Information Processor

As with any information processor, the marketplace consolidates information input and produces informative output.

The most basic sort of information has to do with the simple presence of buyers, sellers, and products. In order for a transaction to take place, sellers and buyers have to be able to find each other. The whereness and the whatness of commerce—what items are for sale, who has them for sale, who wants to buy them—are the first types of information that must be processed in order for a market to function. This processing happens at multiple scales, between countless numbers of parties, and in a manner that is sometimes quite explicit but at other times quite vague.

In times past, the challenge of gathering, managing, and disseminating who-what-where information was handled by the physical existence of the market. A marketplace was very literally a place that concentrated the population of merchants and customers to make it more likely that each could find the other. Aristotle, in *Politics*, describes the need for a city to have dedicated public spaces for particular societal functions, such as eating, worship, exercise, and dispensing, and a square "for buying and selling," which "should be so situated as to be commodious for the reception of goods both by sea and land." The presence of a central market doesn't guarantee that the shoe seller and the shoe buyer will find one another, but by localizing buying and selling activities it greatly increases the likelihood of such a meeting occurring, thereby opening the door to a commercial transaction.

Consider this through the lens of information. Traveling through Greece 2,500 years ago, a traveler in need of shoes didn't have to know the names and locations of cobblers in all the towns along his path. It was enough to know that each town was likely to have its own marketplace—the agora—and that a shoemaker and his wares could be found there. There was also a good likelihood that those who frequented the market knew a great deal about its set-up—food merchants in one sector, furniture in another, and so on—and would be a useful source of information on how to locate a cobbler. Adam Smith described how Scottish bankers used an informational means—repayment history—to sidestep the need to hire an army of agents to track the personal financial health of each of its clients. The agora serves much the same purpose, acting as an information proxy and eliminating the need to compile pertinent details on who sells what, where.

As information tools became more sophisticated, the need for a dedicated marketplace diminished. Foremost among the emerging tools was the printing press. The who-sells-what-where directory approach to information management became more practical, and the need for a centralized market serving as an information proxy became less necessary. The oldest known London business directory was printed in 1677. By the eighteenth century, there were directories in many sizable towns. The location of the shoe shop, the smithy, or the printer could be found in the directory, rather than left to a chance encounter in a central market.

The utility of the directory as a market tool was self-evident. Further developments in printing and communication technology—along with the presence of an educated population that could take advantage of written materials—gave rise to the Yellow Pages as a way to further facilitate connections between merchants and potential customers, and then to additional means of information access, such as directory assistance. Online tools such as local search and social networking, in combination with online shopping, have made a physical marketplace setting even less essential.

Beyond simply finding one another, participants in the market also exchange information on price, of course, and on things that might influence a transaction: product availability, product quality, merchant reliability, consumer creditworthiness, and myriad sorts of other information related to both the product and the shopping experience. Consumers want to know about guarantees, shipping costs, and return policies. Merchants are interested in identifying regular, trustworthy customers, and in understanding consumers' needs. In ancient markets, information between buyer and seller (and would-be buyer and would-be seller) was exchanged face to face. Modern avenues of communication have greatly multiplied the opportunities for information transfer. Advertisements on television and radio and in newspapers and magazines (and on billboards, in catalogs, in flyers, and on websites) provide information on product availability, on product quality, and on outlets where the product can be purchased.

THE

Boſton Directory.

ADAMS Samuel, Hon. Winter-ſtreet.
     Andrews John, merchant, No. 4, Union-ſtreet.
Amory Jonathan, jun. ſhop-keeper, Cornhill.
Auſtin Daniel, grocer, No. 47, Cornhill.
Amory John and Thomas, ſtore-keepers, No 41
     Marlborough-ſtreet.
Ayers Nath. W. India goods, No. 12, Marlborough-ſtreet.
Amory Jonathan, merchant, State-ſtreet.
Alline Henry, notary-public, State-ſtreet.
Armour Enoch, No. 42, State-ſtreet.
Amory Thomas, jun. merchant, No. 36, Long-wharf.
Auſtin Jona. L. and Benja. jun. rope-walk near Beacon-
     hill, and ſtore No. 37, Long-wharf.
Adams & Molineux, auctioniers, No. 9, Merchants-row.
Auſtin Samuel, jun. founder, Market-ſquare.
Adams Daniel, ſhop-keeper, Market-ſquare.
Armſtrong John, painter, No. 8, Long-wharf.
Alexander Giles, merchant, No. 52, Long-wharf.
Archbald Azor G. ſhop-keeper, No. 7, Union-ſtreet.
Alexander Joſeph, hair-dreſſer, Orange-ſtreet.
Adams Abraham, leather-dreſſer and breeches-maker,
     No. 72, Newbury-ſtreet.
Andrews William, houſe-wright, Eſſex-ſtreet.
Appleton Nathaniel, Eſq; United States Loan-office,
     Atkinſon-ſtreet.
Appleton Nathaniel W. phyſician, South-Latin
     School-ſtreet, near the Stone-Chappel.
Archer Moſes, boot and ſhoe-maker, Adams-ſtreet.

Figure 2.1
The Boston Directory of 1789, which contained a comprehensive list of the city's
merchants and distinguished citizens.

Consumers leave a trail of marketing information behind with each swipe of a credit card. The advent of e-commerce over the Internet has enormously expanded opportunities for buyers and sellers to meet, in a manner of speaking, and to exchange information.

But having a meeting place, in cyberspace or in the physical world, is only part of input. Much of the information exchange that the market is processing doesn't take place at the point of a potential transaction between a buyer and seller. A cautionary aside from one townsman to another—that Butcher A doesn't give honest weight, and you're better off with Butcher B—is a significant piece of market-oriented information, even though the exchange may take place miles from either butcher shop. Sellers provide information to potential buyers at every opportunity, regardless of where the buyer is located at any moment or whether there is a likelihood of an immediate transaction occurring. A patient reading *Sports Illustrated* or *People* in a doctor's waiting room isn't likely, during his visit, to buy a car, a bottle of cologne, or a dress advertised in the magazine. Nevertheless, the advertiser hopes that the information provided by the ads will influence future purchases.

The completion of a transaction between buyer and seller is one of the most information-rich events in the world of commerce. Each transaction is a market signal that Product X has been sold at Price Y. Beyond that, a host of other pieces of data survive the transaction to enter the vast information stream of human commerce.

Perhaps as importantly, the *failure* to complete a transaction creates another category of information that is processed by the marketplace writ large. It is hard to think of a non-event as generating information, but each consumers' decision to not buy is a market signal that Product X isn't readily sellable at Price Y. Unsold inventory at the end of a selling season tells as much of a story as do empty warehouse shelves.

Many different types of information influence the actions of buyers and sellers in the marketplace. But only a few major conduits bring the information forward:

Principal actors   The individuals involved in the marketplace bring their personal knowledge to a transaction. At its most basic, the information involved is a straightforward expression of demand ("I want to buy a shirt") and supply ("I have shirts for sale"). But the buyer also brings forward information about his or her desires ("I want a blue shirt," "I want a shirt that says I'm successful," "I don't want to spend more than $100), and the seller offers expertise about the products that best meet the buyer's needs. And buyers have their own expertise ("I'd like a Windsor spread collar and a mitered French cuff), garnered from personal experience and from the knowledge gleaned from other information conduits.

Advertising Information provided by the seller in published form in magazines, billboards, radio, television, websites, and, increasingly, on almost any visible surface in both the real and virtual world, is a major channel for communicating information about products in the marketplace. We are casting "advertising" in the broadest sense, to mean information provided by manufacturers and sellers even when it exists in formats not conventionally thought of as advertising, such as a press release, a conference presentation, or an annual report.

Government information National, state, provincial, and local governments mandate the collection of an enormous quantity of publicly available information that influences marketplace decisions. Some information is directly financial, such as the 10-K financial reports (and a host of other reports) that public companies must file with the Securities and Exchange Commission or the Form 990 that charities must file with the Internal Revenue Service. Local governments collect—and make public—information on mortgages and property taxes. Banks undergo required financial health checkups. Non-financial information too can be an important influence; for example, a finding by the US Food and Drug Administration that a salmonella outbreak originated from a specific processing plant can immediately and powerfully affect the sales and the stock price of the company that owns the plant.

Third-party information Information comes to the marketplace from myriad non-government sources not directly tied to a transaction at hand. *Consumer Reports*, Angie's List, the Kelly Blue Book, a friend's opinion, an analyst's report, and the opinions and experiences reflected in the billions of users' reviews at Amazon.com and elsewhere on the Internet are all sources of third-party information.

Buying a Laptop Computer

Consider the way the aforementioned conduits provide information, and how the information moves through the marketplace, during a single transaction. We have chosen as our example the sale of a laptop computer, though we could as easily have chosen the sale of a house, a car, a shirt, or a few hours of cleaning service. The role that aggregated information plays in the decision to make a purchase, and in the aftermath of the purchasing decision, is intricate, elusive, and hugely important.

The parties involved in buying and selling the computer have already processed an enormous amount of information well before a sale takes place. First, the would-be buyer has identified a want. He is aware of computers and of what they can do; he knows his own desires as, say, a gamer, a writer, a photographer, a music enthusiast, or a spreadsheet analyst; and he recognizes the contribution that a laptop computer can make to fulfilling those desires. He has mentally considered the amount of money he can spend, the type of tasks he performs, the performance and capabilities he needs, peripheral attachments, the overall look and feel he is after, and the cachet that some brand names seem to carry. (He also brings to the process a lifetime of culturally accrued information about shopping, including what money is and how to value it; shoppers forced to deal with an foreign currency quickly come to appreciate how much information they are lacking in dealing with an unfamiliar money system.)

Details about the computer—the ultimate object of the transaction— make up only one category of information that has to be compiled. The buyer has also processed large amounts of data on where to make his purchase, selecting one big-box store, online merchant, or small business from numerous options. The choice brings to bear facts and impressions from previous technology purchases, other purchases, information from advertising, suggestions from friends, family and colleagues, and considerations of convenience and access.

The seller also has processed enormous quantities of information to decide what machines to carry, what equipment packages to offer, what software to bundle, what price points to set, and which computers warrant prime display space in a store window, on a website, or in a Sunday advertising flyer. The mere fact of a buyer and a seller coming together for a potential sale, whether in a store or in cyberspace, already represents a wealth of information that has flowed through and been processed by actors in the market long before a transaction takes place.

Once a sale has been made, however, additional information flows are created and additional information processing occurs. The buyer's experience with the machine (and with its related features like software, technical support, peripherals) forms the basis for his comfort or discomfort with the system and influences his decision to buy a similar model or a different model in the future. The buyer may even cancel the sale altogether and return the computer to the merchant, creating an information footprint for a failed transaction. The merchant uses the information from the sale of this particular laptop as data feeding into her decision whether to restock that model (if it is moving well), to offer an upgraded computer (if newer models with faster chips are available), or to not reorder that model (if sales have been slow or returns have been high). Examining other sales data, the merchant also perceives broader trends, such as a shift from laptops to tablet computers and smartphones.

Much more happens between buyer and seller that expands and reinforces the flow of information. Additional items may be offered at the point of sale, such as a service package for the computer or auxiliary gear. The seller may collect phone, address, and email information to allow future communication and entice further purchases with an offer of points or special discounts; the offers may be custom tailored to the buyer on the basis of his or her previous buying habits. A cookie quietly embedded on the computer the buyer used to make an online purchase may provide a continuing stream of information to the seller about the buyer.

People other than the buyer and the seller are involved. The manufacturer of the computer records the sale and uses that information—along with data on millions of other sales—to make decisions about inventory, manufacturing schedules, technologies to adopt or abandon in future models, prices, geographical distribution, and other things. For a sale made by credit card, the credit-card company is also part of the information flow, and uses the data to understand current patterns of consumers' behavior and anticipate future trends. Auxiliary services, such as software vendors or wireless providers, may also be involved in the transactional flow of information. The seller may provide the buyer's information to third parties that then process the data further and send targeted solicitations (as the third party may see it) or spam, junk mail, and annoying phone calls (as the buyer may see it).

The information processing that has taken place has been carried out in the brains of individuals involved in the transaction; by stores, manufacturers, and software providers that provide the item for sale; by financial institutions that handle aspects of the transaction; and by dozens of other market participants that are involved, however tangentially, in the production, display, promotion, sale, and customer relations surrounding that particular computer. The thousands upon thousands of individual information processors, whether brains or machines, are linked together into the metaprocessor that we call the marketplace.

Perhaps nothing about the above description of an ordinary transaction is very startling, but neither is it trivial. The old saying has it that money makes the world go round, but it's really information making the world turn—including, of course, information about money. Dollars, euros, yen, rupees, and riyal are the molecules of economic activity, but the atoms are the infinite bits and pieces of information that make it possible.

When Information Is Missing, Out of Balance, or Built on Lies

The successes of the information-handling capabilities of the capitalist marketplace notwithstanding, there are also profound information failures in the marketplace.

As in any information-processing system, the quality of the data input is important. The marketplace as information processor is no more immune to the GIGO phenomenon—garbage in, garbage out—than the computer as information processor. In the 1960s that aphorism cautioned computer programmers that their number crunching would produce outputs that were, at best, only as trustworthy as the data that had been entered into the system in the first place. Faulty or spotty information on ground temperature, for example, will result in a faulty weather forecast, no matter how powerful the supercomputer crunching the numbers, or how sophisticated the software making the prediction.

So it is in the world of commerce. Imperfect data about commercial supply, consumer demand, and the in-between steps that make commerce possible can lead to failures in the smooth functioning of the market. The failure can be spectacular and obvious. The collapse of the market in subprime mortgages, which triggered a widespread, long-lasting recession, was largely a GIGO problem (brokers even referred to some types of mortgages as "liar loans", a direct acknowledgment that the information on the loan applications was unreliable). So was the spectacular demise of the Enron Corporation. But even the everyday marketplace, the selling and buying of bananas and blue jeans, will suffer if the information flow isn't somehow "right."

For a long time, economists studying the functioning of markets sidestepped the issue of data quality by assuming that the market operated with perfect or nearly perfect information. Authors sometimes qualified their economic treatises with caveats along the lines of "of course, there's no such thing as perfect information," but market information was assumed to be close enough to the ideal to avoid any major malfunctions. That assumption was important to economists because getting the information right meant that the market worked efficiently, making the best possible use of available resources, and getting the distribution of products and prices right. Capitalism got the information right, which was why it can produce an abundance of shoes, wood screws, and other consumer goods. Communism got it wrong. Or so the prevailing wisdom went.

Joseph Stiglitz (with several others) was awarded the Nobel Prize in Economics in 2001 for his contribution to Information Economics, a field that began to question whether the machinery of the market really was getting the right sort of information fuel. The engine, from Stiglitz's point of view, was running a lot rougher than it should, as he noted in his Nobel Prize lecture:

For more than a hundred years, formal modeling in economics has focused on models in which information was perfect. Of course, everyone recognized that information was in fact imperfect, but the hope, following Marshall's dictum "Natura non facit saltum" was that economies in which information was not too imperfect would look very much like economies in which information was perfect. One of the main results of our research was to show that this was not true; that even a small amount of information imperfection could have a profound effect on the nature of the equilibrium ... .

Boiled down to its essence, the meaning here is that we have long assumed that we get the information right in the marketplace, or at least close enough to right to make for an efficiently functioning marketplace. Stiglitz's point was that the market doesn't get things right as often as we might suppose, and getting it wrong can mean trouble. At the danger of stretching the engine metaphor a bit too far, we can liken an economic market with faulty informration to a car with bad gasoline; it may be able to make the trip, but with a whole lot of unnecessary coughing, pinging, and sputtering along the way.

In the same lecture, Stiglitz noted the near-invisibility of economists' assumptions about information:

[T]he standard proofs of these fundamental theorems of welfare economics did not even list in their enumerated assumptions those concerning information: the perfect information assumption was so ingrained it did not have to be explicitly stated.

This reinforces a theme we noted earlier: that information has emerged from the shadows in economics as in many other fields. What was once an unacknowledged assumption in economic theory became, through the work of Joseph Stiglitz, George Akerlof, and others, a topic of fundamental significance to the discipline: Information with a capital I.

No one takes the concept of perfect information seriously; perfect information is self-evidently impossible. But even when we restrict ourselves to the notion that the market is driven by "good enough" information , rather than perfect information, we are still left with the question "What does good enough information look like?" When we consider not only transaction X between parties A and B but also billions of transactions between billions of parties, what information must come forward in all these transactions in order for the market to operate at its best? It's a difficult question to answer, though we will take a crack at it later in the book. The converse question is much more approachable: "What does information that isn't good enough look like?"

One needn't have a degree in economics to recognize profoundly imperfect information in ordinary marketplace transactions. Common sense will do quite nicely. The seller of a used car may neglect to mention a slow oil leak. The seller of a house may neglect to mention the wet spots that appear on the basement walls every time it rains. A patient visiting a doctor for a specialized medical procedure isn't likely to learn that the doctor has been the subject of twelve malpractice suits for the very same procedure.

Even when information is forthcoming, it is often far from "perfect" in any common-sense view of the term because of the information's complexity. Shoppers can find endless technical specifications for various computers but still face enormous confusion as to the comparability of Computer

A and Computer B, and enormous uncertainty in choosing one over the other.

All actors in the market have their own examples of faulty, incomplete, or confounding information acting as an obstacle to making good choices. A landlord wondering about the reliability of a potential tenant, a home buyer wondering if she has found all the faults in her "as is" home purchase, a Walmart shopper hoping the packaged socks he just bought are comfortable and don't have the bumpy seam at the toes that made the last socks he purchased unwearable—all these market participants are grappling with information that falls short of "good enough" for making a well-informed decision. From an economist's perspective, these situations all contribute to a market operating at suboptimal efficiency. Prices are wrong, the supply of goods doesn't respond well to consumers' demand, and more people could be made better off without anyone becoming less well off (the very essence of economic efficiency).

It is easy to imagine the damage that an individual participant in the market can suffer when missing or incorrect information leads him to rent to the wrong tenant or buy the wrong house. But among our examples it's the uncomfortable socks that most hint at how poor information affects the market. If consumers were fully informed that certain socks were almost unwearable, far fewer people would buy those socks unless the price were to decrease precipitously, in which case some might be tempted to pick them up for use as cleaning rags or as material for sock puppets. Manufacturers, in turn, would have a clear signal from the market that unwearable socks aren't a particularly hot consumer item in terms of demand or profitability. But in the absence of full information, the consumer is drawn to the lower price of the socks and discovers that their quality is low only after the socks have been removed from their packaging and worn for a while. These socks, too, would tend to disappear from the market after a while, except for the fact that a change of packaging and a change of brand name allows their continued sale, without an opportunity for a consumer to recognize them as the same poor products he purchased earlier. The consumer is back to a "garbage in" scenario, because the information associated with earlier purchases is lost when the socks are re-branded.

The example of the socks, though perhaps oversimplified, isn't trivial. The break in the information chain renders the market somewhat impotent by creating a disconnect between manufacturers and consumers.

It is a small step toward Sovietization of the market: Goods are supplied because available manufacturing capacity and materials means they can be supplied, without apparent attention to product quality or responsiveness to consumers' satisfaction. However, it is a step taken without the bureaucratization of the market that was so characteristic of the Soviet economy. For an example of such bureaucratization, let us turn our attention to health care.

3   Health Care Viewed through the Lens of Information

Viewed through the lens of information, participants in the American health-care system have different but overlapping needs, and have different but overlapping frustrations when it comes to meeting those needs.

Patients seek information on their medical condition, be it an infectious disease or a broken bone, in terms of underlying causes, test results, diagnosis, seriousness, conventional treatment options, alternative treatments, and prognosis. Increasingly, patients also want information about the doctors treating them—Who has the most experience with this disease? Who has the best bedside manner? Who won't keep me for three hours in the waiting room? And information about individual practitioners has an institutional analogue: Patients want to know the track record and expected costs of hospitals and clinics. There is also a bewildering mix of administrative information: Is the doctor in my insurance network? Is this procedure covered? Do I need a referral? How many visits am I permitted? How much will all this cost?

For each question in each of the aforementioned areas, the answers can be agonizingly elusive. Symptoms may present themselves with no obvious link to a specific ailment. Finding the "right" doctor may first mean a score of visits to the "wrong" doctor; the same is true for finding the "right" hospital. Understanding insurance requirements sometimes seems to call for a PhD in the topic, and even then it's anyone's guess what the final bill will be for any sort of substantial medical procedure.

Doctors have their own set of informational frustrations. Perhaps the biggest is the sheer challenge of keeping up with medical information in one's specialty at a time when so many disparate sources of information— from disciplines as far-flung as genomics, pharmaceutics, imaging, diagnostics, prosthetics, and nutrition—increasingly come to have a bearing on the specialty. The information-management requirements of insurance companies and government programs—particularly the trend toward electronic medical record keeping—are often seen as burdensome and unproductive. Even worse, some doctors see electronic medical records as a means of limiting physician choice and patient options regarding the preferred course of treatment, since doctors will gravitate toward treatments or medicines pre-listed in the records database, rather than opting for a treatment option that isn't listed, and that may require special justification and added bureaucratic hurdles.

Pharmacists, nurses, insurers, government agencies, medical laboratories, and all others involved in delivering or overseeing health care have extensive information-collection and information-management responsibilities. Each profession relies on information for appropriate decision making, and each has its own particular set of complaints about the difficulties encountered in obtaining needed information and in complying with data-management requirements that seem cumbersome, excessive, and an obstacle to the primary goal of providing health care.

From a marketplace perspective, health care is an odd duck. Price—the great driver of consumer decision making—hardly seems to enter the equation in choices about health care. Doctors, pharmacists, and hospitals don't, as a rule, post price lists for their products and services. Indeed, they would be hard pressed to do so, as each customer (that is, each patient) is faced with a different set of costs depending on whether he is insured, on his insurance company, on the type of coverage, on prior deductibles, and, at times, on his ability to pay. Even if a price list were to be compiled and made available, the difficulty for a layperson of understanding medicalese would limit its usefulness for many types of medical services. And what price point would patients gravitate toward? Patients "shopping" for health care don't always apply the sort of calculus one expects from consumers, and are often motivated by a money-is-no-object mentality when the objective of an economic transaction is restoring health or saving lives.

The American health-care system is broken in several important ways. Efforts at reform have been under way for decades and will no doubt continue in the decades ahead. Asking why the system is broken is likely to elicit a wide variety of responses: that the fault lies with greedy pharmaceutical companies, with overly meddlesome insurance companies, with ludicrous awards in medical malpractice suits, with burdensome government regulations, with our inability to make end-of-life decisions, with patients demanding excessive tests and medicines, or with any combination of the above. Without diminishing the significance of any of these factors, we are compelled to add one more that is generally not expressed: The health-care system suffers from profound information failures at every stage of administration and delivery.

In chapter 2 we laid out the central role of information in a capitalist economy. We emphasized that improving the flow of information improves the overall efficiency of the marketplace in a way that is more responsive to important human values. How does this perspective—the intersection of markets, information, efficiency, and values—manifest itself in the modern health-care marketplace?

The American health-care system is overlain by several large bureaucratic systems, the two largest being the $1,000-billion-a-year government-run Medicare/Medicaid system and the $960-billion-a-year private health insurance industry.[1] These bureaucracies operate as authoritative centralized systems mediating the interactions between those who provide health care and those who are in need of it. They "manage" the health-care system, striving to balance multiple competing goals: providing acceptable care, preventing unnecessary treatments, allocating scarce resources, and controlling overall costs. Health-care providers are highly regulated and are constrained in the type of services they can offer, the procedures they must follow, and the records they must keep. The result is neither a free-market system nor nationalized health care but an odd hybrid system, neither fish nor fowl. From the perspective of the type of automatic and efficient large-scale information processing that the capitalist market does so well, the health-care system is a huge mess. Not that there is a shortage of information! Far from it. But the attempts to actively manage and utilize health-care data suffer from some of the shortcomings of the old Soviet efforts to consciously design systems to manufacture shoes or screws using the data at hand, rather than stepping back and letting the market process the information.

Everyone has had experiences and frustrations with health care. Many of the frustrations are tightly linked to the misfiring of the machinery of information flow.

Consider the informational challenges presented by the following situations:

• A patient enters a hospital for an operation and wants to know in advance what the costs of treatment will be.
• The patient receives a bill from the hospital and has difficulty deciphering the cost items on the bill.
• The patient pays the bill in full, only to receive several follow-up bills indicating that more is owed.

At each step, there is little or no opportunity for marketplace dynamics to function in a conventional manner, since health care is such an atypical market sector.

Participants in the American health-care system will readily recognize these scenarios, whether they have been involved in major operations or minor treatments. The difficulties encompassed by these situations arise from a multitude of factors, among them the complexity of medicine; the inability to predict a precise course of treatment; the competing interests of doctors, patients, insurers, and government programs in defining costs; and the ambiguity of health-care coverage and benefits. The result is an almost endlessly variable yet very familiar set of situations in which missing, unreliable, or confounding information about the cost of medical services acts as a bottleneck to the system's overall efficiency.

But information bottlenecks don't affect only cost information. They occur at every stage of health-care transactions, and they affect every actor in the health-care market. We will list a few more as an illustration of the breadth of the phenomena:

• a mother wondering how her child's pediatrician ranks in comparison with other pediatricians in the area
• an employee faced with choosing among several health plans, and numerous options within each plan, and trying to select the one that is best for his family
• a patient, advised to have a medical test, wondering if the test is really needed or if the doctor is ordering it out of habit, from fear of a lawsuit, or as a result of an undisclosed financial tie to the testing group
• a doctor unsure whether a patient's request for prescription Oxycontin stems from the painful condition reported by the patient or from an addictive need for that habit-forming medication

• an adult patient who needs to know her childhood medical history but has no idea where the decades-old records are kept, if they are kept anywhere at all.

In each of the above-mentioned situations, and in countless other routine transactions in the health-care system, the participants are dealing with information that is incomplete, inaccessible, indecipherable, or wildly out of balance. It is far from the sort of "good enough" information—information meant to approximate the economic ideal of perfect information— that economists suppose is needed for a smoothly functioning market.

In health care, almost all transactions between the end consumer and the service provider are mediated through a third entity—an insurance company and Medicare/Medicaid in the United States, national health-care systems in other countries. In addition, there are large bureaucracies that oversee huge portions of the health-care system. In the United States, the Food and Drug Administration regulates medicines and medical equipment; the Patent and Trademark Office provides long-term marketplace protection for patented drugs, which are also eligible for additional legal protection known as "exclusivity"; the Department of Veterans Affairs oversees services for millions of veterans; the Drug Enforcement Administration restricts the distribution of controlled substances; and medical

3590357	BONE WAX W31G	1	21.70
3590404	SUT VIC 0 J840D	1	52.70
3590756	VITOSS FOAM STRIP 1105	2	3,518.00
3590779	HW TRANS-1	1	6,590.00
3591064	SUT PDS II 1 D-8020	2	186.20
3591164	BONE GFT INFUSE 7510100	1	3,452.00
3592208	INST PROC GENESIS	4	788.00
3593615	SOLN NACL IRRIG 7138-36	1	11.70
3593652	CLIP APPLIER MCS/MSM	1	331.10
3593679	STAPLER SKIN	1	155.80
3593767	TRAY FOLEY 16F W URIMETER	1	61.89
3594582	KYPHX OSTEO INTR SYS T05D	1	2,672.60
3594821	BOVIE CORD DUAL US349SP	2	71.00
3594822	SURGICEL FIBRILLAR 1962	1	356.80
3595004	SURG OR LVL 4	1	8,014.10
3597001	PACK NEURO SNE43NSRSDA	1	400.10
3598097	INST PROC ACCESSORY	4	788.00
3598146	HW SPINAL USA (ENDIUS)	1	13,960.00
3650006	PACU LVL 2 1ST HR	1	856.00
3754796	STOCKING SCD KNEE LENGTH	1	118.40
3754886	SET IV MMED CHECKVAC 265	2	60.00

Figure 3.1

A portion of an itemized hospital bill, as detailed in a 2011 *Wall Street Journal* article.

personnel are licensed by state certification boards and vetted by industry organizations such as the American Medical Association. These many entities, well intentioned as they are, act as an artificial barrier to self-adjusting prices and services. Medicines and medical devices can't come into the market without extensive regulatory compliance and oversight, which impose substantial barriers to entry and limit the opportunities for products to compete in an open market. Extended patent protection for drugs and devices reduces competitive opportunities even further. Prices of pharmaceuticals and other supplies can't self-adjust in an international marketplace, because artificially low costs in some countries in national health-care systems with price controls, or for HIV drugs in impoverished African countries—make for countervailing increases in others.

Prices for medical services vary greatly, without clear rhyme or reason, according to the mandates of a particular insurance program, the financial needs of the organization charging for the service, the ability of the patient to pay, and, quite possibly, the whim of the service provider on any particular day. Indeed, a single entity, such as a hospital, typically has one set of prices in its internal "chargebook," another set for Medicare, another for individual insurance plans (which may have negotiated specific discounts), and still others charged to individual, uninsured patients; is it any wonder that "price shopping" for medical services is nearly impossible? A 2014 study of hospital charges found that a simple blood test for cholesterol varied in price from $10 to $10,169. Though that difference was extreme, it wasn't unusual to find charges that varied by a factor of 100 or more from one hospital to another. The constraints of the modern health-care market make it almost impossible for the marketplace to function in a "sensible" manner.

We aren't advocating making health care more market oriented by removing the constraints. No sensible person would propose a system of health care that didn't have an FDA-like entity or state medical boards to keep things safe. Instead, we are simply acknowledging what seems a self-evident truth: that health care doesn't take place in a conventionally "efficient" marketplace and thus isn't a particularly effective information processor. Our attempts to view the health-care system from a market perspective and from an information perspective are attempts to gain an understanding of some of the strengths and weaknesses of the system, with an eye toward how it can be improved.

Recall the shoes and the screws and the Five-Year Plans of the USSR and ask yourself if American health care is closer to the over-bureaucratized Soviet system or to the freewheeling capitalism of the Western world. There certainly is a built-in cumbersome quality to American health care that leaves one wondering. For all the near-miraculous accomplishments that modern medicine is sometimes capable of, the health-care system, over-all, still has enormous difficulty responding to consumers' demand. On any Sunday afternoon, we can shop for groceries, go to a movie, or meet a friend at the coffee shop. But try to find a doctor! Health care has been singularly unable to respond to that obvious need.

Slowly, almost painfully, the American health-care system is trying to innovate, with the (seemingly market-driven) emergence of urgent-care centers, nurses' stations in chain-store pharmacies, "concierge medicine," and even a few physicians here and there willing to make house calls. We take this as an encouraging sign of the system's increasing responsiveness to market signals. But participants in the health-care marketplace—whether as patients, as health-care providers, as insurers, as laboratories, or as phar-macists—aren't likely to use the word 'efficient' when describing the overall system.

Information Shortcomings: Finding a Doctor

What is the connection between health-care dysfunction and information dysfunction? With so many layers to health care, and so many facets to information, there is no straightforward way to paint a comprehensive pic-ture. But we can glean some insights from grabbing a tail here and an ear there, in the hopes of putting together an overall image of the entire beast, even if it's a sketchy image at best.

The practice of medicine, by necessity, entails a profoundly asymmet-ric information relationship, with health-care providers and insurers pos-sessing far more medical knowledge, more jargon, and more information about the workings of the overall system than do the patients they serve. Decades ago, when patients were likely to turn medical decision making over to their doctors almost completely, the built-in information imbal-ance may not have seemed problematic. But in the current era, with activist patients Googling their every symptom, the information asymmetry is a more apparent issue. Patients struggle to make sense of disease descriptions, biological mechanisms, pharmaceutical activity, treatment options, billing codes, test results, and a lot of related information that medical professionals have spent much of their lives acquiring. As every episode of the television drama *House* made clear, the knowledge imbalance between doctor and patient is profound.

But the imbalance stems only in part from the inherent difficulty of the subject of medicine. Our technological devices are also complicated. A consumer shopping for a new phone or computer often may be at a substantial disadvantage relative to the techie at the Genius Bar, who knows far more about the products than the shopper does. But the complexities notwithstanding, one still has the sense that the technology marketplace works more or less as we expect marketplaces to work, while the health-care marketplace does not. The difference is that the information asymmetries that exist are made much more pronounced by the inability of the health-care system to provide some of the most basic forms of marketplace information.

For one thing, there is a very limited option for patients to shop around. Choosing a doctor has none of the competitive market dynamics of buying a computer. Patients generally know very little about the man or woman tending to their health, beyond a certificate on a wall attesting to his or her accreditation. The health-care system relies on the certification process to ensure that a doctor has the requisite skills, experience, and knowledge to tend to patients. In essence, the various certifications and degrees hanging on the wall of a doctor's office are meant to convey an overall message to patients—something along the lines of "There is no need to delve into your doctor's background, qualifications, or experience, because we have already done that for you, and can attest to his competency." In this respect, patients are a bit like the Scottish bankers of Adam Smith's day, relying on an information proxy to gauge creditworthiness rather than conducting a full-fledged and ongoing investigation of each potential borrower. But the comparison doesn't extend very far. The information proxy for doctors provides only a single piece of information: that this person is, in fact, a doctor.[2] Nothing more than this is offered up—no measures of outcomes, records of complaints, access to malpractice files, assessments by peers, or feedback from other patients—no ranking information of any kind.

Imagine the modern credit-rating system working that way, and that instead of a sliding scale of risk and creditworthiness—one that assigns scores and provides detailed credit reports—lenders got only a single Yes/No piece of reference data. In such a limited information milieu, the modern lending system would be little more than a shadow of itself. Credit would be much less freely available and much more expensive, even for those who rated a Yes from the system, since lending would be skewed toward a presumption that a Yes client was at the most risky rather than the least risky end of the scale. For the No portion of the population, credit costs would be even more astronomical than the most expensive of today's "payday loan" lending businesses—if credit were available at all.

In other words, the information bottleneck chokes off the entire credit system, making it far less efficient and far less responsive to consumers' needs. The system of supply and demand stops functioning, or at best doesn't function well, as the demand for credit isn't met with a commensurate supply. Price doesn't self-regulate the way it does in a smoothly functioning market. Not only the business of lending but the entire economy suffers as a result as credit becomes more difficult to come by, more expensive when it is available, and more cumbersome to obtain even to those who can afford it.

Sound familiar? Health care drags down the economy as well, not because it is so expensive (spending, after all, is what drives the economy forward), but because it has inherent difficulty becoming less expensive, more productive, more streamlined, and more responsive to the needs of those who require the services the system provides. Without fuller information, competition resembling that between McDonald's and Burger King isn't functional. Without robust competition—that great driver toward ever-increasing economic efficiency—another mechanism has to come forward to keep the health-care system on its toes.

Again, we should point out that we aren't advocates of a purely market-driven health-care system. But we do suppose that the overall system is capable of functioning much more efficiently, and that better information tools can be the key to achieving that efficiency. Take the selection of a doctor as an example. In some respects, the health-care system treats doctors as entirely fungible: a pediatrician is a pediatrician is a pediatrician; each one is certified as fully capable of reading a patient's charts, taking a history, providing medicines and vaccinations, making a diagnosis, and recommending a course of treatment. In some situations, the interchangeability of doctors is an asset. A patient on a long stay in a hospital, for example, will be seen by different doctors and nurses on the day, evening, and night shifts and on different days of the week. But new parents needing the services of a pediatrician for the first time may be less sanguine about the "any doctor will do" approach to choosing medical care. They will want to find a doctor not only with good credentials but with a good "style" of practicing medicine.

A patient searching for the best doctor for her particular medical circumstances might turn to the American Medical Association's online Doctor-Finder service, which, the AMA assures visitors, "helps you find a perfect match for your medical needs" by offering quick access to information on more than 800,000 physicians in the United States. The promise of a "perfect match" again raises the specter of "perfect information." But how close to perfect is the AMA's information? From the standpoint of a would-be patient looking for both medical insight and consumer-oriented information, DoctorFinder offers up relatively paltry information in a not especially user-friendly setting.

Each DoctorFinder listing begins with this apparently important caveat:

The information contained in the AMA DoctorFinder report does NOT meet the primary source equivalency requirement as set forth in the credentialing standards of accreditation organizations such as the Joint Commission on the Accreditation of Healthcare Organizations (JCAHO) or the National Committee for Quality Assurance (NCQA) … .

The warning serves as good reminder of the information asymmetry so characteristic of medicine—a service designed specifically for patients begins with a statement that is incomprehensible to virtually all users of the service. Not only does it not convey anything useful to potential patients; it offers up a confounding and jargony message. At best, the wording leaves users who aren't medical professionals with the impression that the information they are about to review is somehow not up to professional standards.

The caveat is followed by a search tool that allows users to search an individual doctor's name, or to generate a list of doctors in a certain area or with a particular specialty, or both. You can pull up an individual doctor's record, which is largely a simple name/city/phone number listing for non-AMA members and a somewhat more extensive listing for doctors who belong to AMA. This is all useful information, of course, but perfect? It answers some important questions, such as "Who practices in my neighborhood?"

DoctorFinder

The information contained in the AMA DoctorFinder report does NOT meet the primary source equivalency requirement as set forth in the credentialing standards of accreditation organizations such as the Joint Commission on the Accreditation of Healthcare Organizations (JCAHO) or the National Committee for Quality Assurance (NCQA).

██████████, MD (Non-Member)

Primary Specialty (Self Designated)(note):
DERMATOLOGY

Location:
Mountain View, CA 94040

American Board of Medical Specialties Certification:
Copyright 2006 American Board of Medical Specialties. All rights reserved.
Dermatology

Figure 3.2
A Doctor Finder listing for a non-AMA-member physician. (Copyright 1995–2015 American Medical Association. All rights reserved.)

DoctorFinder

The information contained in the AMA DoctorFinder report does NOT meet the primary source equivalency requirement as set forth in the credentialing standards of accreditation organizations such as the Joint Commission on the Accreditation of Healthcare Organizations (JCAHO) or the National Committee for Quality Assurance (NCQA).

██████████, MD ☑AMA member
AMA members must adhere to the AMA's Principles of Medical Ethics

Primary Specialty (Self Designated)
(note): DERMATOLOGY
Gender:
Male
Location:
View Map
Los Angeles, CA 90026

Medical School:
UNIVERSITY OF CALIFORNIA SAN FRANCISCO
SCHOOL OF MEDICINE
Residency Training:
LOS ANGELES COUNTY-HARBOR-
UCLA, *DERMATOLOGY*
LOS ANGELES COUNTY-HARBOR-
UCLA,*ANATOMIC/CLINICAL PATHOLOGY*
CHILDREN'S HOSPITAL OF PHILADE, *PEDIATRICS*
Major Professional Activity:
OFFICE BASED PRACTICE
**American Board of Medical Specialties
Certification:**
Copyright 2006 American Board of Medical
Specialties. All rights reserved.
Dermatology

Figure 3.3
A Doctor Finder listing for an AMA-member physician. (Copyright 1995–2015 American Medical Association. All rights reserved.)

"What is the doctor's telephone number?" and (for AMA members) "Where did the doctor go to medical school?" But it offers very little information for answering a question that is likely to be on the minds of most patients: "Which doctor is better for my particular medical condition?" The doctor's specialty is identified, which certainly helps. For the subset of doctors who are AMA members, there is also potentially useful information about educational background and hospital affiliations. But none of this information really gets at the question "How good is this guy?" Nor is there likely to be a standardized set of data points that could answer that question, since 'good' means so many different things in different circumstances—for example, the doctor with the most education about my condition X, or the most experience treating patients with X, or the best outcomes regarding X, or the most amenable "bedside" manner; or the most affordable one; or the one with the shortest waiting time; or one open to non-traditional interventions; or one who is a member of my racial, ethnic, or religious group who can empathize with my particular world view; or a combinations of any or all of the above.

The AMA isn't alone in offering a limited information portal on doctors. Individual insurance companies generally provide similar look-up services for doctors within the insurance network (though their ability to keep the lists up to date generally leaves something to be desired). For users, it is relatively easy to generate directory-style listings that identify doctors practicing a particular specialty or located within a certain distance from one's home or office, but finding meaningful information on the quality of the doctor's practice is difficult.

Commercial services that provide information on individual doctors and dentists have stepped into the void. Some geographically oriented magazines periodically publish lists of the "top" practitioners—two examples are *Washingtonian*'s Best Cosmetic Surgeons in Washington and *New York*'s Top 1,282 Physicians of 2015. Though it isn't always clear how the magazines arrive at their ratings, many of them ask doctors to identify the best of their colleagues in various fields of practice—the practitioners they would choose if in need.

Websites with doctor rankings are also becoming more common. The sites generally provide some or all of the information found in directories—type of practice, location, contact, insurance—and also provide ratings of some sort. (Indeed, the name of one of the more popular sites is RateMDs.)

The ratings take the form of feedback from patients that have used the doctors' services. According to the FAQ page of RateMDs,

The purpose of the site is to be a resource for people who want to find a good doctor or dentist. Where else can you find out what others think of your doctor? When choosing a doctor, wouldn't you like some information first? It also gives you, the patient, a place to voice your opinion. Your opinion will help others find good doctors and dentists … .

The opinion-based information at RateMDs is similar in format to what one finds at Amazon.com for consumer products or at RottenTomatoes.com for movies. And as with those other sites, the ratings and reviews can be quite helpful, in the aggregate, even if an individual review is an untrustworthy attempt to stuff the ballot box with overly positive feedback or to smear a competitor with exaggerated or invented complaints. RateMDs uses several mechanisms to minimize the posting of unreliable content, and to offer doctors the opportunity to respond to a negative posting, to "flag" it as likely to be unreliable, or to ask for its removal.

Dr. Mark Mausner
Cosmetic Surgeon / Plastic Surgeon
★ ★ ★ ★ ★
28 reviews

Dr. Mark Mausner's Latest Rating
I am a former patient of Dr.Mausner and I just called his office to schedule a consultation for an additional procedure. I was shocked and saddened to receive a rec... Read more

Dr. A. Dean Jabs ✓
Cosmetic Surgeon / Plastic Surgeon
★ ★ ★ ★ ⯨
36 reviews

Dr. A. Dean Jabs's Latest Rating
I am deeply grateful to Dr Jabs for my new appearance. I used to have undereye bags that were beautifully corrected by him. My friends tell me how natural my eyes l... Read more

Dr. Roger J. Oldham ✓
Cosmetic Surgeon / Plastic Surgeon
★ ★ ★ ★ ★
7 reviews

Figure 3.4
Examples of RateMDs.com search results and doctor rankings.

The medical community has taken notice. A review of doctor-ranking sites published in the *Journal of General Internal Medicine* in 2012 found that most of the posted reviews were positive, emphasizing the quality of care and service provided by both the physician and his or her staff.[3] A separate review of several thousand negative postings reported that complaints about customer service and poor "bedside manner" were four times as common as concerns about a doctor's skill at medicine.

It remains to be seen whether online services such as RateMDs will be able to fully satisfy consumers' desire for more and better information on health-care providers. No rating sites that we are aware of yet rise to the level needed to fully serve the public, lacking comprehensive coverage of the medical profession, trustworthiness of the information provided, or both.

Even if a site manages to overcome the hurdles just mentioned, there will still be three important areas of missing information when it comes to making a well-informed choice about medical care.

The first area is cost. As much as patients might like to know how much a doctor, a dentist, or a hospital charges for a particular service, the obscurities and vagaries of the medical-insurance complex make transparency of costs an elusive objective. An occasional RateMDs review might mention a particular doctor's "reasonable" rates—a not unhelpful piece of feedback. Sites may also make use of symbols popularized by restaurant reviews—$, $$, or $$$, representing inexpensive, average, and expensive services as judged by patients. But ranking sites aren't likely to provide cost information any more specific than that, lacking access to detailed cost information.

Second, information on the quality of medical care and medical outcomes is even more difficult to obtain. A patient about to receive, say, a knee replacement, would certainly be interested to know the surgeon's overall "success rate"—the percentage of patients that experience trouble-free recovery in the short term and long-term relief from whatever knee problems prompted the surgery in the first place. Even more to the point, the patient would want to know how the individual doctor's record compares with the universe of knee-replacement surgeons. Similarly, a patient about to undergo root-canal treatment for a troublesome tooth would do well to have information on the particular dental specialist's success rate for avoiding post-operative problems, such as an incompletely removed nerve or a post-procedure infection, along with a comparison against other specialists in the field. In both the case of knee replacement and that of a root-canal procedure, the information isn't likely to be available to the patient. For the most part, reliable information on outcomes probably isn't available to the practitioner either, since few doctors methodically follow up with patients for the purposes of collecting data on outcomes.

The third area is what we will broadly label *sanctions*. Some doctors are disciplined by their medical boards for practices considered unprofessional. Others may have dealt with a string of malpractice suits have over the years. News organizations periodically run exposés on doctors with troubling histories who haven't had their license revoked, or who have lost a license in one state and then gone on to practice in another. A story in *USA Today* began in fairly typical fashion:

Dr. Greggory Phillips was a familiar figure when he appeared before the Texas Medical Board in 2011 on charges that he'd wrongly prescribed the painkillers that killed Jennifer Chaney.

The family practitioner already had faced an array of sanctions for mismanaging medications—and for abusing drugs himself. Over a decade, board members had fined him thousands of dollars, restricted his prescription powers, and placed his medical license on probation with special monitoring of his practice.

They also let him keep practicing medicine.

What patients wouldn't want to know such information about the Dr. Phillipses of the world before placing themselves in the care of one of them? Yet such information is difficult and sometimes impossible to come by. Malpractice lawsuits are even harder to unearth, particularly when a suit was resolved by agreement between the parties, rather than by a decision of a court, and the results of the suit were sealed.

Should information on medical sanctions be readily accessible by patients? It strikes us as hard to make any sort of compelling argument for not making such data available, or for not making access to such information as simple as it can be. Yet a confluence of factors—professional resistance, scattershot sources of information, differing formats, difficulties in compiling data, varied precedents for making data public or keeping data private—keep most information on sanctions out of public view.

To repeat what we said earlier, the lack of information to address the questions and concerns of patients as consumers is a bottleneck in the health-care system—a bottleneck that prevents it from behaving more like

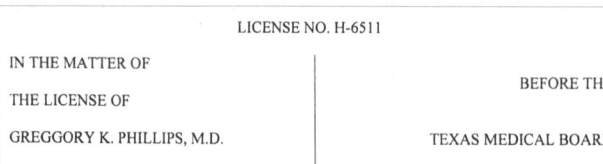

LICENSE NO. H-6511

IN THE MATTER OF

THE LICENSE OF

GREGGORY K. PHILLIPS, M.D.

BEFORE THE

TEXAS MEDICAL BOARD

AGREED ORDER

On the _8th_ day of _February_ , 2013, came on to be heard before the Texas Medical Board (the "Board"), duly in session, the matter of the license of Greggory K. Phillips, M.D. ("Respondent").

Respondent is scheduled for an Informal Show Compliance Proceeding and Settlement Conference ("ISC") on January 23, 2012. However, Respondent has agreed to waive the ISC and instead enter into this Agreed Order. Respondent was represented by Jon Porter. Christopher M. Palazola represented Board staff.

With the consent of Respondent, the Board makes the following Findings and Conclusions of Law and enters this Agreed Order.

BOARD CHARGES

Board staff alleges Respondent prescribed controlled substances to multiple patients without documented medical justification, in violation of the standard of care and Board rules. As such, Board staff alleges the medications were prescribed without adequate evaluation and need. Respondent also prescribed medications, including controlled substances, to family members and close relations in violation of Board rules.

BOARD HISTORY

Respondent has previously been the subject of disciplinary action by the Board as follows:

1.   On October 15, 1999, the Board entered an Order ("1999 Order") suspending Respondent's License and placing him under five years probation due to

Page 1 of 8

Figure 3.5

A portion of a report of a disciplinary action by a state medical board.

a conventional market. If information on patient satisfaction, costs, outcomes, and sanctions were routinely and simply available, each actor in the health-care system would have important incentives to decide how to position his or her practice or institution in a more transparent information milieu. Much as it does in a traditional market, the provision of more and better and readily accessible information would drive continual efficiencies in health care that have yet to be realized.

Hospital Compare

The Medicare program has taken a substantial step forward in consolidating numerous types of health-care data and presenting the information in a manner that is easy to gain access to and to use. The Medicare data pertain to hospitals rather than to individual physicians, but nonetheless offer the beginnings of a model of what a more robust DoctorFinder-type information service might look like.

The Hospital Compare data tool at Medicare.gov provides users a wide variety of metrics on the performance and patient satisfaction at an individual hospital, or as a comparison among several hospitals. After a visitor to the site has selected a hospital or several hospitals, he or she is offered information in a number of categories:

General Information
Survey of Patients' Experiences
Timely and Effective Care
Readmissions, Complications and Deaths
Use of Medical Imaging
Medicare Payment
Number of Medicare Patients

The categories touch on several of the areas we described earlier.

General Information is the equivalent of the DoctorFinder listing—basic identification information for the health-care entity.

The Survey category provides direct rankings based on feedback from patients. (See figure 3.6.)

The Timely and Effective category pertains to level of care offered by the facility. (See figure 3.7.)

Readmissions, Complications and Deaths displays data on medical outcomes in four main subcategories:

30-Day outcomes: Readmission and death rates
Surgical complications
Health-care-associated infections
American College of Cardiology percutaneous coronary intervention (PCI) readmission measure.

Each subcategory offers the same mix of graphical or tabular information as all the others. (See figure 3.8.)

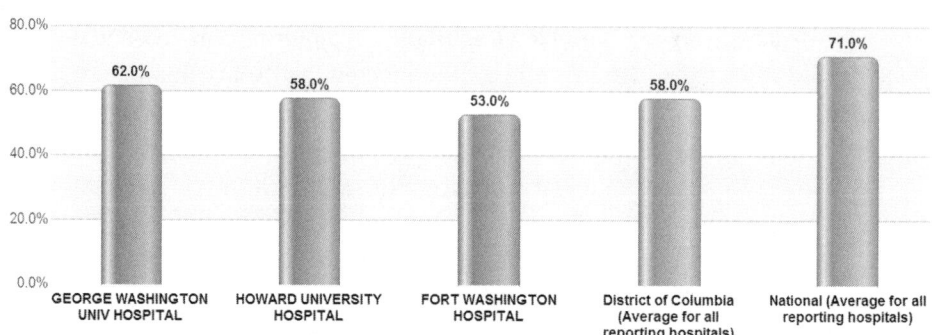

Figure 3.6
Percentages of patients who gave their hospital a rating of 9 or 10 on a scale from 0 to 10.

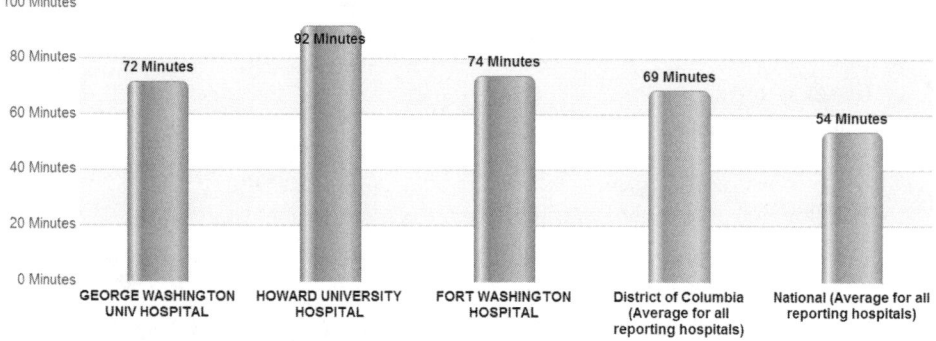

Figure 3.7
Average time patients who came to an energency department with broken bones had to wait before getting pain medication.

The information available through Hospital Compare has obvious utility in providing patients with information about hospitals relative to other hospitals and about individual hospitals relative to regional or national norms. The data are highly informative, although not unambiguously so. Hospitals differ greatly in the communities they serve and the demographics of their patients. An inner-city hospital with a sizable number of gunshot-wound victims and drug overdoses would certainly have different statistical outcomes than a hospital serving a large, suburban geriatric community in an area that attracts retirees. Statistical differences between the

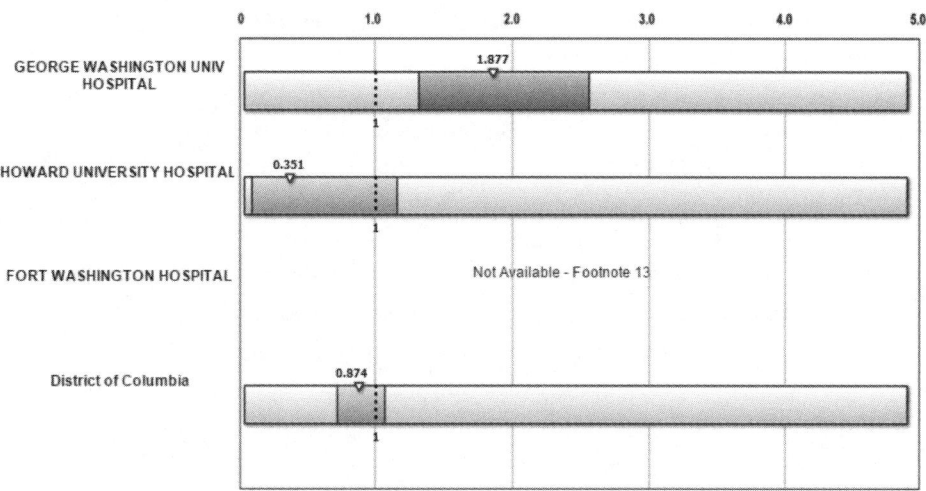

Figure 3.8
Average number of catheter-associated urinary-tract infections at three Washington-area hospitals. (National benchmark for United States is 1.)

hospitals may well be more a reflection of the patient population than of the quality of care provided. Nonetheless, the data that Hospital Compare make available certainly provide prospective patients with some "food for thought" information that can serve as the basis for a well-informed conversation with the patient's primary-care provider regarding which hospital is the best choice.

Hospital Compare is at its least informative when it comes to comparing costs between hospitals. The site offers a difficult-to-find and difficult-to-understand metric on costs, and even once found and understood it is of limited use to many patients. The cost information that Hospital Compare provides is labeled "Spending per Hospital Patient with Medicare" and is described as a measure showing "whether Medicare spends more, less or about the same per Medicare patient treated in a specific hospital, compared to how much Medicare spends per patient nationally." The resulting measure tends to occupy a fairly narrow range of values at most hospitals—probably a testament to Medicare's success at keeping costs relatively uniform throughout its system. The seven Medicare hospitals in the District of Columbia, for example, report per-patient Medicare spending that ranges from 91 percent to 104 percent of the national average for all hospitals.[4] Even for hospitals with larger deviations from the national norm, the information is probably germane mostly to Medicare officials, since it is Medicare that is footing the bill.

For patients, the cost data aren't terribly helpful. For someone not acquainted with the details of the Medicare reimbursement system, the information has limited meaning. Some patients may take the data as a reflection of overall costs and may infer that lower-than-average Medicare costs will translate to lower-than-average costs to the patient. Others may come to the opposite conclusion: that hospitals receiving lower payments from Medicare may try to make up the difference by billing patients excessively. Still others may view the cost information as a proxy for quality of care, and may seek out the costliest hospitals, reasoning that the institutions spending the most are the ones providing the most comprehensive services. More meaningful, from the patient's perspective, would be comparative data on costs borne by the patients themselves; such data, though they exist in the private databases (chiefly of hospitals and insurance companies), are nearly impossible to come by.

Physician Compare

The federal government provides another window into Medicare data at its promising-sounding Physician Compare website. From the name, one might anticipate a site similar to Hospital Compare, with ranking information based on feedback from patients and with comparative statistics on costs, services, and medical outcomes—a system, in other words, that addresses many of the shortcomings of the AMA's Doctor Finder service.

In fact, however, Physician Compare presents rather paltry output, identifying whether a particular doctor participates in any of three Medicare initiatives: electronic health records, electronic prescriptions, and a program called the Physician Quality Reporting System. PQRS certainly sounds as if it may contain useful data on comparative quality of practices, but the Physician Compare site doesn't actually report any PQRS data. Instead, it simply indicates whether a particular doctor participates in that program. None of the information provided is likely to be of significant utility to patients looking for their ideal doctor.

Why such different approaches at the Hospital Compare and Physician Compare websites? The history of reporting Medicare information about individual physicians reflects a complex interplay of a society striving to balance competing interests of many parties: doctors wanting to keep their Medicare data private, medical associations concerned about inaccuracies in the data, investigative journalists seeking to understand a complex and expensive government Medicare program, insurers looking for opportunities to decrease their costs, data-mining firms that provide services to both providers and patients, and of course, patients, hoping to gain some insight into the quality and cost of their care.

The availability of data on individual physicians from both the Medicare and Medicaid programs has fluctuated over the decades. In the 1970s, some information was made public in a manner that identified the doctors charging Medicaid fees well above the national norm. The information shined a spotlight on individual physicians' practices, creating an appearance that some of them were overcharging Medicaid and abusing the reimbursement system. The medical community shot back, pointing out egregious errors in the information, such as naming an individual doctor as the recipient when the amount reported actually represented the income of a group practice.

Lawsuits ensued, many of them filed by the American Medical Association and by state medical groups. In one such case, *Florida Medical Association v. Department of Health, Education and Welfare* (1979), the federal district court in Florida ruled that doctors had the right to keep both their Medicaid information and their Medicare information private, and that a doctor's right to privacy outweighed the public's right to know about the doctor's Medicare records. The decision shut down government releases of information on individual doctors; even requests under the Freedom of Information Act would subsequently be denied. As a result of the court's decision, there was simply no opportunity to use the data to build a Physician Compare website that allowed the use of government-held data to provide a genuine comparison of cost (and other factors) between doctors.

By 2014, the situation had changed abruptly. The federal government announced a "a new policy regarding requests made under the Freedom of Information Act for information on amounts paid to individual physicians under the Medicare program." From then on, the government announced, it would decide on requests for information case by case, weighing the relative merits of releasing the data and keeping them secret. The apparent change of heart stemmed from yet another legal action by Dow Jones & Co., publisher of the *Wall Street Journal*, in a suit asking the court to reverse

Figure 3.9
A headline from the front page of the November 9, 1976 *Washington Post*.

the 1979 *Florida Medical Association v. Department of Health, Education and Welfare* decision. The filing by Dow Jones stated:

Over three decades ago, this court entered an injunction that still serves as a nationwide gag order, severely limiting access to essential information about one of the most important and expensive government programs—Medicare. ... Since 1979, the government ... has closely guarded and withheld from public view multiple databases that are widely considered the best source of information about the disposition of Medicare funds that comprise one-eighth of the total federal budget. One of the databases, the Carrier Standard Analytic File ... is an enormous database of all fee-for-service Medicare Part B claims in the United States. The Carrier File, unique because it contains information about the direct billings of and reimbursements to individual providers, is a key tool for identifying Medicare abuse.

That final sentence, of course, is what Dow Jones was after: unfettered access to a database for the purpose of continuing an investigative series of articles into the inner workings (and alleged failings) of the Medicare system. Dow Jones hoped to continue and expand its investigative series of articles that—even with very limited access to data—uncovered significant waste, fraud, and abuse in the Medicare reimbursement system. The government's 2014 announcement, though, stated that the information in question would be partly available and partly unavailable. It will be up to officials in the Medicare program to decide whether a certain data request is sufficiently in the public interest to warrant a release of information.

Sliver of Medicare Doctors Get Big Share of Payouts

Huge Trove of Health Data Is Disclosed — $21 Million for One Physician in '12

By REED ABELSON and SARAH COHEN

A tiny fraction of the 880,000 doctors and other health care providers who take Medicare accounted for nearly a quarter of the roughly $77 billion paid out to

While total Medicare spending — including hospitals, doctors and drugs — is approaching $600 billion a year, payments to individual doctors have long been

Figure 3.10
A headline and a sub-headline from the front page of the April 9, 2014 *New York Times*.

The tension that led the Medicare program to announce its informational balancing act is the tension between the public's right to know what is in federal files and the protection of an individual doctor's privacy. It is a tension embodied in two laws dealing with information access: the Freedom of Information Act of 1966 and the Privacy Act of 1974. The federal court, in its 1979 decision in *Florida Medical Association v. Department of Health, Education and Welfare*, addressed these laws specifically and came down solidly on the side of the medical community, finding that the release of physician-specific Medicare data would "constitute a clearly unwarranted invasion of personal privacy." In so deciding, the court addressed what had been an ambiguity in the Privacy Act: whether the law applied to individuals as a business in addition to its obvious application to individuals in their private lives.

A more subtle tension in the program's handling of data release is the tension inherent in the question "What entity is the appropriate arbiter of information access?" The federal courts, government agencies, medical associations, and journalists have all wrestled over the issues of access. Missing from the mix are the interests of the general public, a segment of which would certainly value access to such information in a more useful version of a database similar to Physician Compare.

The legal wrangling over access to Medicare information highlights the issues surrounding the release (or non-release) of potentially sensitive data held by the federal government. It serves our purpose, as well, in highlighting the changing information milieu of the past few decades. While consumers can quickly find reviews, price comparisons and records about everything from restaurants and movies to cell phones and frying pans, it can't be said that a very useful information milieu has yet become available in the huge sector of the economy that is health care. Viewed through the lens of a market economy, health care seems to fall short, lacking the efficiency of a smoothly functioning marketplace and lacking the robust flow of information that achieving such efficiency would require.

In the spring of 2014, Medicare did, in fact, opt to release data on payments to individual physicians in response to requests from news organizations. The release was characterized in the press as "10 million lines of data on payments to 880,000 physicians." The sudden availability of new Medicare data after decades provoked a number of familiar responses from the medical community, such as this from the American Medical Association: "Releasing the data without context will likely lead to inaccuracies, misinterpretations, false conclusions and other unintended consequences."

One of the "unintended consequences" of the influx of new information will be a tweaking of the medical marketplace, along the lines we discussed in chapter 2. Consider a few possible (and completely hypothetical) reactions of individual physicians:

I only get a few hundred thousand in Medicare payouts each year; there are doctors receiving millions. I need to find out how to take fuller advantage of the Medicare system.

The doctors getting the most payouts are going to be taking a lot of heat from the government, the press and even their patients. I need to lower my payouts to stay under the radar.

The press is focusing on individual practitioners. Perhaps it's time for me to join a group practice.

No more Medicare patients for me. It's just not worth it.

Ophthalmologists are really raking in the Medicare millions. Maybe I should switch my field of specialty before finishing my education.

This is all a tempest in a teapot. I'll keep doing what I'm doing: taking care of my patients, and submitting Medicare paperwork when needs be.

No matter how any individual doctor responds, the release of the Medicare data will bring about changes to the medical market. Whether the changes will be large or small, or positive or negative, is hard to say. But the availability of new information engenders millions of discrete responses from the actors in the market, each responding according to his or her own value system. The information holds, if not quite the promise, at least the possibility of helping the overall system to achieve better efficiency. A fuller set of information—addressing quality of care, medical outcomes, costs and sanctions, as we described earlier—could lead to an even larger refinement of the entire health-care system.

Nor is it simply the reimbursement data that would bring about a market response. The public availability of Medicare data also provides a wealth of details on an individual physician's medical experience with particular tests and techniques. The *New York Times*, one of the news organizations investigating the 2014 Medicare data release, made the database available for public scrutiny through a simple online interface. Users could enter a doctor's name, or select variables such as ZIP code and medical specialty, to learn not only what the doctor's overall Medicare reimbursements were but also the details of what procedures and services that doctor billed Medicare for.

The desirability of improving the information milieu in health care raises the question of how to bring such improvements about. Medicare's Hospital Compare site consolidated information from multiple sources, providing ready access to information on hospitals in several areas: patient satisfaction, quality of care, outcomes, costs. Is there an entity—or are there multiple entities—that could similarly consolidate information from disparate sources regarding physicians?

Websites such as RateMDs.com take readily available existing information—directories of health-care professionals—and overlay a rating system that allows users to quickly post information about or find feedback on a particular doctor. With a modest amount of effort, such sites could tap into other information sources that are already publicly available—e.g., medical boards' disciplinary actions—and integrate information from those sources into their presentations.

Health-insurance companies have huge databanks of information on costs that could, in principle, be parsed to shed light on who charges how

FRANK S. ASHBURN MD
2013
Ophthalmology
WASHINGTON, D.C.
$591,861 total Medicare reimbursements

Provider's Medicare Services in Detail, 2013
Services **FRANK S. ASHBURN MD** performed on more than 10 patients:

Procedure	Number performed	Number of Medicare patients	Average Medicare reimbursement per procedure	Total Medicare payments for procedure
Removal of cataract with insertion of lens *Surgeries and procedures* CODE: 66984-F	293 Top 20% nationally	196	$579.92	**$169,917**
Eye and medical examination for diagnosis and treatment, established patient, 1 or more visits *Exams and medical services* CODE: 92014-O	1,541 Top 20% nationally	1,443	$95.84	**$147,689**
Eye and medical examination for diagnosis and treatment, established patient *Exams and medical services* CODE: 92012-O	1,305 Top 20% nationally	811	$68.74	**$89,706**
Eye and medical examination for diagnosis and treatment, new patient, 1 or more visits *Exams and medical services* CODE: 92004-O	217 Top 20% nationally	217	$121.14	**$26,287**
Laser repair to improve eye fluid flow *Surgeries and procedures* CODE: 65855-F	86 Top 20% nationally	72	$273.14	**$23,490**

Figure 3.11

The 2014 public release of Medicare data provided detailed profiles of reimbursements for medical procedures, along with the number of times a doctor performed each procedure and the number of patients involved, as shown in this excerpt from the interactive database of the *New York Times*.

much for what procedure, particularly when doctors submit full bills of services charged even though they will receive only partial reimbursements from the insurance company. One Web-based application, GoodRx.com, makes use of available data from numerous sources to present comparative information on the costs of prescription medicines (but even in that case, the cost data are confounded by the complexities of insurance coverage for the medicines in question). The cost of doctor and hospital services could readily be presented in a similar manner.

Insurance companies also have enough data to present a statistical picture of how well particular doctors' patients fare in the years after their knee operations or root-canal treatments. Other insurance companies that provide liability coverage to physicians and to others in the health-care industry keep the data on how often an individual practitioner, group practice, or hospital is sued for malpractice, how those suits are resolved, and how much the insurers paid out as a result.

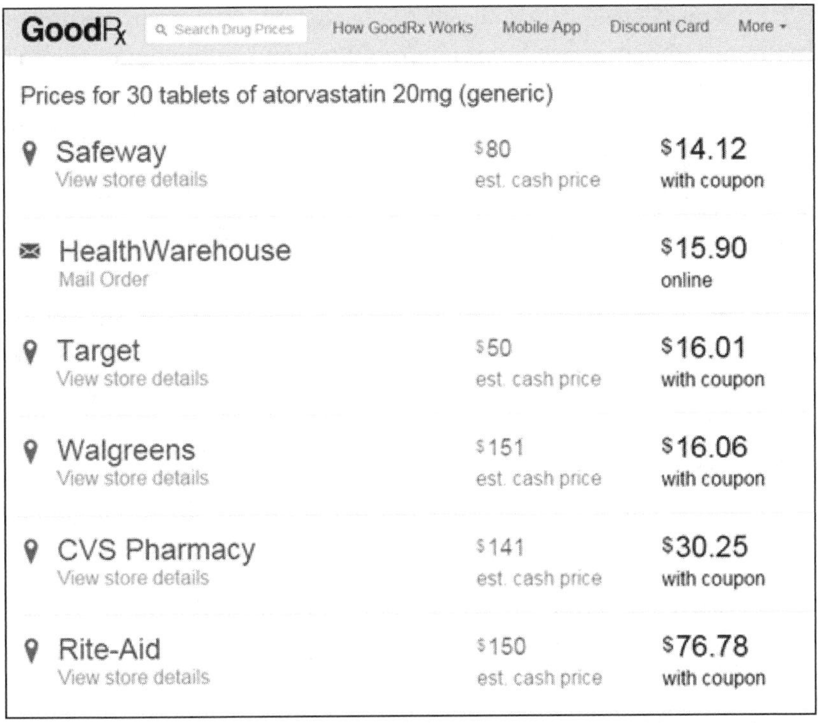

GoodRx	Q Search Drug Prices	How GoodRx Works	Mobile App	Discount Card	More ▾

Prices for 30 tablets of atorvastatin 20mg (generic)

⦿ **Safeway** View store details	$80 est. cash price	**$14.12** with coupon	
✉ **HealthWarehouse** Mail Order		**$15.90** online	
⦿ **Target** View store details	$50 est. cash price	**$16.01** with coupon	
⦿ **Walgreens** View store details	$151 est. cash price	**$16.06** with coupon	
⦿ **CVS Pharmacy** View store details	$141 est. cash price	**$30.25** with coupon	
⦿ **Rite-Aid** View store details	$150 est. cash price	**$76.78** with coupon	

Figure 3.12
GoodRx.com quickly compares costs of medicines from neighborhood sources.

One emerging source of information is data on *influence*: the amounts of money pharmaceutical company pass on to doctors and medical facilities— gifts, speaking fees, free travel, and the like—as part of corporate marketing efforts for particular products. Public release of such data was required by a number of legal settlements regarding possible corruption or unfair prac- tices in the pharmaceutical industry. ProPublica, an investigative journalist organization, compiled and published the data in a lookup service on its Dollars for Docs website.

With the passage of the Physician Payments Sunshine Act (a component of the Affordable Care Act), payments to doctors became subject to manda- tory reporting. The data are reported annually, and the Medicare program publishes the information at its Open Payments website (www.cms.gov/ openpayments). (ProPublica reports that the increase in data transparency has been accompanied by a decline in the amount of overall payments from pharmaceutical companies to the medical profession. It remains to be seen whether that trend continues as even more information is released under the Sunshine Act provisions.)

'Sunshine' isn't the operative word in another medical database maintained by Medicare, the National Practitioner Data Bank. Created by law, and in operation since 1990, the NPDB keeps tabs on some of the sanction information we described earlier, particularly the actions of medical boards to revoke or restrict doctors' licenses to practice. The database is accessible to some government agencies and medical professionals. It isn't available to members of the general public, but obviously it could be an important source of information with which to compile more meaningful profiles for public consumption.

Should the American Medical Association, the American Dental Association, or the counterparts of those associations in other disciplines make the effort to compile available data, solicit new data from other groups, and provide much more comprehensive information on health-care providers? Should the AMA's DoctorFinder service genuinely provide the sort of information that would help a prospective patient make the "perfect match" between his or her needs as a patient and a consumer and the doctor best equipped to meet those needs? Professional medical groups are logical organizations to take on the task of amassing, consolidating, and presenting cost, outcome, ranking, and sanction information about individual health-care professionals. Certainly the AMA is in a position to address its concerns about Medicare data being released "without context" by bringing to bear additional information sources that make better context possible.

Existing commercial efforts, including RateMDs and similar services already in existence, could also extend their reach to include additional information. And, of course, information-management firms such as Google and Amazon have the necessary skills, sophistication, and resources to step into the mix relatively easily.

We will leave it to each organization to explore these questions. We'll simply note that more and better market-style information in the world of medicine looks to be an emerging trend and an important means of lessening the effects of information bottlenecks. It may well be that remaining relevant to patients in the Information Age will entail providing something much more substantial than office hours and a phone number.

4 Corporate Transparency

In the corporate world, the centerpiece of information availability is a company's annual financial statement, chock full of data on costs, earnings, properties, credit, liabilities, and much more. The Securities and Exchange Commission's website offers a succinct statement on the role for financial reports:

We all remember Cuba Gooding Jr.'s immortal line from the movie Jerry Maguire, "Show me the money!" Well, that's what financial statements do. They show you the money. They show you where a company's money came from, where it went, and where it is now.

Do they? Do modern financial reports truly accomplish these goals? In select cases, the answer is clearly No. Before the dramatic implosion of Enron in 2001, Bethany McLean, an investigative reporter for *Fortune*, wrote a prescient article titled "Is Enron Overpriced?" McLean (who later would write a book titled *The Smartest Guys in the Room: The Amazing Rise and Scandalous Fall of Enron*) pointed to the extreme difficulty of making sense of Enron's financial statements:

[F]or all the attention that's lavished on Enron, the company remains largely impenetrable to outsiders, as even some of its admirers are quick to admit. Start with a pretty straightforward question: How exactly does Enron make its money? Details are hard to come by because Enron keeps many of the specifics confidential for what it terms "competitive reasons." And the numbers that Enron does present are often extremely complicated. Even quantitatively minded Wall Streeters who scrutinize the company for a living think so. "If you figure it out, let me know," laughs credit analyst Todd Shipman at S&P … .

Enron was the darling of Wall Street, named numerous times (oddly enough, by *Fortune*) as America's Most Innovative Company, and no one was capable of making sense of its financial reports. The SEC's pronouncement notwithstanding, whether Enron's financial reports answered any of the "show me the money" questions such reports are supposed to address is questionable. Its reporting raised a sort of if-a-tree-falls-in-the-forest question: If a company reports its finances, and no one can understand the report, has it really told us anything of significance?

Of course, Enron's accounting sleight of hand was tied to a deliberate and illegal effort to hide the firm's true operations from regulators and the public. But even legitimate financial practices often fall into the "impenetrable" category. The same sort of criticism that was leveled at Enron was also directed at the "too big to fail" insurance giant AIG, whose near demise threatened not only the company but the entire US economy. *Time* noted:

[I]t was awfully hard for outsiders—and even insiders—to understand the gravity of the company's problems. "You can read through every financial statement in the world and have absolutely no clue as to the risks they are taking." says Leo Tilman, a former Bear Stearns strategist ... .

Investors, analysts, and regulators may hope to get an in-depth understanding of a company's operations by reading through corporate financial statements, but, as the cases of Enron and AIG make clear, it really isn't at all apparent that the reports show us what we want to know. Corporations, after all, have a fiduciary responsibility to maximize profits and a legal responsibility to file the reports that the SEC (and other authorities) require. They have no legal obligation to provide details about their finances beyond what the rules require.

By looking through an annual report in a bit of detail, we can get a feel for what public companies currently report and how close the information comes to showing you the money. We will use the coffee-shop chain Starbucks as an example. According to the company's 2011 annual report, it had $11.7 billion in sales, $7.4 billion in assets and $1.7 billion in earnings, numbers that reflected strong year-over-year growth and substantial profitability for the firm. The company has certainly shown us the money, at least in these very broad-brush strokes.

Starbucks offers a very straightforward business model for our purposes. In contrast with Enron or AIG, there is little mystery about how Starbucks makes money. It sells coffee. Lots of coffee. The company's annual report begins this way: "Starbucks is the premier roaster, marketer and retailer of specialty coffee in the world, operating in more than 50 countries." It is no surprise, then, that the international coffee market plays a large role in

Starbucks' year-to-year finances and overall business strategy. The annual report devotes a considerable amount of ink (or more accurately, pixels) to the interplay of the company's operations and the international coffee market:

Starbucks is committed to selling only the finest whole bean coffees and coffee beverages. To ensure compliance with our rigorous coffee standards, we control coffee purchasing, roasting and packaging, and the global distribution of coffee used in our operations. We purchase green coffee beans from multiple coffee-producing regions around the world and custom roast them to our exacting standards, for our many blends and single origin coffees.

This being Starbucks, not just any coffee beans will do; there is a price to be paid for insisting on quality:

Although most coffee trades in the commodity market, high altitude Arabica coffee of the quality sought by Starbucks tends to trade on a negotiated basis at a premium above the "C" coffee commodity coffee price. Both the premium and the commodity price depend upon the supply and demand at the time of purchase. Supply and price can be affected by multiple factors in the producing countries, including weather, political and economic conditions. Price is also impacted by trading activities in the Arabica coffee futures market, including hedge funds and commodity index funds [and] by the actions of certain organizations and associations that have historically attempted to influence prices of green coffee through agreements establishing export quotas or by restricting coffee supplies."

The result of all these factors, says Starbucks, is considerable economic uncertainty—"The price of coffee is subject to significant volatility"—that has a profound influence on the company's overall business performance.

Commodity price risk represents Starbucks primary market risk, generated by our purchases of green coffee and dairy products, among other things … . Risk arises from the price volatility of green coffee [, which] directly impacts our results of operations and can be expected to impact our future results of operations … .

In order to manage some of the market's volatility and ensure adequate supplies, Starbucks enters into contracts with coffee merchants:

We buy coffee using fixed-price and price-to-be-fixed purchase commitments, depending on market conditions, to secure an adequate supply of quality green coffee. Price-to-be-fixed contracts are purchase commitments whereby the quality, quantity, delivery period, and other negotiated terms are agreed upon, but the date at which the base "C" coffee commodity price component will be fixed has not yet been established … . Until prices are fixed, we estimate the total cost of these purchase commitments.

In short, Starbucks is buying high-quality coffee at a premium above main-stream coffee prices and is operating in a market that is subject to volatility and even to a degree of manipulation by "certain organizations" that act to influence coffee prices. The fate of Starbucks' finances is inexorably linked to the international market for premium coffee beans.

All this provides important context for where and how and on what Starbucks spends its money, and highlights the central importance of the coffee market to corporate performance. A would-be investor, hoping to be well informed about the company's business, might well wonder about the details of this critical market segment: How much coffee does Starbucks buy? How much does it pay for the coffee? At this point, the "show me the money" aspect of the report begins to falter. Starbucks' annual report offers a bit of insight—but only a bit—into these questions, and the information provided is unnecessarily convoluted:

As of October 2, 2011, we had a total of $1.0 billion in purchase commitments, of which $193 million represented the estimated cost of price-to-be-fixed contracts. All price-to-be-fixed contracts as of October 2, 2011 were at the Company's option to fix the base "C" coffee commodity price component. Total purchase commitments, together with existing inventory, are expected to provide an adequate supply of green coffee through fiscal 2012.

The neat figure of $1.0 billion worth of contracts is suggestive, but also rather ambiguous. It is tempting to assume that these are all contracts for coffee beans, but the text doesn't quite say that. The billion dollars represents not purchases during the year covered by the annual report, but commitments for future purchases over some unspecified period of time. It is tempting, again, to suppose that the contracts cover a year's worth of purchasing, but the report doesn't explicitly confirm that. A significant portion of the cost—$193 million—is an estimate of prices not yet pinned down without any discussion of likely variability. There is no mention of the quantity of coffee purchased or the average per-pound price that Starbucks pays, meaning there is no opportunity to compare this company's costs against what others pay for premium coffee.

There isn't, in other words, an answer to the question "Where did their money go?"—at least, not an answer that offers up clear details on how much Starbucks spent on its major "raw material."

Bits and pieces of other data about Starbucks' coffee-buying are scattered throughout the annual report:

• A table of Inventory Values shows $677.8 million for coffee held in inventory at year's end—$431.3 million worth of unroasted coffee, $246.5 million worth of roasted coffee.

• A table of Contract Obligations details a total of a little more than $6 billion in contract obligations extending out five years or more. Most of these are lease obligations for the company's many storefronts, warehouses, and offices. About $1.1 billion worth are short-term (less than a year) purchase obligations.

• A footnote adds the detail that 94 percent of the short-term obligations—about $1 billion worth—are for the purchasing of green coffee.

So again—if we assume that people are willing to work their way through the scattered numbers—there is the strong suggestion that Starbucks spends about $1 billion a year to purchase raw coffee beans, without specific confirmation that the figures actually apply to annual purchasing.

Why make readers of the financial statement work so hard to find inconclusive numbers about expenses on coffee? Why wouldn't Starbucks simply come out and state, clearly and unambiguously, how much coffee it purchased in a year, the price it paid, and the type of price variability it encounters?

One possibility is that no one cares. Some investors will look back at last year's performance and will be content knowing Starbucks' operating margins and overall profitability, without a need to know about details of its premium-above-base-C coffee buying habits. For these investors, at least, it may be enough to know that Starbucks' $11.7 billion worth of sales generated earnings of $1.7 billion.

But if interest among would-be investors is the standard by which to gauge the information content of an annual report, one can't help but wonder at the proliferation of arcane, almost trivial detail about Starbucks' operations. Its wholly owned roasting and distribution facility in York County, Pennsylvania is 298,000 square feet in area, and the area of the one in Renton, Washington (leased, by the way) is 125,000 square feet. There was $46.9 million floating around in unused Starbucks Cards, and income of $30.2 million from property sales.

Starbucks incurred $33.3 million in "interest expense," $11.8 million in lease-related "asset retirement obligations," $15 million in R&D expenses, and $37.3 million in foreign income taxes. The annual report provides a simple and straightforward accounting of these particular costs, but they're small potatoes in comparison with the presumptive billion-dollar coffee expenses, only vaguely accounted for.

Another possible explanation is that Starbucks has something to hide and doesn't report the details of its coffee buying because it doesn't want anyone to know. Perhaps it doesn't want investors to recognize the degree to which it is sensitive to commodity price fluctuations. Perhaps it doesn't want competitors to know how much it pays for its premium beans. Perhaps it is mired in a culture of corporate secrecy that precludes offering up the details about its business other than the absolute minimum amount of information required to be presented. Certainly would-be investors who remember Enron's deliberate obfuscation of its accounts couldn't be blamed for wondering about financial reports from other companies.

A third possibility, and the one we subscribe to, is that investors, analysts, regulators, and anyone else interested in Starbucks' finances for any reason all want to know the details of the company's business. Starbucks isn't bent on hiding or obscuring those details. The reason it doesn't present a clear picture of its business operations is that the structure and requirements of an annual financial report are, at once, so specific, so hidebound by regulation, convention, standard operating practices, and innumerable guidance documents, and so convoluted as to render clarity a forgotten art. Starbucks' annual report doesn't offer a full overview of the company's business because it doesn't have to, and because the members of its financial reporting staff are so thoroughly preoccupied with crossing innumerable i's and dotting innumerable t's that delivering plain-spoken, coherent financial information about the company's operations falls by the wayside.

So it isn't just Starbucks pulling down a confusing, crazy-quilt screen over its data that obscures its financial reporting. The fact that Enron's financial reporting was "impenetrable," even to financial specialists, provided some frustrated quotes for journalists, and raised an eyebrow here and there, but no one seemed to treat it as anything out of the ordinary. Obscurity in an annual report is business as usual. We can imagine that Enron's annual report used confounding presentation as a deliberate strategy to obscure the company's unsavory operations. But the truth is that almost all annual financial reports are, to varying degrees, silent on many important financial details of a company's performance, and many of them are quite incomprehensible.

Now let us return to one of the SEC's essential questions to be addressed by a financial report—"Where does the money go?"—and speculate about what Starbucks spends its money on while conducting its business. Three cost areas immediately rise to the surface: raw materials (coffee, milk, sugar, etc.), pay for the staff, and rent for leased properties. Starbucks' annual report addresses these major expenses in a fractured and inconsistent fashion. Coffee expenses, as we detailed above, are presented in a vague manner, with a suggestion that Starbucks spends about $1 billion a year on its principal commodity. The report is silent on the amounts spent on other commodities. Lease and rental costs—a corporate expense on a similar scale to coffee buying—are specified as $749.9 million. Labor costs (Starbucks has 149,000 employees) aren't mentioned anywhere in the report. Again, this isn't (as far as we know) any sort of insidious attempt to hide important details of the company's finances. It doesn't seem very likely that Starbucks has any nefarious intent in failing to provide details (or any information at all) on its overall payroll. Instead, its annual report presents the big picture on overall costs—payroll is in there somewhere—along with an odd and scattered collection of details about those costs that include some rather minor expenses while ignoring some major cost items.

Starbucks spent $10,175.8 million on "operating costs" in 2011. Its annual report "breaks out" the costs as shown here in figure 4.1. Cost of Sales and Occupancy is almost half the total pie, and Store Operating Expenses a huge chunk of the other half. Neither category is very well defined in the annual report. (Again, there are only bits and pieces of details about what is and what isn't included in any category.) The "breakout" of costs is really no more revealing than the" "un-broken-out" statement of overall operating costs. Is the presumptive $1 billion expense of coffee purchases a "store operating expense," or a "cost of sales," or somehow divvied up between the two? "Occupancy" certainly sounds as if it would include leasing costs, but might that also be considered to belong to "store operating expenses"? Labor costs? Who knows which parts of the pie include employees' salaries or health insurance. Accountants and analysts may be able to make some reasonable guesses as to which costs are where, but why should guesswork be a necessary part of reading an annual report?

Starbucks didn't create these cost categories willy-nilly. Its financial data are presented this way in deference to standardized financial reporting guidelines that create generic categories such as Cost of Goods Sold

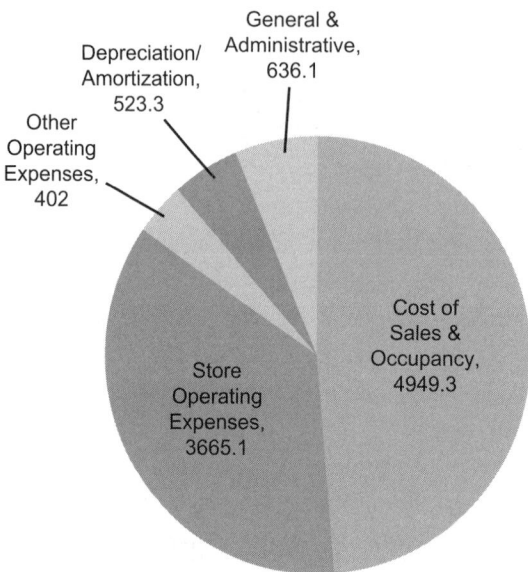

Figure 4.1

(which Starbucks has labeled Cost of Sales and Occupancy) and Operating Expenses. But there is tremendous variability between firms in what costs are included in which categories. And though the use of quasi-standardized categories may serve the purposes of the accounting profession, they aren't particularly helpful in answering the basic questions that a financial report is supposedly intended to address.

If one major purpose of a financial report is to answer the SEC's question ("Where does the money go?"), Starbucks' annual report could be much more straightforward—and, we believe, much more informative—if it were to answer that question directly. As an illustration, we have made up some numbers (a necessity, since Starbucks hints at some of these numbers but doesn't actually provide most of them) to present data on how the company spends its money. Our numbers are presented in table 4.1. This is a direct and more common-sense accounting of how Starbucks spends its money—a straightforward answer to the question "Where does the money go?"

The purpose of our alternative accounting is to present a more straightforward description of the major items that a company spends its money to acquire. In Starbucks' conventional accounting, purchases of goods and services take a back seat to categorical presentations of expenses that—while

Table 4.1
Hypothetical expenses for Starbucks (billions of dollars).

Coffee	1.1
Other supplies	0.6
Property leases	0.9
Labor	5.1
Marketing	0.14
Taxes	0.42
Services	0.75
Debt service	0.05
Acquisitions	0.6
Utilities	0.5
Total expenses	10.16
Labor breakout	
Hourly	2.1
United States	1.1
Europe	0.6
Elsewhere	0.4
Salaried	1.0
Benefits	0.8
Bonuses	0.6
Retirees	0.6

providing useful information—obscure the company's expenditures on real-world stuff. In a family's budget, for example, dividing expenses into categories such as Mom, Dad, Tommy, and Cheryl paints a useful picture of who the family is spending money on, but provides no information on *what* the family is buying. Similarly, Starbucks' report puts expenses into accounting categories without specifying what the company is actually purchasing. Our alternative budget for Starbucks is the equivalent of a family budget that itemizes the costs of actual goods and services such as clothing, rent, food, and phone bills.

What does Starbucks spend its money on? Half of its annual costs (in our imagined universe) are for labor. In contrast with the Cost of Sales and Occupancy information in the annual report—which also accounts for about half of all expenses—we have provided a further breakout for this huge piece of the pie. Of the $5.1 billion in total labor expenses, $2.1 billion goes to hourly wages, about half for employees in the US and half for

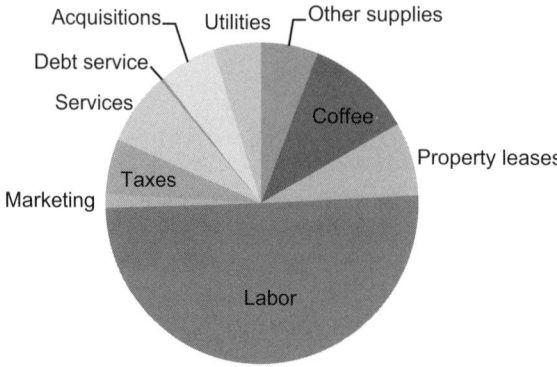

Figure 4.2

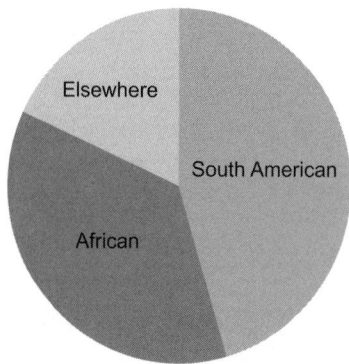

Figure 4.3
Origins of coffee.

employees elsewhere. Another $1 billion goes to salaried employees. Other large pieces of the pie are also accounted for: benefit expenses, bonuses, and retiree costs.

Coffee is another substantial portion of expenses, and in figure 4.3 this too has been broken out, into subsections detailing the geographic origins of the coffee that Starbucks purchases.

The rule of thumb we used to guide the presentation of data in figure 4.1 is that slices of the pie larger than 10 percent of revenue—for Starbucks, about $1 billion—are broken down into smaller components. This ensures a reasonable level of detail for financial items and avoids the absurdity of having one category of items account for a huge, ill-defined chunk of

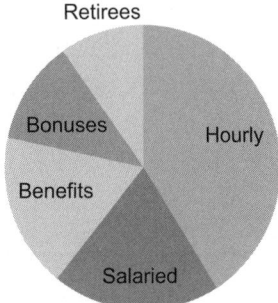

Figure 4.4
Labor breakout.

the pie chart. We focused here on expenses, as an example of alternative accounting, but the same approach would be taken for income and assets.

We don't mean these data as replacements for the traditional presentations of Cost of Sales, Operating Expenses, and the other categories that Starbucks (and other companies) use in their financial reports. To the extent that such presentations serve necessary accounting purposes, they should be retained for the benefit of the analysts, bankers, regulators, investors, and others who make use of the information.

Nor are we proposing that our imagined presentation of Starbucks' expenses is the preferred presentation. There are many ways to examine financial data in detail, even at the billion-dollar level: geographically, by business-unit details, by product classifications, by material flows, by personnel divisions, by accounting categories, and so on.

We are suggesting that traditional financial data should be augmented with a straightforward presentation such as we have just described: a clear-cut accounting of where a company's money comes from and where it goes, with a focus on self-evident business categories such as labor, property, and raw materials on the expenses side of the ledger. This is what we believe 'transparency' really means in financial accounts: not simply more data, but different data—information that presents a clear, common-sense picture of what a company is, what it does, and how it operates.

Transparency in Financial Reporting: a Few Principles

We have a few principles to offer for enhancing the information content of financial reporting, along with some suggestions for the types and levels of detail of information to report. First, the principles:

Size matters.   Large companies should provide a large amount of information. A billion-dollar company should operate with considerable transparency, a ten-billion-dollar company with even more transparency. A hundred-billion-dollar company should be a veritable glass house. Entities that are considered too large to fail are the very entities that are too large to operate in financial obscurity.

Large operations should report.   Any division, subsidiary, joint venture, or operating unit that is, itself, a large business entity should report in as much detail as if it were a stand-alone company.

Invisibility is untenable.   Regardless of whether a company is public or private, foreign or domestic, or regulated by the SEC, the FDIC, the OCC, the FRB, the CFTC, the CFPB, or a counterpart of one of those agencies in another country, or by no one in particular, companies with substantial financial presence should provide substantial amounts of publicly accessible information.

Information trumps regulation.   It is more valuable to have a clear picture of what a business entity is doing than it is to attempt to use regulations to control business operations that operate largely in secrecy.

Plain English (or plain French, or plain German, or plain Mandarin) is crucially important.   If a financial report is impenetrable, it is not transparent in any meaningful sense, no matter the quantity of financial data provided. In addition to whatever financialese is necessary for consistent and comparative reporting, companies should provide detailed descriptions of their practices and finances in language that non-specialized audiences can readily understand.

Large companies, then (and of course the meaning of 'large' must be specified), should make certain kinds of information universally available to market participants. For the sake of discussion, let's say that, for entities with annual sales or assets under management of $1 billion or more, the following types of information should be available:

A general and plainly stated description of the company   What the company does, who the owners and senior managers are, where it is located, and the size and scope of its operations and workforce should be stated. This sort of overview—along with all the information described below—should be available for the company as a whole as well as for each sizable (billion-dollar-or-more) subdivision.

Organization   The company's organizational arrangements and the connections between the company and its subsidiaries, joint ventures, and other components should be laid out, with a description of the rationale (e.g., operational efficiency, minimizing tax obligations) for the various organizational pieces.

Performance   How the company fared in the past year, and in recent years, should be made clear, and projections for the years ahead should be offered. Significant factors that have been or will be affecting performance should be mentioned.

Income   The obvious "Show me the money" questions should be answered. Explain where income comes from, detailing the relative role of product sales, sales of services, investment earnings, interest, rentals, real estate income, lawsuits, licensing arrangements, currency trading, and other types of income. Distinguish actual income received from statements of the present value of future anticipated income. The descriptions should be sufficiently detailed so that no one category amounts to more than 10 percent of total income or is larger than $1 billion.

Expenses   The relative roles of total personnel costs for salaries, bonuses, benefits, pensions and retirement, costs of materials, equipment costs, real estate costs, taxes, licensing costs, legal costs, insurance, debt service, and energy should be presented in detail, along with other areas of substantial spending. (In our Starbucks example above we took a first crack at such a presentation.) Again, no one category should amount to more than 10 percent of total income or exceed $1 billion.

Finances   The relative roles of cash, liquid assets, illiquid assets, issuance of shares, and hard-to-value assets in the company's overall finances and accounting should be explained. Detail and discuss the existence of off-balance-sheet transactions and the potential of their becoming assets or liabilities. Articulate both short-term and long-term financial obligations. Explain who the company is in debt to, the amounts involved and the nature of the debts, where the company makes financial investments, and the nature of the investments (stocks, bonds, funds, currency, etc.). Include a description of unusually complex or innovative financial arrangements and accounting methods, and their role in overall company finances.

Risk   Where the company's financial exposure lies, and the range of potential exposure (from anticipated to extreme events), should be described.

What are the downsides of investments, particularly those that are highly leveraged, or where risk of a loss exceeds 100 percent of the amount invested? Under what circumstances are debts callable? What requirements are there for having collateral or cash at the ready? Explain the company's protective strategy for its finances—types of financial insurance, coverage provided, and perceived gaps. Detail involvement in relatively new types of financial vehicles that may not yet be well categorized in terms of overall risk. What risks does the company face that are tangential to its main business operations, such as lawsuits, strikes, environmental liabilities, or government investigations?

Labor and compensation   Specify who collects top-tier salaries at the company and how much is their compensation in terms of pay, perquisites, and bonuses. What is the range of the highest salaries relative to the company average? How many employees does the company have, and how are they categorized? How much non-employee support (by contractors, freelancers, or temporaries) does it use? How many employees are in the lowest range of salaries? How many are in the middle range? What sort of salary clauses are used to protect salaries (e.g., golden parachutes) or to restrict them (e.g., bonuses tied to performance)?

Tax returns   Large companies should make their tax returns public.

Some readers are sure to find the above list problematic, in whole or in part, for any one of a number of reasons, including these:

• It's too onerous. These requirements would have to be implemented through new regulations. Companies already face substantial reporting burdens, and calling for additional information simply means that fewer resources are available with which to carry out a firm's actual business.

• It's duplicative. Any large company already provides a substantial amount of reporting to its shareholders, and often to government bodies and to the public. There is nothing to be gained by insisting on repackaging information that is already available merely to give it a different format.

• It's too intrusive. Publish tax returns? Companies are entitled to privacy, no less so than private citizens.

The first two objections don't strike us as particularly substantial. The third has more heft to it. However, we suggest that the benefits of greater transparency and more coherent information in financial reporting—particularly the benefit of a market that functions fairly, efficiently and openly—far outweigh any of the costs associated with adding the type of information we have described.

Let's consider these objections one at a time.

Is the information we are calling for too onerous? Bear in mind, we are addressing the largest companies in the world, firms with resources that rival those of countries. Observers of the stock market speculate about which company is likely to become the world's first trillion-dollar corporation; a number of firms have already surpassed the halfway mark and are growing rapidly. Only a few countries have gross domestic products that pass the trillion-dollar mark. The information we have identified isn't hard to come by from a corporate point of view, and, as we have described things, there is plenty of wiggle room to give companies flexibility in exactly how much information they provide and in what format they provide it.

Given the "size matters" principle just described, a billion-dollar company would provide far less detail in its reporting than would a ten-billion-dollar company, and both would have far less to report than a too-big-to-fail hundred-billion-dollar operation. What's more, we have laid out a principle that information trumps regulation, and have left open the possibility that as additional information reporting becomes the norm, regulatory controls of corporations can be relaxed—a tradeoff that we think many companies would welcome.

As to the objection that information is duplicative, we go back to the question raised about Enron: How does the company make its money? Despite mountains of reporting from the company, the most fundamental question about how Enron earned its income couldn't be answered, even by expert industry observers and financial analysts. Enron even prided itself on its black-box approach to business, in which its methods of earning money were kept secret from potential competitors. The seeming openness of public companies, and the mandated insistence in recent years on greater transparency and reporting, has not (yet) resulted in a steady flow of information that can answer straightforward questions such as those we have presented here.

Today an enormous amount of information is reported by most sizable companies, but there is a dearth of useful data to support the marketplace by answering the questions that are of most interest to market participants: what a business is, how it operates, and in what ways its finances are at risk.

As for the reporting being overly intrusive, this is an issue that raises fundamental questions about the status and responsibilities of companies in the modern world, the role of external oversight, and the appropriate balance between privacy and transparency.

Companies are required to provide certain financial information in a publicly accessible format. These same companies are entitled to keep financial information in their tax filings secret. Why? Why is public provision of some types of financial information deemed necessary while other types of financial information are protected as private and not subject to public scrutiny?

At one time, corporate tax returns were considered public documents. A variety of legal and policy decisions—especially those that personalized corporations, treating them as if they were individual citizens—eventually closed the door on public access to corporate tax returns. But we can find little reason why the returns of large corporations should be secret. Taxable income is calculated using a very different set of standards and rules than are used for accounting income, as reported in financial statements. As a result, earnings reported in a financial statement can be substantial while earnings reported on a tax form can be much smaller or even negative. Making both types of reporting publicly accessible would open a window on corporate finance that has been tightly closed for the better part of a century.

With roughly 25–30 percent of large corporations (and two-thirds of all corporations when smaller companies are included) paying no income tax in any given year, a more detailed understanding of how this comes about would be in the public interest. More than that, it could be information that makes the market, as a whole, more efficient, making it in everyone's self-interest—even in the self-interest of the corporations that would be doing the reporting.

Scholars who study the prospects of public disclosure of corporate tax forms don't all agree that disclosure would be beneficial. But there is widespread agreement that disclosure would have a considerable influence on the behavior of the actors in the marketplace, particularly the behavior of the companies affected by disclosure, the regulators and analysts with an oversight function, the politicians who craft tax and financial policy, ordinary investors scrutinizing a company's finances, and the general public interested in the fairness (or lack of same) of the tax system. That such

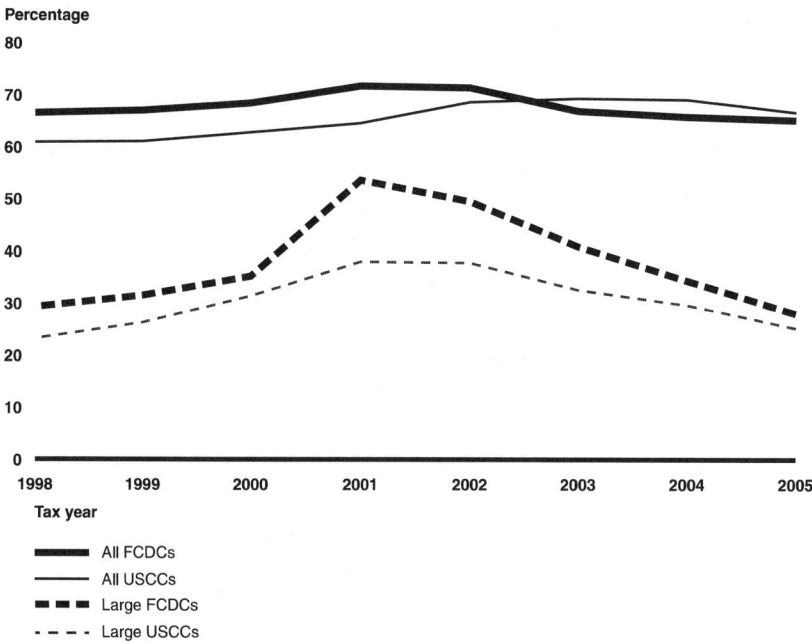

Figure 4.5
Percentages of FCDCs (foreign-controlled domestic corporations) and USCCs (US-controlled corporations) that reported no tax liability in tax years 1998–2005. Source: GAO analysis of IRS data. ("Large" FCDCs or USCCs are those with assets of at least $250 million or gross receipts of at least $50 million. Differences between all FCDCs and all USCCs were not statistically significant in the years 2002–2005.)

agreement exists is, once again, a reminder of the power of information to bring about real change in the behavior of individuals and organizations, and in the overall operations of the economic, financial, and tax systems.

Of course, changing behavior just for change's sake is hardly a compelling reason to require corporate disclosure of tax filings. But the reverse is also true: Secrecy for secrecy's sake—secrecy perpetuated simply because it is a long-standing habit—also stands as a less than compelling argument for preventing disclosure of the tax returns of the largest corporations.

Americans insist that their presidential candidates make their tax returns public, and refusal to do so raises the question "What does he or she have to hide?" We could ask the same of our largest corporate citizens.

Product Information and Corporate Secrecy

Companies keep many things other than their tax returns secret, of course. What would happen if the most famous corporate secret of all time—the formula for Coca-Cola—were to become known?

The formula, which for many years wasn't even committed to writing, is currently written down and kept at the World of Coca-Cola exhibit in Atlanta, in a vault worthy of Fort Knox.

The dramatic aura of secrecy stems more from the marketing department than from the lawyers protecting the company's intellectual property, but still keeping the secret is central to Coca-Cola's way of doing business. With a secret formula, Coca-Cola creates a mini-monopoly for itself. No other company can sell a can of Coke, or even something nearly identical to Coke, because no other company has the magic formula. Other soda companies compete with Coca-Cola the way railroads compete with airlines: as an alternative product that meets a similar consumer need with a very different offering in the marketplace. Pepsi-Cola competes with Coca-Cola as a carbonated, cola-flavored beverage to quench your thirst, make you more popular, and infuse your life with a heretofore unknown vitality, but its manufacturer can't claim to be using the same formula that Coca-Cola uses.

From the point of view of Coca-Cola as a company, the value of maintaining a mini-monopoly (it has absolutely cornered the market in Coca-Cola) is self-evident. But forces outside the market generally frown on monopolies—at least, big ones such as Standard Oil, AT&T, DeBeers, and Microsoft. The trust busters among us believe that monopolies create market inefficiencies by lowering supply, raising prices, and stifling innovation—all consequences that flow from the lack of a fully competitive market. Is it possible that Coca-Cola's mini-monopoly has the same effect on a smaller scale?

You can answer that question by imagining what would happen if Coca-Cola's secret formula were suddenly to become public. Supermarket brands of cola would be able to claim to be just like Coke, or at least to be based on exactly the same formula. The dynamics of competition in the soda aisle would change, even if only modestly. Generic colas wouldn't simply be competing with other generic colas; they now would be in head-to-head competition with Coke. The Coca-Cola company, of course, would respond in some fashion—perhaps with an advertising blitz to further reinforce the brand, taste tests proving how superior Coke is, and incentives to super-markets to give Coke prime end-of-aisle display space. The company might also bring the price of Coca-Cola products closer to the prices charged for generic colas.

For the Coca-Cola company, the outcome of a loss of secrecy wouldn't be particularly desirable, but it wouldn't be earth-shaking. It is highly unlikely that the company's sales, profits, or market share would be affected signifi-cantly. But its central product would face more direct competition. Con-sumers would benefit from more choice and perhaps better prices. Overall, the market is tweaked just a bit and would function with slightly enhanced efficiency.

Put more generally, the primary motivation for corporate secrecy is to make competition more difficult. The less information a potential com-petitor has—about my secret formula, my production process, my cost of energy, my contracts with suppliers and clients, my tax incentive deals, my currency hedges—the better my odds of maintaining my mini-monopoly and fending off direct competition. But as much as companies dislike active competition, it is universally understood that competition is a very good thing. Might a more open flow of information, though equally disagreeable to individual companies, be beneficial to the market as a whole?

Corporate secrecy is such a deeply ingrained practice that it hardly ever gets a second thought until secrecy is breached by Chinese cyber-snoops, embarrassing internal email messages are leaked by a whistleblower, or a company's contracts are revealed during a legal case. Secrecy is routine and is continually reinforced, whether by simple tradition or with formal legal documents. We even grace secrecy with numerous terms of art. 'Proprietary information', 'confidential business information', 'trade secrets', and 'non-disclosure agreements' are all names for intentionally kept secrets and for mechanisms to protect such secrets.

As information comes to the forefront, we find ourselves with a jury-rigged information milieu in the corporate world. We vigorously insist on an ill-defined principle of transparency in some corporate dealings, and we vigorously protect a massive edifice of corporate secrecy in other dealings. We would argue that it is time to take a fresh look at the entire flow of information from the corporate world, and to reconsider what additional information should come forward, what protections should be relaxed, and, conversely, what information should be less forthcoming and better protected.

Antitrust regulators in the United States and elsewhere expend considerable resources on preventing large companies from becoming super-large and overly dominant in a single sector of the economy. This type of preventive activity makes sense and helps ensure a robust and fully competitive marketplace. Yet we can't help but wonder if the combined effect of millions of discrete mini-monopolies, like that enjoyed by Coca-Cola, doesn't exert an overall influence on the marketplace that exceeds the influence of a more classic full-fledged monopoly? We don't know the answer to that question, but we feel that committing to finding an answer is worthwhile and important.

Unintentional Secrets

So far, we have discussed intentional secrecy—that is, the deliberate withholding of information in the form of trade secrets, proprietary processes, and the like. We suspect, however, that unintentional secrecy is even more significant in determining what is and what isn't known by producers and consumers and the many third parties, such as regulators and analysts, intent on understanding the market.

By "unintentional secrecy" we mean the information that falls by the wayside during the almost countless number of transactions required to bring a product to market. It isn't information that's a trade secret, necessarily. It's more a case of "don't ask, don't tell," as information that isn't essential to a product's marketability, or that may be detrimental to market success, disappears along the supply chain.

Consider a (very incomplete) chain of events involving the raw materials for a toy that shows up in toy stores (or in Happy Meals) around the world. A chemical company, say in Taiwan, manufactures the raw resin that will form the plastic body of the toy. A manufacturer of printed circuits in Japan produces the microchip that supplies the toy's voice and blinking lights. A Chinese paint manufacturer makes the colorants. Another company in China manufactures the tiny button battery that will power the toy's special effects, and still another prints the packaging.

Each ingredient that goes into the toy has its own complex back story. Suppose, for example, that the white paint from the Chinese factory was originally ordered by a computer manufacturer for use in the housing of a desktop computer. The paint was then shipped to a distributor. The distributor was intending to deliver it to the computer manufacturer when the news arrived that the computer manufacturer has gone out of business. There was then a warehouse somewhere in China full of pallets of paint with nowhere to go. After a few quick email messages and a heavily discounted price offering, the paint was rerouted to the toy company. And did we mention that the paint contained lead?

The story above is hypothetical, but similar stories are all too real. Children's toys have repeatedly been pulled off the market for containing lead. Although we aren't privy to the details of the contracts that exist between toy distributors in the United States and toy suppliers in other countries, it seems likely that virtually all companies require their suppliers to import only items that comply with US law and to specifically ensure that the imports don't contain lead. Those provisions notwithstanding, though, lead-tainted toys repeatedly show up at US borders and often make it onto store shelves and into consumers' homes.

Clearly there is a breakdown of the flow of information somewhere along the chain of commerce. Company A manufactures paint that contains lead; company Z doesn't want to have anything to do with that toxic paint; yet

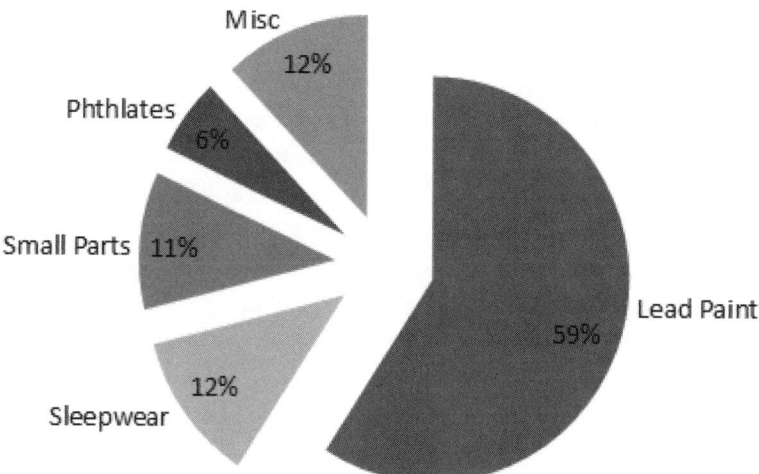

Figure 4.6
Consumer Product Safety Commission actions on import violations for children's products.

as the paint passes through companies B through Y, the fact of the lead content somehow drops from sight. At some point, a commercial transaction takes place in which the material is simply categorized as white paint, and the details of its composition are ignored. The information is lost. No one upstream of the loss tests the paint to determine its true content. The toys are tainted. The information regarding toxic components of the paint drops out of the marketplace—deliberately or otherwise.

Information is easily lost during market transactions, but it is also important to keep in mind the flip side of this story. Most toys make it to market lead-free. Somehow, the information is preserved throughout the supply chain. The message from toy sellers that lead isn't an acceptable ingredient makes its way down the supply chain to hundreds of merchants, and confirmation is passed back up the chain to the seller that the toys arriving on their shelves are in fact lead-free.

The system breaks down, though, when the presence of lead in the paint becomes a marketplace secret. It's hard to say in any particular case whether such a secret is intentional. In the example we invented above, the paint loses its provenance and has no real identity, and no one in the chain of events has specific knowledge of its composition. It becomes generic paint, and nothing more. No product sheets, no safety data, no useful information to speak of. Information about the presence of lead disappears. Whether that disappearance happens by design or by happenstance makes little difference from the point of view of the end consumer.

When withholding information is so seemingly natural and acceptable, it is easy to overlook the simple truth that secrecy is the opposite of transparency. If more and better information makes for a more responsive, more honest, more efficient market, then missing information is actively gumming up the works. Whether the information goes missing as a result of a company's intentionally keeping it secret (as with Coca-Cola), as a result of a company's merely not reporting it (as with Starbucks), or as a result of a company's creating an unintentional secret (as with the lead-contaminated toy), the end result is a market that doesn't function as well as it should. When the market failure involves toxic chemical contamination, more than economic efficiency is at stake. Lives are at stake.

For the sake of discussion, let's accept for a moment the premise that more and better information in the marketplace is desirable. The closer we can get to the economist's notion of perfect information, the more fully realized the market becomes. This raises an obvious question: What sort of information? What are the missing elements to marketplace information that are needed to make the market run more effectively? What information will bring us closer to perfection?

These questions are rarely asked. "Perfect information" has stood for so long as an abstraction (and, as Stiglitz reminded us, as a largely unexplored assumption of modern economics) that there has been very little attention to the question of what perfect or greatly improved information actually looks like. We obviously need to know about lead-contaminated toys. It's safe to say that, as a general rule, the market should retain information regarding legally mandated requirements such as lead-free toys. But do we really need the formula for Coke to make the market more efficient, or are there other, more preferable types of information that we can inject into the market to help make the world a better place?

Let us return to the example of Starbucks to explore these questions in a bit more detail. We have already added new facets to the company's financial reporting to create a flow of information that, in our opinion, better serves the needs of the public and makes for a more effective market. But is there more information that might be added to bring the system even closer to the ideal?

Starbucks itself has provided part of the answer to that question. In addition to its annual financial report, Starbucks produces a second detailed report, titled the Global Responsibility Report. The purpose of that report, which the company has published annually since 2001, is to make public the company's commitments and progress in the area of social responsibility:

As we have grown to now more than 18,000 stores in over 60 countries, we recognize that commitment to corporate citizenship is also a business imperative. We can use our scale for good, and catalyze change across entire industries so that Starbucks and everyone we touch can endure and thrive.

There is nothing terribly unusual about a corporation embracing a goal for social good. Henry Ford saw his automobile factories as a great force for social progress, a sentiment echoed later on by the famous (but misquoted) statement "What's good for General Motors is good for the country." What distinguishes Starbucks' effort in this area is the provision of information about the broader societal aspects of its business. Starbucks articulates the good it hopes to achieve, sets goals, measures progress, and reports, every year, on how well it is doing in relation to its goals. Noble stuff, but is it really, as Starbucks states, a "business imperative"? The report elaborates a bit on this:

[N]ever before have we seen the marketplace and today's consumers have such a deep interest in and knowledge about what companies stand for and how they are living up to their promises. Not only is standing for something beyond making a profit the right thing to do, it is the way business must be conducted in the 21st century. Only by doing business through the lens of humanity can an organization establish a crucial reservoir of trust with its people and its customers. At Starbucks, it is a trust we must earn every day … .

A corporation is a collection of individuals, and individuals are entirely capable of doing great good. But Starbucks makes it clear that the collective conscientiousness of its management and its employees isn't the only motivation for the company's good deeds. Another motivation is the expectations of the marketplace. As far as Starbucks is concerned, turning its back on social issues would be bad for business, damaging the "crucial reservoir of trust" that the company has established in the eyes of the public. The Global Responsibility Report is its attempt to document the ways in which Starbucks is responsive to the concerns of both current customers and potential customers.

Put another way, the report is a market-driven provision of information. It doesn't cover every social, environmental, and cultural issue known to humankind. Quite the reverse, it selectively covers discrete areas that have been identified as the company's priorities in terms of good corporate citizenship. Starbucks' efforts in this regard are given form and substance by an invisible hand that selects some issues and some types of information, and rejects others, entirely on the basis of the demands of the consumer market, much as a product offering such as Frappuccino is shaped by the likes and dislikes of Starbucks' clientele.

If the invisible hand can bring forward the information the public wants, it is possible that we don't need an exact or explicit answer to the question "What does closer-to-perfect information look like?" Given the right opportunities, the market itself can make its desires known on this topic. All that would be needed is the mechanism to "hear" the market's desires about information and respond accordingly.

For Starbucks, the broad meaning of providing better and more socially relevant information on its operations focuses on three areas that consumers' concerns have repeatedly identified as having high priority: ethical sourcing, environmental stewardship, and community involvement. To a lesser degree, the report also focuses on workplace and diversity issues and on corporate governance.[1] These areas of focus, for which Starbucks has committed to voluntary annual reporting, provide a partial answer to the question we posed earlier: What additional information is needed to bring the market a bit closer to perfect information? The market itself creates the answer for Starbucks, as the firm takes the pulse of the social concerns in its sphere of operations (the concerns of its managers, employees, customers, suppliers, public-interest groups, competitors, and the communities in which it operates), processes all that information in the vague yet compelling way in which the marketplace works, and creates its social-responsibility "products," including broad goals, specific performance targets, and the manner of communicating its activities to the public.

The areas that Starbucks chose to target aren't unusual. Many other companies produce similar reports (usually under the heading of a corporate responsibility report or sustainability report), and most of the reports focus on similar themes: environmental protection, ethical sourcing, community involvement, and worker issues such as safety, opportunity, dignity, and avoiding the use of child labor. This shouldn't come as a surprise, since the same set of public concerns are likely to be expressed in many different areas of the marketplace, and to lead to similar sets of social reporting activities. Just as market demand drives a similar set of features in mobile phones from many different manufacturers, so too will social reporting be driven in a relatively uniform direction.

In fact, these areas have been codified, in a manner of speaking, in a formal reporting structure that is widely used by large companies in crafting their social-responsibility reports. A non-profit organization called the Global Reporting Initiative issues guidelines for reports that provide performance indicators for reporting on the three pillars of sustainability (Economic, Environment, and Social), with the latter category broken down into subareas of labor, human rights, society, and product responsibility.

Like the financial reports they are modeled on, the corporate responsibility reports produced by Starbucks and hundreds of other multinational corporations provide information that is responsive to a wide range of interests and needs. On the one hand, the reports include more information than anyone can make use of—no one participant in the marketplace wants, or needs, or could utilize every piece of information in a financial or sustainability report. But such reports cannot contain enough information to serve the collective needs of all market participants.

Improving Product-Specific Information

Annual reports are a step forward in bringing the market a bit closer to a state of perfect or pretty good information that can, in turn, make for a more efficient and effective market. But the information provided in once-a-year reports is paltry in comparison with that provided by the main source of information in the marketplace: the information attached to the goods and services that are bought and sold. An investor interested in owning stock in a car company may well seek out the reports from Toyota, General Motors, and Ford, but a shopper looking to buy a car turns elsewhere for the information she wants. An annual report (whether financial or sustainable) may highlight the excellent durability or style or gas mileage of a car company's fleet as a whole. A shopper isn't buying a fleet, however, but is purchasing an individual car, and needs to know the specs for the specific model she is considering.

Better information in the marketplace, whatever that ultimately comes to mean, will inevitably be attached to the products and services in the marketplace, much more than originating in detached sources of information such as annual reports. Of course, there is a pragmatic limit to the information that can readily be associated with an individual product, if for no other reason than that there is only so much room on the packaging. Two quick trips, one to the supermarket and the other to Amazon.com, can tell us much about the limits of, the strategies associated with, and the expansive possibilities created by closer-to-perfect information about individual products.

Supermarket products generally come with at least two important pieces of information readily available. The first is product identity, which consumers glean from packaging and store labels or from simple familiarity. (We know apples when we see them, even in the absence of a sign identifying them as such.) The second is price. Supermarkets know that shoppers are generally highly conscious of whether a particular item is a "good buy," and devote considerable manpower to posting price information on signs, on shelves, and on products.[2] If consumers have no interest in information beyond price and product identity, then they are shopping for what economists call a commodity (a product with no differentiation from one supplier to the next), and there are few if any considerations other than price.

But like another abstraction we have been discussing, perfect information, commodity products aren't typically found in the real world, and certainly not in supermarkets. Shoppers expect, and supermarkets provide, a wide range of additional information about even the simplest of products. Apples are distinguished by variety. American shoppers can choose among Fuji, McIntosh, Delicious, Rome, Gala, Granny Smith, and about half a dozen other common varieties; many additional varieties are found in other markets in other parts of the world. Stores usually specify the origin of the apples (e.g., "from Washington State" or "locally grown"; because some shoppers prefer local produce, stores may even identify the individual orchard. Stores may also offer suggestions as to what uses certain apples are well suited for (e.g., "perfect for baking"). If the information isn't yet adequate for making a decision, a helpful produce worker may be at the ready, paring knife in hand, to cut a slice of an apple so that the shopper can assess its taste, texture, and aroma.

Some of the apples carry an additional identification, "organic," which is both a piece of information in its own right and a sort of information proxy covering a wide range of inputs. (Some stores identify non-organic produce as "conventional," but most do not.) To many shoppers, "organic" equates to "no pesticides." Official guidelines for certification as organic, however, specifically prohibit synthetic pesticides, but also restrict use of synthetic fertilizer, hormones, antibiotics, and genetically engineered products. Organic farms in the United States also follow soil-conservation, seed-handling, and crop-rotation practices required by the US Department of Agriculture. The label "organic," then, is a simple representation for a complex set of conditions surrounding the growing and marketing of fruits and vegetables. Much as a single letter on a student's report card quickly and conveniently summarizes an entire semester's worth of information about the student's academic accomplishments, the single word 'organic' tells us much about an apple.

An ordinary piece of produce, then, comes with a significant quantity of information, even though an apple is essentially unadorned (except for those annoying stickers, which largely serve to provide information to checkout clerks and scanners rather than to shoppers).

Elsewhere in a supermarket, the opportunities to convey product information expand enormously with product packaging, which typically includes verbal and visual content intended to both inform and persuade. The basic information content varies from product to product, but typically includes the following:

company name (e.g., Nabisco)
brand name (e.g., Oreo)
product identity (e.g., chocolate sandwich cookies)
unit value, both English and metric (e.g., net weight 1 pound/453 grams)
packaged content (e.g., three stay-fresh packs)
nutrition information
ingredients
non-ingredients (e.g., contains no trans fats)
safety information (e.g., produced in a facility that also processes peanuts)
expiration or "best if used by" date
recycling symbols
other product symbols (kosher, organic, ENERGY STAR, UL)
contact information (e.g., company's URL or phone number)
place of origin
product directions
guarantee
bar code
printer's color squares (for color quality control)

And that's just the basic information. Most modern product packaging excels at marketing. Products tell a story ("ingeniously simple, crisp and light"), make a claim ("new and improved"), offer a promise ("satisfaction guaranteed"), or catch our eye with an array of colors and images. An Oreo box may feature an image of a cookie almost joyously splashing into a glass of milk. Whether explicit or merely suggestive, product packaging is replete with informative messages that both instruct and entice the shopper. Though the examples above are all from the United States, the phenomena we describe should be familiar to shoppers in supermarkets around the world.

As informationally rich as a supermarket shopping experience can be, the experience of shopping online is even more so. A visit to the multimerchant online shopping website Amazon.com reveals a new world of information possibilities.

In an important way, shopping at Amazon limits the flow of information. Shoppers can't pick a product off the shelf, heft it in their hand, give it a squeeze, or smell it for freshness. Photos may show a product at all angles and various zoom levels, and allow shoppers to alter colors and features, but shopping at Amazon is still a limited experience involving a generic representation of a product rather than the actual product. The opportunities for direct sensory interaction with products are limited, although the "Look inside" feature at least gives a semblance of an ability to browse if one is shopping for books.

Amazon attempts to sidestep these limits by providing an encyclopedic offering of auxiliary information on each product it sells. Unlike supermarket shoppers, faced with a take-it-or-leave-it choice of product pricing, customers at Amazon can quickly compare prices from multiple merchants, and can consider information on special offers such as free shipping or rebate programs. Often there are detailed text descriptions and photographs (and sometimes there are video or sound clips) to familiarize consumers with a product's features and uses. Technical specifications are provided for electronic products. Articles of clothing are displayed with customizable colors and fabrics. Magazines can be leafed through. Shoppers can select from inventories of new and used merchandise.

If you are shopping for a lamp, for example, Amazon's customization features allow you to quickly sort through thousands of available products and narrow down your purchasing options. You can customize the site's display by specifying a height, a brand, a material, a color, a style, features, a price, a seller, and even how recently a lamp was posted on Amazon's website. You can add a lamp to your "wish list" and automatically keep track of new offers, sales, and upgrades as other merchants offer the same item or existing merchants change their prices.

Perhaps most tellingly, shoppers can also sort their lamps, or any other products, by customers' ratings and reviews.

The Reviews feature at Amazon (and at most other major online retailers) expands and formalizes a source of information that is only sporadically available in a supermarket setting: the opinions and experiences of other shoppers. Amazon customers can post reviews of the items they have purchased and rate the goods on a scale of five stars. Sellers too can be rated, so that an online merchant with particularly good customer service might appear as a five-star seller (or close to it) while merchants providing a less satisfactory customer experience won't be able to display as many stars. Amazon even provides a facility for the reviews to be reviewed. A comment that is inappropriately rude, vengeful, or profane, or that appears to be self-serving spam, can be flagged by other viewers for review and possible deletion by Amazon. Conversely, reviews that are pegged as particularly valuable rise to the top of the list, with the best reviews prominently displayed on the Amazon product page. Thus, not only are the products being ranked by visitors to Amazon's website; the reviews are being ranked as well.

The ability of both Amazon and visitors to the site to distinguish high-quality and low-quality reviews with a reasonable degree of accuracy is important to the success of the system. A site overrun with largely untrustworthy content would quickly (and understandably) lose the confidence of the buying public.

We are back, once again, to something like a report-card model of providing information. Amazon's star rating system acts like schools' A through F grades, so that even a product with hundreds of individual reviews can be assessed almost instantly. On the other hand, shoppers wanting additional details can read the individual reviews for more information—akin to a teacher's written comments on a report card—with the added luxury of having multiple reviews to choose from and knowing that the reviews themselves are ranked according to their overall utility.

5   Something Is Missing

The online information milieu for shoppers is rich. Amazon alone reportedly offers more than 180 million products and, as we just detailed, provides extensive information on most of them. Nevertheless, there is still a substantial disconnection between the information needs of some consumers and the information provided by online retailers. A shopper purchasing a shirt on Amazon can find a lot of information about the shirt's price, fabric, color, size, comfort, pattern, stitching, shipping and return options, washability, and durability, and about the service reputation of the merchant. But Amazon and other online marketers generally don't provide information to answer questions such as these:

Was this shirt made by child labor?
Does it have a small global warming "footprint"?
Are the dyes toxic?
Was the workplace a firetrap?
Are the workers treated with dignity?
Am I funding a warlord by purchasing this item?

Let's call these questions about a product's *sustainability*. Information that addresses these questions provides insight into how much a particular product contributes to or subtracts from the overall well-being of the world, with consideration given to the product's economic, social, workplace, health, and environmental impacts.

We have made repeated mention of so-called perfect information, and of the importance of information to the efficient functioning of the market. Now we can return to a question we asked earlier: What sort of information? What are the types of information that should be added to routine marketplace transactions to bring the information milieu closer to the ideal? What does good enough information look like?

Information on the sustainability attributes of products would go a long way toward improving the information milieu. We say this not simply because we would like to see more of this type of information, but because the market is calling for it. The efforts thus far to provide better information have been well meaning but piecemeal. Corporations' sustainability reports provide little or no information about individual products. Labels and certifications such as Fair Trade (for coffee) or Green Seal (for cleaning products) pertain to only a small portion of global trade.

But imagine that the marketplace were to routinely provide information that would answer questions about sustainability—information that would flow with each and every product as reliably as price information and product identity. For the moment we will put aside two big questions—why the market would want to make this information available, and how it might do so—and focus on what the overall effect might be.

Shoppers buying something in our imagined system—a shirt, a clock, a can of soda, a soccer ball, a sofa—now would get a sustainability score with every product. Much like Amazon's five-star rating system, the sustainability score could be simple but could be layered with deeper tiers of information. Each rating could be linked to much more comprehensive information that would be available to anyone who cared to delve deeper. Each shopper, for each product, would be able to unearth detailed information on the product's sustainability, to take a quick look at the product's sustainability rating, or to ignore sustainability information, much as shoppers now do with the nutrition labels on food products.

It is important to recognize how fundamentally different this information milieu would be from the current one. In the sustainability marketplace, each and every product would be rated. In the current market, ratings like those we listed above are very rare. Some products carry certifications through programs such as Fair Trade or Green Seal, but they are rare exceptions to the rule, and are typically sold at a substantial premium, much as organic foods are. The vast majority of products on store shelves provide no such information. They exist in a vague in-between state in which nothing is known about the attributes that contribute to or detract from societal well-being.

We look to the global economic system to make the world a better place—commerce creates wealth, and wealth creates well-being. But we know very well that commerce has a dark side—that it has the potential to destroy ecosystems, kill workers, enslave children, poison rivers, and so on. A market that embraces a "don't ask, don't tell" approach to sustainability attributes has no opportunity to utilize information in the service of bettering the world. A market that adopts sustainability information on the fringes, with an occasional Green Seal claim, brings about, at best, improvement at the fringes. A market that incorporated sustainability information at its very core would be a market that could change the world.

Again, imagine the marketplace in which the items for sale would be given sustainability ratings of one to five stars. Not only premium items would be rated in this way—not only the stuff sold in the high-priced stores where shoppers can afford to pay more to shop "clean and green." Every single item, in every single online or brick-and-mortar shop, would carry a sustainability rating, as reliably as it carries a price tag.

Sustainability ratings would become important and perhaps decisive in some shoppers' purchasing decisions. A consumer concerned about global warming or fair labor practices, an activist wanting to take activism down to the level of every purchase, or a father hoping to instill a caring attitude in his children might seek out five-star sustainability items.

On the other hand, no one would be obligated to take the information to heart. A shopper looking to buy a shirt could choose any item he wanted, even a one-star shirt made by underpaid workers in an unsafe firetrap of a factory in Bangladesh that dumps highly toxic dyes into the Buriganga River. The shopper could buy that shirt and can shrug uncaringly at its detrimental aspects, or, more likely, remain blissfully unaware of them. He wouldn't have to pay the sustainability rating any mind; he could ignore it as readily as he might ignore the calorie count on a box of donuts.

But what about Walmart? Which shirts would that giant multinational chain choose to carry to stock in its thousands of stores around the world? Walmart isn't an impulse shopper and isn't dragging three unruly kids through a store as it makes its purchasing decisions. Walmart pays extremely careful attention to the items it places on its shelves. Would it stock the one-star shirts? Give this some thought for a moment. Put yourself in the shoes[1] of the Walmart manager making purchasing decisions as to which shirts to carry. What weight, if any, would you give to the sustainability stars? What factors would come into play in making that decision?

We don't, for a moment, imagine that Walmart would immediately subscribe to a five-star-only policy, or carry only the highest-rated products in each of its product lines. Shoppers want what they want. If the latest and coolest iPad or smartphone had only a two-star rating, Walmart would carry it anyway. But it isn't difficult to imagine a sort of rising tide for all products once a sustainability rating system was in place. It already works that way with conventional product ratings. Neither Apple nor Samsung would be content to see its devices receive consistently low product ratings from consumers on Amazon or any other shopping site. Consumers' dissatisfactions would lead to quick upgrades to their products to bring them into line with customers' expectations.

Similarly, neither Apple nor Samsung would want to surrender the competitive advantage of higher sustainability star ratings. Each would want to outdo the other with multi-starred products, demonstrating to consumers that its electronics were not only full-featured but also planet-friendly.

The existence of the star rating system—the addition of better information to the market—changes many decisions, even if it isn't clear in advance whose decisions will change or in what manner. But it is important to recognize that the changes would come about only if the star system were to become almost universal, applicable to all products in all geographic locations. Sustainability stars would have to work on a scale and in a manner that would parallel the market's other great information tool: prices.

Differences in prices don't create a competitive dynamic in the marketplace. It is *information* about differences in prices that makes that happen. If a consumer can buy Product A in Los Angeles for $15 and the very same product in New York for $5, the Los Angeles merchant only feels competitive pressure to lower prices if shoppers are aware of an alternative, better price for the same item. If Product B fills the same need as Product A, and sells for only $1, then both the LA and NY merchants may have to rethink their product pricing if consumers know of the alternatives and change their buying habits as a result.

Despite the oversimplification of this description, at its core is the fundamental mechanism for the workings of the capitalist market, in which constant exchanges of information about shops' offerings, consumers' desires, products' prices, and alternative products create a quasi-equilibrium that helps the supplies of products to equal the demand for them and keeps prices for similar products reasonably competitive. There will always be a market for high-priced items in places (such as the north coast of Alaska) where delivery is difficult, or in shops (such as Tiffany and Prada) where price is a secondary consideration to luxury, service, and status. But the luxury market occupies a small niche of global commerce, while the bulk of transactions focus on keeping costs to a minimum.

If all products were subject to the sustainability star system, a similar dynamic could kick in. Consumers could consider (or not consider) the star ratings of what they would buy, and could choose (or not choose) alternatives partly on the basis of those ratings. Each participant in the shopping community would give the stars as much weight as he or she deemed appropriate in each transaction. Through billions of transactions, sustainability attributes would reach their own market-driven equilibrium. To the extent that the attributes were important to shoppers around the world, the entire world would begin to respond.

We are now back to the almost magic way that the capitalist marketplace offers up shoes in styles, colors, sizes, price ranges, and variations unimaginable in a Soviet-style system of central planning. With a sustainability rating system in place, the market could work similar magic, sorting through billions of pieces of information about the things consumers hold dear—about our collective human values—and responding accordingly to satisfy consumers' demand.

If all consumers were to steer their purchases toward five-star goods, death-trap factories in Bangladesh might become a thing of the past, global warming might begin to abate, toxic substances might no longer be found in toys, and gemstones mined by ruthless warlords might no longer be on the market. If, as would almost certainly be the case, only *some* shoppers were to give weight to the sustainability stars for *some* purchases, at least *some* progress would be made toward making the world a better place.

Sustainability star ratings would provide the information that could make the connection between the widely held values of sustainability and the millions of individual products that make up the modern consumer marketplace. If the values of sustainability—values such as ensuring that workplaces are safe—are widely and deeply held in the population at large, then a sustainability rating system can be expected to have a broad and deep effect on market dynamics. Conversely, if the vast numbers of consumers give no more than lip service to sustainability values—if the stars are simply ignored—the effect would be muted.

The star system also can be thought of in terms of its influence on innovation in the capitalist marketplace. Innovation conventionally revolves around lowering the prices of products and adding features to products that are attractive to consumers. A sustainability star system would take societal values that appear to be widely held and deeply felt and bring them down to the level of individual products, so that the forces that drive innovation forward could be brought to bear in responding to those values with all the creativity the marketplace can muster. To the extent that the stars truly reflected values that were fundamentally important to shoppers, the innovative forces unleashed would be powerful indeed.

A Simple Example: BGH

An example might help make this all a bit more concrete. Rather than tackle the entire marketplace and all aspects of sustainability, let's consider a simpler situation: the sale of milk, and a single attribute of milk that is occasionally of concern to consumers. Dairy farmers sometimes use bovine growth hormone (BGH)—a product of genetic engineering—to increase milk production of their cows. Not all consumers are comfortable with the notion of chemically stimulating cows to produce more milk than they would under natural conditions, or with the use of genetically engineered growth hormones that, some feel, might be present in the milk they are drinking.

As a result of the use of BGH, and consumers' backlash to its use, the market for milk has become segmented. Two types of milk are sold: milk that is clearly marked as produced on farms that do not use BGH[2] and milk that isn't marked as to whether it comes from farms that use BGH. To our knowledge, no milk is labeled as from cows that *have* been given BGH, even though, in view of public concern about BGH, one might expect there to be such a label. In other words, there is "no BGH" milk, and there is "no information on BGH" milk, but no one is selling "yes, we use BGH" milk.

Shoppers have become segmented as well. Three types of consumers have emerged: those who will only buy no-BGH milk, those who dislike the idea of BGH but not to the point of actively shopping for the no-BGH variety, and those who don't care about BGH one way or the other. And once again, just as there is no yes-BGH milk on the shelves, there are no consumers actively searching out milk from yes-BGH cows. From an information standpoint, that's how we describe the milk market as it currently exists. In a moment, we will elaborate on the same market as it would appear with more complete information. But we would be remiss if we didn't first acknowledge the fierce controversies that have revolved around the informational aspects of BGH labeling.

The makers of BGH, who sell it to some milk producers, don't want other milk producers labeling their products with language such as "BGH free." From the perspective of the BGH manufacturers, such labels imply that BGH somehow makes the milk less wholesome. Consumer advocates and some milk producers, on the other hand, take the view that shoppers have a right to know about how their milk has been produced, particularly when a significant portion of those shoppers are concerned about artificial hormones and about the fact that dairy cows are being hormonally induced to go into a sort of biological hyperdrive in order to produce more milk.

We approach the matter from an entirely different angle, looking at it in terms of better information in the market. As we have said repeatedly, the market can never achieve a state of perfect information, but it can certainly get closer to perfection through the provision of better information. Providing straightforward information about the use of BGH would, in fact, move the milk market a step closer to the informational ideal. Controversies aside, could such information make for a more efficient market?

That question brings us back to a system of sustainability stars, or at least a simplified version of it: a hypothetical rating system that would apply only to milk and that would have, instead of five stars, only two ratings: Yes and No. The BGH label (which probably would be a bit more graphically sophisticated than the one shown here in figure 5.1) would be affixed to every bottle and every carton of milk offered in every market in the world. Would the market work better for it?

Figure 5.1

Several things would change right away. The very large market segment of no-information milk would vanish, as all milk would be either no-BGH or yes-BGH. The effort a shopper would have to expend to know the status of milk would be reduced almost to zero. Without the label, a shopper might have had to visit a certain store to be assured of no-BGH milk, or might even have had to become familiar with a store's policies regarding dairy products. Now the information would be readily and simply available. For the sizable group of shoppers who cared about the issue but who in the past couldn't be bothered to make the effort to seek out no-BGH milk or to discern the status of "no-information" milk, the bar would have been lowered, and relevant information would be at hand.

For marketers, the information would provide an important guide to product placement. Markets for milk would quickly differentiate themselves through consumers' buying habits. Shoppers in Argentina might strongly prefer no-BGH milk, while shoppers in Brazil might not make much of a distinction. More likely, local preferences would emerge—for example, consumers in East Los Angeles might strongly prefer no-BGH milk, while over in Westside 75 percent of purchases might be of yes-BGH milk. Milk distributors could use the market data to provide precisely the products that were favored in each area. Dairy farmers could also adjust to the information, creating the right supply to meet the local demands of the market.

Milk prices would self-adjust on the basis of the new information. If no-BGH milk were purchased by a very small number of shoppers as something of a niche specialty, it probably would be sold at a premium price. If, on the other hand, no-BGH milk were widely preferred by consumers, its price probably would be close to that of the yes-BGH milk with which it would be competing.

The price of milk wouldn't be the only price that would self-adjust. The price of BGH itself would respond to shifting demands as the dynamics of the milk market became clearer. If yes-BGH milk were to lose market share, the manufacturers of BGH might choose to lower the cost of the hormone to encourage more widespread use. On the other hand, if the labeling didn't change the demand for yes-BGH milk—that is, if consumers didn't appear to base their purchasing decisions on the new bit of information—the manufacturers of BGH would have a powerful additional marketing tool with which to sell their product, as they would now be able to use market data to assure dairy farmers of a robust market for yes-BGH milk.

Thus, several things would have contributed to a market for milk that would work "better," in some sense, than the market that functioned with less information about BGH. Even if the improvements would be marginal, they are worth articulating:

• Shoppers would have easy access to information on BGH on all milk cartons and could more readily buy the type of milk they preferred.
• Farmers, distributors, and grocers would get clear market signals about the demand for milk produced with or without use of BGH.
• BGH manufacturers too would get clearer signals from the market.
• The prices of yes-BGH and no-BGH milk would adjust in each local market according to the demand from consumers for each kind of milk.
• The price of BGH would adjust in a more informed market.

In addition, the presence of a BGH label would provide continual feedback on the level of consumers' concern about BGH. But the label might seal its own fate over time. A complete lack of response by consumers to whether milk producers used or didn't use BGH might indicate that there is no further need for a BGH label, since consumers don't really care about its presence or absence. If a large number of consumers avoided purchasing yes-BGH milk, the use of BGH at dairy farms might be phased out, and again there would be no need for a BGH label. It is in the middle ground, where some consumers do and some consumers don't respond to BGH-related information, that the label would serve an ongoing purpose.

An important feature of the hypothetical market improvements articulated above is that, in isolation, they aren't very impressive. They are marginal improvements in market efficiency, at best, and can perhaps be thought of more as changes to the market than as clear-cut improvements. A change in the price of BGH, for example, will be an "improvement" to the manufacturer if the manufacturer can sell it an increased price, but the increase is obviously no improvement as far as the buyer is concerned. An economist may see the change as the market "getting things right," or at least more nearly right than before, but for the individual participants in the market the only obvious improvement is the newfound ease of distinguishing yes-BGH from no-BGH milk—an improvement that, like the others, is in the eye of the beholder. A more significant change is in the market's new-found ability, which information makes possible: The invisible hand of the marketplace can now respond to a social issue that is of concern to a significant portion of the population.

Tweaking the Market

We can compare the list of advantages of BGH information against the more familiar advantages of having access to information about price. The advantage of knowing what something costs allows individual shoppers to make informed choices about whether to purchase it. For a consumer buying a carton of milk, the advantage of price information offers, at best, the prospect of saving a few dimes by shopping at one store instead of another. But easy access to price information for milk is also what communicates a "price signal" to the market writ large, leading to competitive pricing between stores and creating an information milieu that continually adjusts the supply of milk and the demand for it. No central Ministry of Dairy Products is needed; the adjustments are spontaneous.

The advantages of competition in the marketplace are similarly elusive, at least at the level of market participants. No matter how enthusiastically we embrace competition as central to the modern market system, the last thing a manager of a Burger King wants to see is a McDonald's opening up across the street. Direct head-to-head competition between the restaurants might compel the Burger King manager to lower his restaurant's prices or to spend limited capital on upgrades to its décor and its kitchen equipment. Whatever advantages may arise from the newfound competitive environment are difficult for the hard-pressed manager to appreciate, and customers may not even notice the small price adjustments that occur as a result.

At one level of economic activity, then, the benefits of competition or pricing information—the mainstays of the capitalist market—are difficult to articulate and, once stated, may not seem impressive. Only when one steps back from an individual transaction or an individual establishment and looks at the larger picture of the economy as a whole, painted by trillions of transactions by billions of consumers at millions of establishments, do the benefits become more clear. The never-ending series of tweaks to the economy keep the overall system in tune, even though any individual tweak, on its own, is fairly trivial.

So too with the role of sustainability information in the economic system. The BGH example is nothing more than a tweak—a minor change to a minor commodity with only the smallest of consequences. Only when the information milieu is extended to millions of products and billions of transactions can the enormous capacity of such information to bring about change be appreciated. All the tiny, virtually insignificant shifts in the marketplace, when compounded over many orders of magnitude, add up to broad changes in the world writ large.

The market creates compelling global positives as well as dire negatives. Introducing sustainability information into the market does nothing less than change the world, shifting its balance of positive and negative attributes and remaking it as a more accurate and honest reflection of the values held by its billions of inhabitants. The provision of information isn't a guarantee of greater sustainability, just as BGH information is no guarantee of a shift in the type of milk consumed and just as warnings on cigarette packages are no guarantee that people will change their smoking habits. But in each case the information allows the market to more directly reflect the value system of those doing the shopping. Each pack of cigarettes purchased reflects a complex calculus of individual values, a highly personal (even if largely unconscious) weighing of all the negatives (health effects, cost, stinkiness) against all the positives (looking cool, social engagement, indulging a habit, satisfying a craving, making a statement). The same goes for BGH information ("Who do I believe: Monsanto and the FDA, who say BGH is perfectly fine, or the governments of Canada, Japan, and the European Union, all of which have banned the use of BGH?") and all the other attributes of sustainability that could be added to the five-star sustainability indicator we have been discussing.

We ask the reader's indulgence for one more hypothetical example. Imagine a label on clothes that conveys yes-or-no information about child labor. Like the BGH label, the child labor label is universal, applied to all clothing items around the world, not only a tiny specialty segment of "Fair Trade" clothing. Stretch your imagination even further and imagine the label to be reliable—a No genuinely conveys a high degree of credibility that no children were involved in the clothing's manufacture. This information tweaks the market in much the same way as does the BGH label. Its reach is much broader, however, affecting not only a single product line (milk) but the thousands of products making up the clothing sector. More importantly, its effects extend directly to the human beings manufacturing clothing around the world. Each additional attribute that comes under the sustainability umbrella, each class of products included, and each geographic area involved extends and multiplies the number of tweaks occurring and their overall effect.

People care about sustainability attributes—greenhouse gases, child labor, worker safety, genetically engineered hormones, toxic chemicals—a lot. Or a little. Or not at all. Each person has his or her own value set that is brought to bear in reacting to the information at hand. What's more, personal values change as new information comes to the fore, or as personalities adjust to new circumstances in life. To the extent that the global population embraces sustainability, that embrace will be reflected in a market that robustly provides information on sustainability. Before consumers can react to sustainability attributes, though, the information about these attributes must be present, more or less universally, in our economic system.

The eventual extent of the effects, and their particular nature, depends on the collective human values of billions of shoppers around the world.

6 Where Does Sustainability Information Come From?

If society were to decide to inject sustainability information into the economic system, where would such information originate? How would it be managed? Who would ensure its credibility?

For a simple informational demand, such as a BGH notice on a milk carton, the mechanisms involved would be relatively simple. The dairy farmer producing the milk knows with certainty whether or not BGH is used on the farm. That information would have to be retained through the small number of steps involved in bringing the milk from the farm to the supermarket. As milk was aggregated from individual farms to delivery trucks, intermediate cooperatives, and processing and packaging plants, BGH-related information would have to be retained so that the milk could be sold in the supermarket with the appropriate "Yes BGH" or "No BGH" indicator.

For something like a five-star sustainability indicator, though, the information milieu would be much more complicated. The process of assigning the stars and preserving the underlying information, as millions of products made their way through the commercial stream, would necessitate some choices about very complex issues. For some items of information, such as BGH use, the challenge would be the straightforward one of preserving information from the point of origin through a final sale. But other types of information have to be created before they can be preserved. A product's contribution to greenhouse gases, for example, isn't a self-evident piece of information, the way BGH use is. If a product's sustainability rating is to be based partly on greenhouse-gas contributions, then seemingly a protocol would have to be established to document how the contribution is determined, rated, and presented. In this respect, greenhouse gases are like other more familiar but equally non-obvious product attributes, such as calories-per-serving, gross vehicle weight, or toxic constituents. Information about such attributes can be provided readily enough, but it is only useful in the context of a fairly standardized means of determining what information is to be presented.

Existing product information comes from a number of sources, and as a result of various directives and practices. The original manufacturer is obviously an important source of product information, but so are merchants. Industry associations play a role by creating uniform standards to which categories of products must adhere. A camera's ISO (film-speed) setting and a router's 802.11 (wireless) designation are examples of industry standards—standards that were arrived at through an arduous international consensus process. Government requirements play a similar role in mandating that certain information, such as nutritional labeling, appear on certain products. And product reviews—whether from journalists, organizations, bloggers, or commenters—play a large (and, no doubt, increasing) role in bringing forward information on individual products.

The information milieu, then, is a hybrid sort of creature, a combination of centralized and formalized information requirements that mix together with a hodgepodge of ad hoc information from numerous unfettered sources. This same hybrid mix can form a basis for providing sustainability information to the market. Yes, a formalized metric for documenting a product's contribution to greenhouse gases may be needed, but this is also an attribute that can be addressed through less formalized approaches. Because there are many facets to marketplace information, there are also many ways we can begin to create broad and comprehensive sustainability information.

One of the most effective starting points would be actions taken by a very large purchaser. This could be a private-sector buyer, such as Walmart or Target, or a public buyer, such as the US government or the European Union. These entities, spending tens or hundreds of billions of dollars each year, have the budget power to establish purchasing standards and reporting specifications affecting broad swaths of the global market.

Let's begin with the private sector. Suppose that Walmart announced to its suppliers a policy along the following lines:

Beginning in 20XX, all products sold at Walmart should include a URL where consumers can find sustainability information on the specific product, and can post their own observations about products' sustainability.

There are many variations on what a sustainability policy might look like, how it would be worded, and the specifics of what, in fact, was required of suppliers, but for the moment, we will stick with the above hypothetical and work through some of its meaning.

The crucial phrase, of course, is "sustainability information." What does that mean?

In a rigidly constructed information system, each element of sustainability would be well defined, as would the type of data to be presented. Some sort of reporting authority—a corporation, a government agency, an international organization, or a "blue ribbon panel" of experts—would specify what is to be reported and how to report it. An example of this approach is the Global Reporting Initiative, which has codified sustainability reporting in great detail for different areas (e.g., economic, social, environmental) and for different sectors of the economy (e.g., financial services, airports, electric utilities, food processing). In the case of "market presence," for example, GRI calls for reporting a "range of ratios of standard entry level wage by gender compared to local minimum wage at significant locations of operation."

In a completely open-ended system, on the other hand, the term 'sustainability information' would mean whatever the manufacturer of a product thinks it means, and the website for the product would contain information the manufacturer deems relevant. If the manufacturer thinks information about greenhouse gases is relevant, such information will be included in whatever format the manufacturer deemed fitting. If greenhouse gases don't seem significant, no information will be forthcoming. In a more structured system, Walmart would lay out the specifications of the types of information that should be included, providing specifications for what type of greenhouse-gas information should be reported, when it should be reported, and how the data should be generated. A hybrid of these two approaches would include a *de minimis* set of standardized information on sustainability, along with any additional information that seems worth including on an *ad hoc* basis.

For any of these scenarios, visitors to a product's sustainability-information website would have the opportunity to post comments about the overall quality of the information reported and the types of information that aren't—but should be—included. The presence of greenhouse-gas information might get a lot of favorable feedback from consumers, for example, whereas the absence of information on child labor might elicit a large number of negative comments. It isn't hard to envision a system that evolves—one that starts with only a few structured elements, then solidifies over the years as consumers' use of the sites and collective comments on useful and missing information help to clarify what kind of sustainability information is most desired by users.

Walmart could establish its policy as an absolute: "Provide sustainability information if you want to do business with us." Or it could craft its policy as an incentives-based policy: "Only products with sustainability information are featured in our ads, get preferential store displays, are put on sale, etc." Or it could make the policy entirely voluntary: "We would like to see a link to sustainability information, but really it's up to you if you want to provide it."

Of course, Walmart is highlighted here as an example, and, as the world's largest merchandiser, an example chosen for obvious reasons. But other large retailers also could serve as examples. So could large purchasers, such as the US government, which could announce a policy of purchasing only goods that include sustainability information.

Whoever makes that first move, and however it is structured, an announcement along the lines of what we have been discussing carries an unmistakable message: Sustainability information is now a necessary component of doing business. An equally important if more subtle corollary to the message is that the public's response to a company's sustainability information will be an important consideration in future transactions. Those two elements—sustainability webpages for individual products, and the opportunity for feedback from consumers—are the informational requirements needed to bring sustainability squarely into the marketplace. They aren't equivalent to the simple five-star rating we described earlier, but they constitute an enormous step in that direction. The link to sustainability information for a product is the Web-enabled analogue to the BGH label we imagined for milk. It serves a similar function by eliminating the marketplace option of staying silent. Once sustainability information becomes an expected and normal part of a marketplace transaction, consumers are able to respond to that information as a direct reflection of their individually held values, and of the weight that each person assigns to those values. And now not only can consumers make their market preferences known (by buying or not buying products partly on the basis of sustainability information); by using whatever commenting or ranking mechanisms are built into the sustainability-information websites, they can also weigh in on the sustainability information itself.

In short, undesirable products will tend to disappear from the marketplace, as they always have. The reason Edsels are no longer available is that consumers didn't want to buy them. The difference now is that sustainability information can be woven into consumers' choice about what is or isn't desirable. BGH milk will disappear from the market if consumers—once they have information about BGH—treat it as they treated Edsels. In much the same manner, undesirable forms of information can be expected to diminish as consumers' preferences about what makes for a good presentation of such information become known. It isn't beyond reason to suppose that a five-star sustainability ranking system could emerge spontaneously from the push and pull of consumers' demands, although reason also dictates that an externally imposed, consciously designed ranking system might be needed to bring such a system into being in the near term and have it be applied consistently throughout the market.

Sustainability Information: An Example

We can apply the BGH example more broadly to illustrate what sustainability information—one variant of it, at least—might look like, and how the market might respond to its presence.

Suppose that Walmart or Amazon or another large market presence—Target, Tesco, Carrefour, Alibaba, the US government, NATO, the European Union, the United Nations—announces its expectation that products will henceforth include sustainability information. The announcement adopts the hybrid approach we described above. The nature and the extent of the information will largely be at the discretion of each product manufacturer, but should include, at a minimum, the following three elements:

identification of the factory or facility where the product originated
steps taken to minimize the "carbon footprint" of the product
steps taken to ensure workers' safety and dignity.

Each product has a Web address at which anyone interested can access information on the product's sustainability details and visitors can comment on the quality of the information provided.

Such a system could easily involve detailed forms, guidance documents, and instructions, but that isn't what we have in mind, at least not for this particular mental exercise. Our system is simple: a statement of expectations, and a list of minimal requirements, no more elaborate than the one just presented.

Imagine that you are a merchant with a product or a service that you have marketed to Walmart[1] in the past, and that you have now become aware of Walmart's new policy. You have to decide whether you want to continue marketing through Walmart. If the answer is Yes, you are obliged to respond to the new sustainability policy, which means evaluating the information you have available and making several decisions about each of your products:

Do I have the information I need—about the manufacturing facility, greenhouse-gas footprint, and worker conditions—to respond to the new policy and prepare a sustainability report, or do I have to gather additional information?

Am I satisfied with the information as it is, or do I want to be able to tell a better story on sustainability than the information currently allows?

What additional information on sustainability, beyond the minimum, do I want to provide, if any?

Where will I post the information on the Internet?

What type of online feedback system should I provide for users' comments?

No matter how you choose to answer these questions (along with any auxiliary questions that you infer), your responses will differ from one product to the next, and will also be very different from the responses of other suppliers providing information for *their* products. Some suppliers will, no doubt, provide very perfunctory information; others will provide elaborate detail on the sustainability-related aspects of their products. Some will address only the three elements that Walmart identified; others will range far and wide over the broad landscape of products' sustainability. Some will provide accurate information; others will inflate their sustainability claims, lie outright, use boilerplate language with little meaning, and make mistaken claims about their products. And no doubt there will be responses that are hard to imagine ahead of time but that will add further variability to the overall information system.

In the absence of a standardized format (which Walmart doesn't provide in this particular hybrid example), the sustainability-information webpages also will be highly variable, both in presentation and in the feedback and commenting options they give consumers.

We can reasonably expect a great degree of variability in consumers' feedback to the sustainability pages. Walmart sells many thousands, perhaps millions, of discrete products, and now each of them will have its own sustainability webpage. Many of the pages may never have a single visitor; others will have page views but no consumer feedback. Conversely, highly trafficked pages will be visited thousands of times a day and will amass an enormous amount of feedback from users.

This would be a messy, somewhat chaotic system. The market, though, has a wonderful capacity for bringing order to the chaos of millions of individual decisions, and it can do so here as well, not only with the webpages but also with the products on the shelves of Walmart's stores. We have deliberately started with a loosely structured "capitalistic" version of a sustainability information system, one with a minimal degree of planning and centralized organization, in order to emphasize the self-organizing possibilities that are inherent in an information-rich system.

Sustainability at Dupreshi

Suppose that a facility accepts Walmart's conditions and decides to take the minimalist approach by posting a webpage—one sustainability webpage, out of hundreds of thousands of pages for the individual products that Walmart carries—with three short descriptions of the three required elements:

Factory identification: This item was made by the Dupreshi Garment Company in factory #345.

Carbon footprint: We have requested that all our suppliers and shippers take steps to minimize their emission of greenhouse gases.

Worker safety and dignity: Dupreshi follows applicable laws in all its facilities and subscribes to the United Nations' Guiding Principles on Business and Human Rights.

As we mentioned earlier, it is possible that this particular page will never be viewed and will never receive any feedback. But the page may have a steady viewership and receive plenty of feedback. Under the right circumstances, it may even go viral. Over time, the entire spectrum of visibility may unfold. A page may languish in obscurity for a year or two, then attract attention for one reason or another and receive a lot of commentary and notice, then fade back into quietude years later.

Suppose that, after a long period of quiet, a viewer posts an anonymous comment:

I work at Dupreshi Factory #345 at 185 Lamatia Road in Chittagong, Bangladesh. Do not believe what you read here. Working conditions are terrible and dangerous. Many workers are children no more than 10 or 11 years of age. Last week a young girl crushed her arm in a packaging machine and was told to leave and not come back. She has no medical care for her injury.

This is followed soon after by a second comment:

It's not just the Dupreshi workers who are made to suffer. I live 100 meters from their Chittagong factory, and the stench from the factory is unbearable. It's so strong, it makes the whole community sick. I don't know what chemical it is, or what causes it, but we have complained time and time again to the owners, to no avail.

What happens next? Even if 99 times out of 100 the answer is "Nothing much," it isn't at all difficult to imagine a scenario in which the comment leads to a response of some sort. Perhaps someone posts the comment on her Facebook page, urging her friends not to shop at Walmart. A community organizer in Chittagong might urge other workers to post their observations about working conditions at the factory on the webpage. A reporter might telephone Dupreshi and Walmart and ask for a comment, or might arrange to visit the factory. Walmart might decide to review its supplier relationship with Dupreshi. And, of course, the company itself might respond directly:

These are nothing but lies, and were probably put here by our competitors to cause trouble and discredit us. No children work at our Lamatia Road factory. No one was injured and fired. Our neighbors have not complained. Dupreshi operates with the highest degree of responsibility for our workers and for the environment.

The dialogue raises obvious questions about the truth of the situation at Dupreshi. But even in the absence of clarity, the exchanges have added to the information on the factory. The original sustainability report identified the facility only as Factory #345, but the subsequent commentary added a street address that was confirmed by the company's response. We see here the tiniest of informational tweaks: the addition and validation of a piece of information that wasn't previously available.

What of the diametrically opposed claims about Dupreshi's operations? Regardless of which set of comments is closer to the truth, the resulting dialogue brings a modicum of additional scrutiny to Dupreshi, leading customers, communities, journalists, and merchants to examine their respective relationships with the company in more detail. The attention, while no guarantee of change, increases the likelihood that Dupreshi will, at the very least, amend its sustainability report to provide more than the absolute minimum of information on its products, which will lead to further informational tweaks. In response to increased scrutiny (or even the possibility of it), Dupreshi might even go several steps further to change its manufacturing operations, tweaking its products as well as its sustainability information.

Variations on the above scenario will play out millions of times for millions of other products, and therein lies the potential of sustainability reporting. The simple provision of marketplace information may bring many small changes that may lead to enormous changes overall. Over time, small improvements to the system, such as improved location information, can result in much fuller accounts of a product's sustainability attributes and significant changes in how those products are produced.

The hypothetical sustainability system we have imagined here has a few straightforward features that magnify its potential:

Large-scale participation   The incentive for participating in the sort of sustainability system we have described is access to markets worth many billions of dollars that service many millions of consumers. A small merchant attempting to implement such a system with his suppliers would have little leverage to make it happen. A buyer operating on the scale of Walmart or the federal government could not easily be ignored.

Easy and open access   The sustainability information is meant for anyone with an interest in it. Think of it as a Sunday newspaper's advertising insert, chock full of unstructured but useful information and available for everyone to see. Except, of course, the information is online. It is accessible not only by directly visiting the Web link for the information, but through general Internet searches that display the information in routine search results. A search on Dupreshi would turn up not only the sustainability page highlighted here, but also all other pages submitted by the company for any of its other products that it markets through Walmart.

Ability to add observations and comments   Viewers can not only read a product's sustainability webpage, but can also add their own observations and comments, whether from the perspective of a consumer, a worker, a neighbor, or an investigator, or from any other vantage point that brings a person or an organization into contact with the information.

Dynamic updates   Walmart called for information on location, greenhouse gases, and working conditions, all of which Dupreshi provided. But users' comments delved into another subject deemed important enough, by at least some participants, to be worthy of comment: the pollution of the surrounding neighborhood attributed to the factory. The added information creates the possibility of subsequent responses as well as an impetus for revising future sustainability reports—for this one Dupreshi product, for other products from the same company, and for products from other suppliers—that address the new sets of concerns.

Self-correcting information   Bad information will undoubtedly come forward, but the attentions of tens or hundreds or thousands of viewers, along with viewers' comments and ratings, will ultimately separate the wheat from the chaff. Untrustworthy information will lose out to high-quality information based on collective decisions in an information marketplace in much the same way that eight-track tapes lost out to cassettes.

In our thoroughly hypothetical situation, we can make market participants say or do anything we please in response to Dupreshi's sustainability report, just as we crafted the report itself to suit our purposes. Likewise, we can have Dupreshi respond—or not—as we see fit. The exercise has value in making concrete the ways in which participants can create and react to sustainability reports, but it also puts undue focus on a single product from a single company and on the small number of individuals who take an interest in the information provided by the company about that one product. In the process of focusing on a single drop, we risk losing sight of the ocean.

Dupreshi's response may be interesting, but the big story will be the response of the market as a whole. What happens in the world when thousands of companies inject into the market sustainability information on millions of products? The answer is straightforward: A market that is awash in sustainability information (and *only* a market that is awash in such information) will respond to that information in a manner that collectively reflects the values of the billions of market participants. The market is the blender that mixes together the endless number of consumers' reactions— "I care a lot about this, a little about that, and not at all about this other thing"—and sorts them out with its vast information-processing capabilities.

Can a "free-market" information system really work this way? Is it possible for a sustainability reporting system to actually present useful and trustworthy information when anyone can post to it? Common sense may seem to answer that it isn't possible—or at least, not very likely—that a crowdsourced system would prove reliable. But experience says otherwise. Wikipedia is an open online encyclopedia to which anyone can contribute. Individuals can, and do, try to "game" Wikipedia by posting scurrilous, misleading, or simply goofy information. But the online community and the rules under which Wikipedia functions are both robust enough that the end product is perhaps the most useful and widely used reference tool in the Internet. Crowdsourced information can be trustworthy.

Our suspicion, then, is that the direct provision of sustainability information will make the world a more sustainable place, because the bulk of the individuals in the market really do care about issues ranging from worker welfare to global warming. The complex web of dynamics that have the potential to alter Dupreshi's way of doing business or to rebalance the use of BGH in milk production will operate millions of times to move the market toward more fully and more accurately reflecting the values of all its participants.

Though there is no way to know in advance exactly how such a system would unfold in all its details, we can speculate about some of the ways in which it might present itself over time:

• Business operations would become more transparent. As companies make affirmative statements about individual facilities doing X, Y, or Z to advance sustainability, questions will arise about the accuracy and honesty of the statements. Some companies will respond with more of an open-door policy so that sustainability claims can be more readily verified.

• Factory workers would have an important voice. No one knows the actual conditions in a factory better than those who work there, but few workers have the means of voicing concerns about manufacturing conditions. Sustainability reporting will provide an open and anonymous forum in which concerns can be aired publicly.

• Third-party verification would become more commonplace. In much the same way that online businesses offer assurances by posting shopping safety and security seals like Better Business Bureau Accredited Business, PayPal Verified, or McAfee Secure, we would expect to see the emergence of a robust business of third-party vendors to validate the information in sustainability reports.

• Sustainability reporting would evolve rapidly. Even with the helter-skelter approach described here, with minimal guidance as to what a sustainability report is or what information it contains, the issues that bubble up to the surface will alter the appearance of subsequent reports and move them toward a similarity of focus, content, and style. Even in the absence of a central, universally recognized list of sustainability issues, the feedback loops we have described will help crystallize the appropriate set of reporting criteria.

Those are the informational building blocks needed to bring sustainability squarely into the marketplace. It is not yet the simple, five-star rating we described earlier, but it is an enormous step in that direction. The link to sustainability information for a product is the Web-enabled analogue to the BGH label we imagined for milk, and it serves a similar function by eliminating the marketplace option of staying silent. Once sustainability information has become a requirement (or at least a near-requirement), consumers will be able to respond to that information as a direct reflection of their individually held values, and of the weight that each of them accords to those values. And not only will consumers be able to make their market preferences known (by buying or not buying products partly on the basis of sustainability information); they will also be able to weigh in on the sustainability information itself by using the commenting or ranking mechanisms built in to the sustainability-information websites.

Undesirable products will tend to disappear from the marketplace, as they always have. The difference now, though, is that sustainability information will be woven into consumers' choices.

The sum total of all this will be a market shift toward sustainability—a shift as substantial as the underlying consumers' sentiment and oriented toward the features that the buying public deems most important. The shift may be very sizable, and indeed we suspect it will be. On the other hand, it may be relatively minor. After all, it isn't possible, from our parochial perspectives as we sit here in Washington D.C., to effectively gauge the overall sentiments of a market composed of billions of individuals making trillions of decisions. But once the appropriate information on sustainability is put forward, the market itself will make its collective sentiments known.

What of the five stars?

Earlier, we speculated about the advantages of a simple reporting system that would rate each product on a five-star sustainability scale. How—and where—does this fit in?

Visit almost any large buying site on the Internet, and the ratings are right there. For example, the four-out-of-five-stars rating for an AT&T phone (figure 6.1) represents the accumulated feedback from several hundred customers' reviews. A would-be buyer can read the full reviews, but can also get information in an instant-overview format through the star system. The option to provide a star-based ranking is a built-in feature of the system, but the actual ranking is the sum total of the inputs from users.

The same sort of approach could be used for sustainability rankings. The entity managing the sustainability sites (we are still using Walmart as our example here) can design the pages to include free-text submissions of information, observations, facts and opinions, and can provide the option for a simpler "rate this product's sustainability" feature, with users clicking

210 Corded Phone

★★★★☆ ☑ (356 customer reviews)

List Price: $18.79

Price: $9.30 & FREE Shippir

You Save: $9.49 (51%)

Figure 6.1

on one to five stars. The overall product-sustainability rating would be based on the total of combined user ratings, just as is the case with the AT&T phone's product rating.

The actual rating could be a straightforward sum of all users' ratings. It could also rely on input from users as only one of several factors leading to a star rating. Walmart could include other sources of information, such as a sustainability questionnaire submitted by the manufacturer for each product or input from a third-party certification organization, as a way of establishing an initial rating.

There are obviously many variations on how the rating system could be constructed, managed, and presented. Like the shopping sites themselves, the sustainability rating system probably would change as suppliers, merchants, shoppers, and other interested parties all learned about and became more familiar with the system. As initial weaknesses are identified—people will, no doubt, try to "game" the system with submissions intended to artificially boost or lower a product's ranking—these will be dealt with as the system grows and adjusts. For example, Walmart might decide to introduce an opportunity to rate the ratings, mirroring another feature that is common on shopping sites. (Was this review helpful? Thumbs up or thumbs down.) The written reviews deemed most useful by users would receive more visibility than other reviews; if the reviews include a star rating, then that rating could be given more weight than would a rating from an unhelpful review.

The Internet is clearly the ideal tool for making all this product-specific sustainability information available. That the Internet is a powerful mechanism for dispensing information is obvious. Less apparent is the powerful role the Internet can play in achieving a dynamic, geographically robust consensus among all market participants as to what information about each of the millions of items of commerce should be put forward.

Products should carry a simple webpage address that any interested party can visit to learn more about the attributes of the product that bear on social values. The webpage wouldn't be a product description page, such as one now finds on Amazon.com and on the sites of other online merchants (though it could certainly include links back to such commercial sites). Instead, it would be the product's sustainability page, which would focus on the types of environmental, social, and community issues that generally fit under the umbrella of the term 'sustainability'. Although we have envisioned a process that begins with one merchant (Walmart) initiating the provision of information, ultimately the sustainability pages should be available for all products, no matter where or how they are sold.

The webpage could describe where and how the product is made, where it is sold, the environmental impacts of its manufacture and use, the conditions under which the workers do their jobs to produce the product, and other important information. The webpage would allow visitors to the site to post comments and reviews. It also would have a rating mechanism so those same visitors could assess how well the information provided addresses any of their social values and concerns.

We will even go so far as to recommend setting aside a corner of the Internet for this activity. A Product Sustainability Information Protocol could be created to provide a unique set of addresses for sustainability pages. The Internet address could be identified with a PSIP:// header. A simple 4-by-4 alphanumeric construction, such as PSIP://S3RT.57BK provides more than a trillion combinations, which should be more than enough to get the process started. The URL is neat and compact, and can easily fit on almost any item in commerce. Every product for sale now would have a unique link to sustainability information that could be accessed as quickly as one can type in its eight-digit URL.

High-Quality Information in the Market

In essence, our proposition is this:

Information fuels the global marketplace. For the market to be at its best, the information must be of the highest quality. Information can be of high quality only if it informs consumers about things they care about—including the state of the world.

Put simply:

Better Information = Better Economic Performance = A More Sustainable World.

The market can move forward with information of middling quality, just as your car can run on gasoline even after a troublemaker has poured some water into its gas tank. The water degrades the quality of your fuel and lowers your vehicle's overall performance. Too much contaminated fuel and the car won't run at all. If the gas is only moderately degraded, however, the car will still run, though with varying amounts of chugging, pinging, coughing, and sputtering.

In our view, the Soviet economic system failed largely because the information "fuel" it needed was too heavily contaminated. The Soviet economy lacked the ability to generate the high-quality information that the market needed to function. The capitalist system operates much more effectively, chiefly because information generation and information flow are of much higher quality—more robust, more timely, more pertinent, and simply better—than they are in centralized economies. Neither communism nor capitalism functions at peak performance, however, and information shortcomings are a large part of the reason for their inability to do so.

The Soviet Union's Five-Year Plans were attempts to consolidate and respond to known information, but were also, by their very nature, obstacles to gleaning timely information and responding accordingly. A production schedule for factory output in 1955, designed in the 1950 Five-Year Plan and based on data from the 1940s, couldn't be successful without a mechanism for being highly responsive in the interim to new information. A particularly bad storm in one part of the USSR immediately changed the demand for boots, and no pre-determined production schedule could anticipate such demand or effectively respond to it. Changes in production had to await the next meeting of the Central Committee of the Footwear, Leather, and Leather Goods Industry, which then made a recommendation to the All-Union Artificial Hides and Film Materials Industrial Association, which then ... . You get the picture, we're sure.

It wasn't the accuracy of the information in the Five-Year Plan that was the main problem. The bigger problems that the Soviet system faced were that information was slow to materialize and that a lot of information was simply missing. Even if the planning process had been based on the best demographic numbers, supply-chain data, and consumption projections the world had ever seen, the plan would still have been information-poor when it came to responding to the demands of the market, and fairly blind and deaf to the types of new information that materialize constantly—like a sudden storm—in any dynamic economic system.

We know from experience that the capitalist economy does a far better job of reading the tea leaves of consumers' demand, understanding what is needed in the market, producing the right numbers and types of goods— wood screws, boots, shoes, phones—and getting them to the markets in which they are needed. Capitalism responds to information in a way that central planning cannot. The machinery of capitalism has hummed along, fueled by high-quality information, whereas the Soviet system sputtered and came to a halt.

But capitalism, as effective as it has been, still sputters and coughs from an informational fuel mix that is missing some significant ingredients. It can be made to operate much more effectively, and an important step in making that happen—our proposition—is to introduce better information into the marketplace to improve overall economic performance. This raises questions, however: What is meant by 'better'? What makes for "better performance" or "better information"?

Economics is very different from its sister disciplines in the hard sciences. The gravitational constant and plate tectonics are entirely independent of anything that human beings might want or feel about how things should be in this world. In fact, human beings could disappear from the planet entirely and these physical constants and geologic forces wouldn't be affected in the least. But remove humans from the marketplace and the marketplace itself disappears. Economics is essentially all about human desire. Narrowly construed, it is about what people want to buy and how much they are willing to pay for the things they want. In a more expansive view (only slightly more expansive), economics is about the things people *value*: not only what products they want and what prices they are willing to pay, but how those products comport with the personal values of each individual shopper: how a product comes into existence, what materials are used in its manufacture, how producers interact with workers and communities and with the planet in the course of making things.

Buying a pair of shoes, for example, can be seen as a simple desire: I want new shoes. But it's actually a far more complex set of desires: I want shoes of a particular style, color, brand, comfort, performance, durability, and price. I want shoes that other people will look at and say "Cool shoes!" I want good service and a flexible return policy. I want fast delivery and a comfortable shopping experience, whether I'm dealing with a brick-and-mortar store or an online merchant. And in addition, I want to buy the shoes with a clean conscience, even if I'm pretty vague about what I mean by that.

The marketplace has elevated one human desire—the desire to not pay more than one has to for a certain item—above all others, and does a reasonably thorough job of providing high-quality information about that particular aspect of our collective value system. But it falls short in other areas of our collective interests, particularly regarding social values. Even if we imagine that 99 percent of the world's consumers want BGH-free milk, or goods made without child labor, there is no way the market can respond to those consumers' desires, because high-quality information related to those values is simply not available. If the information were to come forward somehow—if information about the use of BGH or child labor were to adhere to each product—the market would become more responsive to our collective human desires.

Not everyone responds to the information in the same way, of course. If information on child labor were universally available for all products, some shoppers would reject goods made with child labor and others would ignore the information. Some shoppers would, no doubt, seek out such products, perhaps on the notion that by purchasing them they would be helping to support an impoverished family somewhere in the world. But whatever the choices made, the availability of the information permits participants in the market to respond as they see fit. As a result, the market not only becomes more efficient, it becomes a more complete and accurate reflection of the things that people actually want.

Thus, making the world a bit "better" is, at least in part, a matter of articulating human desires. A better market and better information are inextricably linked to one another, and both are tied to the things we want for ourselves and for the communities we live in, whether local, regional, or global. Defining our human desires will help in identifying the type of information the market needs to operate in peak fashion. Improving the information in the market will help us crystallize what our collective desires really are.

How to bring the right sort of information forward is the big challenge. Human beings are nothing if not diverse; there is no single list of the things people care about that covers all desires or that manages to give the right "weight" to how significant a specific desire may be. And humans are complex, so that any list of "things people desire" would grow very long very quickly. Isolating BGH, child labor, and deforestation as topics for which people have certain desired outcomes is well and good, but the isolated focus sidesteps hundreds of other topics of concern. Perhaps the most significant problem is that the people who bring goods forward in the global market aren't necessarily forthcoming, particularly with information that may seem less than flattering or that might be taken as being at odds with the values held by large segments of the population. If Dupreshi fired the underage employee whose arm was mangled by a packaging machine, it has no interest in making that information public.

The sustainability page for Dupreshi's products would be the vehicle for bringing such information forward.

Dupreshi's motivation for providing the information is clear: It wants to sell to Walmart, and Walmart—at least in our example—requires it. But why would Walmart or any other purchaser want to create a system for collecting and disseminating product-specific information on sustainability along the lines we have described?

Almost all large companies, particularly public-facing companies that interact directly with end consumers, are now grappling with the question of what to do about societal values. A great deal of effort is already being directed toward sustainability in the form of corporate reporting, product certifications, third-party audits of the supply chain, sustainable philanthropy programs, revisions to product specifications and contracts, and development of new metrics for proactively identifying unacceptable situations and for reporting progress toward sustainability goals. Walmart does all these things, and so do many other corporations.

Companies embrace sustainability goals in response to a broad set of motivations, not the least of which is that corporate managers are human beings who want to do the right thing for their company and for the world at large. They also act in their own conventional self-interest, embracing sustainability as a means of protecting and enhancing their corporate reputation and as a way to let customers know that—in many senses of the word—the company is a safe place to do business.

The globalization of both commerce and information exchange has made it increasingly difficult to maintain such an aura of safety. It isn't enough for Walmart's stores to be safe, with the requisite security guards, sprinkler systems, and the like. Each product on Walmart's shelves should have the same aura of safety. A child's toy made with toxic heavy metals isn't safe, nor is a collapsible stroller that can pinch a finger or a toe. But a sweatshirt sourced from an overseas firetrap of a factory is also not safe for its workers or for a shopper who will regret buying the sweatshirt at Walmart should Walmart's connection to that factory ever become clear.

Merchants will pursue better, finer-grained, more reliable sustainability information to make things safer for customers, for workers, for communities, for the environment, and for the merchants' bottom lines.

Really?

Is a five-star sustainability rating system really a workable concept? There are numerous reasons to suppose that it is not, particularly when it is envisioned along the largely unstructured lines we have described.

The main reason is one of information quality. Manufacturers posting their own sustainability information have every motivation to emphasize the positive features of their products and minimize (or omit entirely) mention of anything negative. Self-aggrandizing webpages amount to propaganda rather than useful/reliable information. Inviting anyone in the world to rank a product's sustainability with one to five stars, or to post textual information about the product, provides additional opportunities for misinformation: paid commenters who post artificially inflated glowing reports and always give five-star feedback, product competitors doing just the opposite and deliberately criticizing a product without a valid reason, dissatisfied consumers who simply want to "badmouth" a company by downgrading its products, and commenters who post to the wrong site or about the wrong product or who are misinformed about a product's sustainability attributes.

A reviewer of an early draft of this book worried that the problem of information quality was overwhelming, and that a sustainability rating system such as we are suggesting was unrealistic and probably unworkable. We have reason to feel much more hopeful, however.

Wherever rating systems exist, the prospects of gaming the system through faulty information exist. This may seem to be most true for the type of sustainability rating system we have written about—an open-ended system in which anyone and everyone can participate, no matter how well or how poorly informed they may be about the topic at hand. Despite the apparently fatal design flaw of a "crowdsourced" system, rating systems with such universal access exist and manage to function credibly.

We have mentioned one such system already: users' reviews and star ratings at Amazon.com. It isn't a naive system, with all users' posts and all star ratings treated equally. By actively soliciting feedback from customers who have purchased a specific product, Amazon increases the frequency of posts from users who have actual experience with a purchased item. The use of "Was this review helpful to you?" voting allows the site to identify and highlight both the most valuable negative reviews and the most valuable positive reviews. The "Report abuse" link below each review gives both sellers and buyers an opportunity to flag inappropriate postings for further review (and possible removal) by Amazon. A "Questions and Answers" feature offers a means of soliciting more direct feedback on how well a product functions in the real world. A separate system for rating merchants and for rating individual products also adds to credibility; purchasing a product from a merchant that has received thousands of ratings (Amazon posts the number received) and has an overall rating of 4.8 stars lends a strong air of legitimacy to the business, as it would be extremely difficult to consistently "game" the system thousands of times over.

Amazon's experience is worthy of note, as it is one of the world's largest online merchants, but it isn't the only model of a credible crowdsourced rating system. Rotten Tomatoes uses a star-based system for movies and separates the reviews of casual moviegoers from those of professional film critics. Users of the site can choose whether to trust the masses or to give more weight to the opinions of the critics. The e-commerce company eBay uses a somewhat different system than Amazon for rating products and merchants, but has also produced a system that potential customers find useful.

Credibility is possible even in the absence of star ratings and users' comments. Twitter has become an important tool for journalists, particularly those trying to track real-time developments of fast-breaking news stories. Even though anyone can post anything to Twitter, journalists have shown themselves to be reasonably adept at sorting the wheat from the chaff, verifying their sources of fast-breaking information, and avoiding the embarrassment of passing along false Twitter posts as newsworthy items.[2] One important (we're tempted to say near-miraculous) source of information is the crowdsourced online encyclopedia called Wikipedia. Anyone with an inclination to do so can contribute to or edit that widely cited reference work. Against all expectations, Wikipedia produces content that is largely credible and appropriate to encyclopedia-style entries. There are lapses in quality, to be sure, but they aren't so grave as to invalidate Wikipedia as one of the Internet's most valuable, widely used reference tools.

The point we are making isn't that any of the aforementioned systems can serve as a perfect model of a sustainability rating system for the world's commercial goods. It is simply that crowdsourced systems that self-regulate and provide meaningful information are possible.

Even in a rating system that convincingly provides reliable and credible information about products' sustainability, a challenge to the system still remains: What sort of information, exactly? What constitutes "sustainability"? What information, on what topics, should be reported? As we noted earlier, it is certainly possible to prescribe required information elements in advance, much as requirements for reporting taxes or filing a corporate annual report are specified in great detail. But we are partial to self-organizing systems, and again we point to Wikipedia as a quasi-model. There is no master list of encyclopedia entries to be written. Either the collective participants opt to create a Wikipedia entry for someone or something or they don't. Some articles have great depth; others are deemed "stubs"— essentially placeholders for topics of potential interest that are waiting for additional user-supplied information. The focus for sustainability attributes can be similarly crowdsourced, along with particular data elements and reporting criteria for each attribute.

Ultimately, tackling the issues of credible definition (about what sustainability means) and credible content (about how products promote sustainability) requires some sort of—for want of a better term—policing mechanism. Some entity is needed to decide that some information stays, some gets deleted, some remains obscure, and some rises to prominence, and that one product warrants five stars but another product only two. The entity could be the corporation managing the sustainability website— Walmart, in our hypothetical example. It could be a government agency acting in some sort of regulatory capacity. It could be a cadre of elite experts with deep knowledge and experience in matters of sustainability. Or it could, as we have suggested, be the largest "entity" of all: everyone. The same entity that makes Wikipedia work, that populates Amazon and Rotten Tomatoes, and elects parliamentarians and presidents can also drive the sustainability system forward in a workable fashion.

Impact

Information doesn't have to be seen to bring about changes. The simple possibility that it might be seen can be potent. A manufacturer creating a sustainability page (or more likely, multiple sustainability pages) for its product line will engage in a type of "what if" exercise to attempt to antici- pate the reactions of market participants all along the supply chain—bulk buyers, shippers, local communities, workers, advertisers, and consumers— in the event that they visit a product's sustainability page. The anticipation alone can be a compelling influence on behavior, even if it turns out that the website is never viewed, just as the possibility of an income tax audit can influence the taxpayer's behavior even if an audit never actually occurs.

The precise nature of the changes that might be made in response to postings to a sustainability page aren't knowable in advance. A manufac- turer might certainly change its production process or the safety proce- dures in its factory in order to be able to make honest statements about a lowered global-warming impact or enhanced safety measures associated with its product. Or it might engage in various kinds of subterfuge, from greenwashing ploys (in which the only thing that changes is the language) to outright lies, in order to make a product appear to be more favorable to sustainability than it actually is. Or it might decide to do nothing and let the chips fall where they may.

Whatever preliminary, anticipatory decisions are made, the process of bringing about change in the marketplace has only begun. Some sustain- ability pages will get visits, and it's a safe prediction that some will receive thousands or even millions of views over time. The views serve as a spot- light (the world is paying a good deal of attention to this particular prod- uct) and as a metric (product X is getting 10 times the attention of product Y). The sites provide feedback, identify societal concerns, and act as a gauge of collective comfort, or lack thereof, with the particular product.

The technology needed to host and manage millions of sustainability pages is nothing out of the ordinary. The challenging part of creating this is institutional: who participates in such an undertaking, who decides what information to provide, who provides information, and who manages the whole thing? And there are important "why" questions as well: Why would anyone what to participate in creating sustainability pages for any and all products?

We hope that the presentation thus far has been interesting enough to spark some ongoing attention to the desirability of moving forward and broadly improving the quality of information, especially sustainability information, available in the global market. Ultimately, it will be public discussion of these questions that provides the actual answers. However, there are steps that can be taken by some of the larger players in the market—steps they could take more or less unilaterally—that could jumpstart the entire process.

A small number of entities are so large a presence in the global market that their purchasing decisions are enough to influence the decisions of millions of businesses around the world.

Walmart sells almost half a trillion dollars worth of goods a year through 11,500 stores operating in 28 countries (as of 2015). By many measures, it is the largest company in the world. It already operates large and complex websites featuring thousands of products. Despite their size and complexity, those sites function quickly and smoothly, providing shoppers substantial amounts of information that can help them to make informed purchases. Walmart could readily add a link on each product page leading to a related page with sustainability information for the product. But before that could be done, the pages would have to be filled with relevant sustainability information from the products' manufacturers, arranged in whatever format Walmart might put forward. There are numerous approaches that Walmart could take to making this happen. We offered up a hybrid approach as a hypothetical example, but there are many variations on how such a scheme might work. Here are a few possibilities:

Formatted   Have companies fill in a form providing the precise types of sustainability details that Walmart deems significant.

Free-form   Leave the submissions open-ended, so that the manufacturers self-identify information they deem relevant to sustainability.

Hybrid   A mix of the two approaches, with some standardized reporting, followed by open-ended text.

Mandatory   Require sustainability submissions in order for items to be carried by Walmart.

Voluntary   Make reporting optional.

Optional, but ...   Products that provide sustainability information receive preferential treatment of some sort. For instance, only products that have a PSIP Web address can be featured in Walmart ads.

Go for broke   Set up a formal reporting mechanism, and have all manufacturers enter their information

Ease in Solicit PSIPs for a limited number of suppliers, such as suppliers of clothing items, and gradually expand the system to suppliers of other products.

The US government buys about as much commercial goods as Walmart sells. Federal procurement amounts to about $500 billion per year. The government could take measures similar to those described above for Walmart, asking or requiring suppliers to submit sustainability information in order to be eligible for government procurement or to receive some sort of preferred procurement status. The government isn't as light on its feet as a private company in its ability to implement a PSIP system, but it certainly has the appropriate weight and influence as the largest buyer of goods in the world.

Amazon.com, though not (yet) quite the behemoth that Walmart is, is still the most influential online merchant and has pioneered many interactive methods of reviewing, commenting, and ranking that would be useful in the sustainability context. It would be interesting to have Amazon offer a link on each product page to sustainability information that manufacturers could optionally provide (though requiring some sort of information submission is certainly a possibility). The many merchants that operate through the Amazon site could also be given tools to help them work with their suppliers, with the aim of creating similar information pages. Other large online merchants, such as the Japanese firm Rakuten (owner of Buy.com and other sites) and Taobao.com (an Alibaba Web property that is considered the Chinese equivalent of Amazon), could take similar unilateral actions.

An entity needn't be a global purchasing giant to exercise substantial influence on the market. In the US, individual states spend billions on procurement, and they could introduce a provision similar to that suggested above for the federal government. Well-known merchants could do the same—CVS, Walgreens, Safeway, or Target in the United States, Tesco, Carrefour and similarly positioned mega-retailers in other countries. Merchandisers with substantial audiences—the National Football League, FIFA, the Olympics—could similarly take measures on their own to implement a sustainability information system. The United Nations, though not involved in procurement on the scale of other entities, could nevertheless introduce a system that could have a substantial symbolic presence.

Sustainability information brings the marketplace several important steps closer to the economists' ideal state of affairs: complete information, perfectly accessible to all. Building a mechanism to incorporate information about human values serves to redefine the notion of economic value. We can recast Adam Smith's well-known quote on self-interest this way: It is not from the benevolence of the butcher, the brewer, and the baker that they no longer rely on child labor, but from their regard to their own interest.

7 Finding Things Out: Foraging for Coherence in the Information Age

We are bombarded with sensory input, yet we somehow manage to make sense of the world. Information comes to us in raw form through the five well-known senses (sight, hearing, smell, touch, and taste) and through other sensing mechanisms that don't fall neatly into the primary senses: a sense of balance, a sense of time passing, and the ability to distinguish temperature, for a few examples. In our waking state, the flow of information is constant and voluminous. At times, the onrush of incoming information can be overwhelming, especially when we find ourselves in unfamiliar and dangerous circumstances. A first-time driver in heavy traffic reels from the onslaught of traffic lights, cars, horns, pedestrians, street signs, reflections, bicyclists, intersections, car radios, cell phones, passengers, potholes, puddles, solid white lines, dashed yellow lines, external conversations, internal conversations (the kind we have with ourselves), and everything else that demands attention—and also everything that should be ignored—so that attention can be paid to the most meaningful inputs.

Yet in time the tsunami of information input subsides to mere ripples. We develop experience-based rules of thumb—heuristics—that are largely unconscious and unarticulated. We use them to make our way forward, whether through traffic or through life. We manage, most days, to process all this information selectively, safely, and, for the most part, automatically, setting intelligent priorities without much apparent effort, and without descending into confusion and chaos. We call this process *foraging for coherence.*

We have chosen the word 'foraging' deliberately. Foraging behavior is one of the most fundamental survival skills for living creatures. Human beings wouldn't live very long if the quest for food and water were based solely on a random walkabout through the environment in the hope of stumbling across edible plants, catchable game, or drinkable water. Foraging is the strategic questing for these things, combining sensory input, instinctual behaviors, remembered experience, and sheer cleverness to increase the odds of successfully locating sustenance. Ecologists, borrowing numerous concepts from economics, have postulated that foraging behavior, whether among humans or other animals, can be explained as an organism's attempt to optimize its efforts. Reduced to its simplest components, foraging means that creatures seek to maximize their intake of energy while minimizing the output of energy needed to secure food. In effect, the food forager conducts an unconscious cost-benefit analysis of the energy lost in searching against the possible energy gains of finding a food source.

In the real world, food searches are, of course, considerably more complex than a simple input-output consideration of calories, as food seekers need not only energy but also nutritional diversity and, if they are foraging connoisseurs, diversity in tastes and palatability. Ecologists who study optimal foraging in animals are sometimes struck by the sight of a foraging organism that passes up a seemingly abundant and accessible food supply. Researchers attempt to identify factors other than nutrition—the possible presence of a predator, for example—that come into play in the cost-benefit calculus. The urgency of the quest also comes into play—a desperately hungry forager must embark on a single-minded exploration for food, and must make do with whatever energy source is at hand. A well-fed forager, in contrast, can roam the countryside with several objectives, not only looking for food (and being selective in what it does or doesn't eat) but also seeking out other items of interest (a mate, a water hole, a source of raw materials) or simply heading out for a good explore.

There is a tendency to think of foraging as something that animals and primitive people do. For modern humans, foraging for food is limited to raiding the refrigerator or finding a good restaurant. But we also forage for coherence, and do so constantly in our waking moments. We are information-seeking creatures, and we adopt many of the same strategies, and rely on the same intellectual skills, as we do (or at least as our ancestors did) when foraging for food in the wild.

A great deal of human creativity is directed at our foraging behavior. Our ancestors invented specialized items for food foraging: bags and baskets for carrying, tools for digging, weapons for hunting. They also developed information tools—words, maps, markings—that could be used to locate sources of sustenance, to gauge the type, quality, and abundance of what is available, and to pass that information to others. Information is central to successful foraging. Even ants, among the simplest of creatures, have evolved sophisticated mechanisms for communicating the location of food sources to other ants, using self-reinforcing pheromone signals that spontaneously transform a colony's search activities from the chaos of helter-skelter search patterns into the well-structured trails of ants efficiently transporting food from a found source back to the colony.

Evolution has taken our species in a technological direction, and our information tools have developed and expanded well beyond the use of helping to find food. A fantastic convergence of technologies—in combination with the discovery that information, on its own, serves as a central, dominant theme and a unifying principle in fields as diverse as communications, biology, economics, and quantum mechanics—have led us to rethink the role that information plays in individual lives and in creating larger structures out of collections of individuals.

If the Information Age has a champion, it is almost certainly Google, a company with the self-described mission to "organize the world's information and make it universally accessible and useful." Google is the information-foraging tool par excellence, or at least would like to be seen that way in the face of competing information-foraging applications from the likes of Bing, Facebook, Yahoo, and even such upstarts as DuckDuckGo. One feature of the Information Age is that we now do much of our foraging for coherence online.

Google offers—and all sophisticated search engines now offer—ready-made heuristics to help manage our information-foraging behaviors. Just as a novice driver is challenged by the task of setting priorities (Should I watch the car, the light, or the bicyclist off to my right), a person searching for information on the Internet is challenged by an almost overwhelming number of choices. Should I begin my search for information at Wikipedia? At the *New York Times*? At the White House website? Bloomberg? CNN? StumbleUpon? Instagram? Should I focus on books, newspapers, technical journals, legal documents, video broadcasts, images, or government databases? Or should I post a question on Facebook and get facts and opinions from friends, family members, and assorted online strangers?

Google and other search engines attempt to sidestep the need to find answers to these questions, or even to ask them in the first place. Their built-in algorithms do much of the deciding for you, selecting the high-est-priority search results from a constantly expanding universe of online information of all shapes and sizes. Google's algorithms replace some of your heuristics; the search engine identifies relevant materials, lists them for your consideration according to priority, and displays bits of text, thumbnail-sized images, webpage previews, trending news stories, and other cues to help you zero in on the information sources that are most responsive to the question you are exploring—or so Google hopes. Search engines are even tending toward responsive technology that learns from an individual's search terms and from what sites an individual has visited. A responsive search engine fine-tunes future search results to provide relevant materials on the basis of individual preferences and previous search history: a search on 'SEC' returns the Securities and Exchange Commission's website to a financial professional, but it returns the Southeastern Conference's site to a basketball fan.

The sophistication of today's search engines removes a lot of the "grunt work" from information foraging. Recall the steps, both mental and physi-cal, that would have been necessary in the pre-Internet age to locate a copy of the full text of the Declaration of Independence. The task wasn't terribly difficult, but neither was it trivial. You probably would have begun with books in your house. Perhaps you had an encyclopedia, or even a diction-ary, that included the full text. It also might have been found in a history textbook from a high school or college class. But if it wasn't to be found in your house, you probably had to go to a library and search the card catalog, or to a bookstore and search the US History shelves. Since descriptions of books didn't provide deep details on contents, you had to make a judgment call and select books that seemed likely to contain the text of the Declara-tion. Perhaps you found a title such as Great Documents in American His-tory, and your several hours of information foraging seem to have paid off: the text of the Declaration is at hand, if the book is available.

In comparison, consider an online search conducted by means of a modern search engine such as Google. It takes seconds to type 'Decla-ration of Independence' into the search box, and the very first result is likely to be the full text transcript of the original document at the web-site of the National Archives of the United States. Google is so efficient at searches of this particular kind that it isn't even necessary to type the full three words; three or four letters are enough for Google to suggest (if the "suggest" feature is enabled) that you are searching for the Declaration of Independence. Google "knows" that 'Declaration of Independence' is the likely search term, rather than Declaration of Human Rights, Declaration of Sentiments and Resolutions, declivity, declaim, declaratory, or any one of dozens of other 'decl' words. Google's huge database of search terms recognizes that 'Declaration of Independence' is a common search term, especially for searches that originate in the United States, and so its suggestion algorithm gives that phrase priority over other possible search terms. Even for erroneously entered search terms—for instance, 'Decoration of Independence'—Google is smart enough to get you to the correct result almost instantaneously.

Search engines have freed us from relying on many of our deep-rooted heuristic devices when we are foraging for coherence, at least when we are online. (When unplugged, we are forced to negotiate the information landscape the old-fashioned way.) But we aren't free of heuristics. The Information Age creates a demand for each of us to develop personalized search strategies that don't have the advantage of having been tested and refined over decades or centuries. Online behavior is something new, and without effective shortcuts and rules of thumb it can be daunting. In fact, the intersection of driving and Information Age technology offers up a compellingly cautionary tale: One often hears of drivers unquestioningly following their GPS directions, only to wind up hundreds of miles off course or perhaps stranded in dangerous and unfamiliar territory. A park ranger in California coined the phrase "Death by GPS" in reference to the more extreme examples of this phenomenon. (Go ahead, Google it.)

Foraging for information online calls for searchers to develop their own set of tricks for getting the job done efficiently—that is, getting the desired information with a minimum of effort. There is a bit of an art, for instance, to scanning a page of search results. Much as the search engine would love to have it be the case that the first search result is the one you're looking for, we all know from everyday experience that such isn't always the case. Rather than read through the first few hundred words on a search-results page (or the first few thousand, depending on the search settings), search engine users learn to make quick sense of, and judgments about, the information presented to them.

With almost any search engine, a search on 'apple' produces a page of links, almost all of which have to do with Apple Inc. and its products. If you happen to be looking for information on apple as a fruit, a quick scan of the page gives you plenty of clues that little if any information that you would find useful is available. The words on the page (iPhone, iPad, Samsung, patent, AAPL, billion) are distinctly non-pomaceous, and the words you would expect to see (fruit, red, crunchy, delicious) are missing. The images on the page suffer from the same shortcomings.

As you evaluate the available information and decide on your next steps as a searcher, your foraging mechanisms and newfound heuristics are already at work—indeed, had been at work since your initial selection of an information space (online, rather than offline) and of a particular search tool with which to begin your exploration. When you are foraging for coherence, the recognition that a first set of results falls far short of the goal calls for a refinement of your foraging/searching strategy.

One obvious refinement is a change in your search terms. A search on 'apple fruit' gets you exactly the results you're after. However, there are other options. Depending on your search habits (that is, your heuristics), an alternative refinement may be the option of choice. For example, you might use a browser's Find function to locate the word 'fruit' on the search-results page as a rapid way of bypassing all the Apple technology links.

But suppose your search was about neither computers nor fruit, but about the music company called Apple that you remember from your youth, the one started up by the Rolling Stones. A search on 'apple' is a dead end, for obvious reasons, but so is a search on 'apple rolling stones', which gives a lot of results about music by the Rolling Stones available through Apple's iTunes store, and about the singer Fiona Apple as she is written up in *Rolling Stone*, but nothing about a music company called Apple.

Your first effort at foraging for information was unsuccessful, your second was no better, and subsequent stabs at new search terms aren't working either. You now are faced with a small-scale version of the hunter-gatherer's dilemma: Continued searching may involve more effort than it is worth. If the cost-benefit analysis turns negative, or merely runs the risk of turning negative because future success is far from guaranteed, it may be time to assess how badly you want to find information about the Rolling Stones' Apple music company.

Now heuristics come into play again. If you are an experienced searcher, you may try a different tactic: Instead of searching the entire Web, narrow things down, and search for 'apple' on Wikipedia. The online encyclopedia offers disambiguation pages for many of its topics, and some disambiguation is just what you need. Sure enough, the Apple disambiguation page at Wikipedia—http://wikipedia.org/wiki/Apple_(disambiguation)—has a heading for Companies (the second heading, after Fruits and Plants) and lists Apple, Inc. for computers and Apple Corp., "a multimedia corporation founded in the 1960s by The Beatles." Aha! So it wasn't the Stones after all! Memory is a tricky thing!

Primary Documents: A Challenge in Information Foraging

The Declaration of Independence and the origins of Apple Corp. raise interesting search challenges for anyone seeking primary resources on either of them—that is, sources that refer directly to the topic at hand and were created at the time the topic itself came into being. The Internet, for all its glories, is particularly weak at dating the materials it makes available. Most electronic documents have several dates associated with them, including an original creation date, dates of republication, the date on which an electronic version was created, a date of the original posting to a webpage or a database, and dates of subsequent website updates. Many materials mention various other dates that may or may not have much to do with the actual date of the document itself, and which may be rife with words and numbers that resemble dates but aren't. The human eye and brain do a pretty good job (heuristics, again) of sorting through these bits of information, isolating dates that truly are dates, and selecting the date most appropriate to the document itself. Search engines, for all their sophistication, are poor at this particular task.

Searching the Internet for date-specific documents, then, calls for a particular set of skills that enable one to avoid having to mull through thousands of possibilities, one at a time, to identify the document date. Since some of our traditional information-organizing and information-searching skills have been rendered fairly obsolete by the Internet (when is the last time you referred to the Dewey Decimal System?), we have to develop new skills—new heuristics—if our foraging tasks are to be effective and efficient.

Suppose you are interested in finding primary sources about the assassination of President Abraham Lincoln—documents that reveal events as they unfolded to nineteenth-century Americans in the hours, days, weeks, and months after Lincoln was shot. In other words, you are searching for

documents created in 1865, rather than for documents that merely reference the 1865 date of Lincoln's assassination.

A search on "Lincoln assassination" turns up ample materials (more
than 9 million, according to Google's "results" number, though what that
number means is anyone's guess). However, a scan of the search results
doesn't readily suggest a site that carries the actual documents of the day. As
is so often the case, a Wikipedia article tops the search results. It offers up a
few primary documents, such as a thumbnail image of a police department
blotter listing the assassination, but there is no clear indication as to which
materials, and which links, lead to materials from the time of the assassination itself, as opposed to documents looking back in history at the event.

A link to the "Lincoln Assassination" pages at the Library of Congress
looks worthwhile, but the landing page is primarily modern-day text, and
not until one has clicked through to the Ephemera Gallery does one find a
small collection of documents posters, articles, prints, and other items dating back to 1865. Even the Assassination page at the Abraham Lincoln Presidential Library, as promising-sounding a source as that may seem, turns up
nothing in the way of primary materials.

How *does* one forage through the vast online landscape of information
when the quest is date-sensitive and the Internet isn't?

It is here that our newly developing foraging heuristics come into play.
A simple brute-force search will eventually turn up the sort of primary
materials you desire—click on dozens (or hundreds) of links from your
search-results page and, bit by bit, you will be able to compile a collection
of nineteenth-century sources. That simple foraging technique is adequate
for the large bulk of searches that take place on the Internet. Occasionally,
though, a simple Google search doesn't do the job. Experienced searchers generally develop more sophisticated strategies for identifying primary
source materials more rapidly and with far less effort than the brute-force
method requires.

There are many different strategies, and the choice of a foraging
method—whether you are searching for information on Abraham Lincoln
or on this season's hot holiday toys—depends entirely on the strategies
you have developed in the course of your searching. Your knowledge of
the topic, your knowledge of search techniques and tools, your personality,
your temperament, and your experience converge to suggest a search strategy that, with a bit of luck, will turn up the results you want.

For historical primary documents, any of the following search strategies could be fruitful:

Change the search terms. Fine-tuning a search with terms such as "Lincoln assassination primary documents" will turn up some links to sites that specialize in collections of original materials, whereas a search for "Lincoln assassination newspapers" or "Lincoln assassination reward poster" uncovers particular types of primary documents.

Change the search tool. There are many databases that allow the searcher to specify a date range. The Google Scholar search tool provides this function at no charge; a search on "Lincoln assassination" returns several thousand documents, and the customized date range tool quickly narrows these down to several hundred primary documents from 1865. The online Digitized Newspapers collection at the Library of Congress offers similar capabilities, producing millions of search results from 1865. Subscription services such as NewspaperArchive.com and Proquest Historical have similar date-specific search functions. *Harper's Weekly*, available online, was a popular nineteenth-century magazine that provided, then, and still offers now, detailed coverage of the events surrounding Lincoln's death. Even without dates, using Google Image or Bing Image for any of the aforementioned searches returns materials that can be quickly scanned and enables one to make a reasonable judgment as to the date of each item.

Ask for help. Social networking tools offer a way to ask people, rather than algorithms, to point you toward information sources. A Facebook request to your network of friends and colleagues (and others) for primary documents on Lincoln's assassination reaches out to individuals who know you and who can gauge the sort of documents that might be of greatest interest. Participation in online history forums and email messages to librarians, historians, archivists, or collectors are other means of reaching out in cyberspace for direct assistance in finding materials.

Go offline. As was the case with a search for the Declaration of Independence, going to a library or a bookstore and perusing a few books on the assassination is another means of identifying documents pertinent to your search.

Mix and match. No one is constrained to a single search strategy, of course.

260   HARPER'S WEEKLY.   [APRIL 29, 1865.

Figure 7.1
Illustrations of the assassination of Abraham Lincoln in an 1865 issue of *Harper's Weekly*.

These variations on search techniques are no less applicable to finding a good restaurant in town than they are to pinpointing historical documents. Sometimes a simple search request at Google, Bing, or Yahoo is all that's required, with not much needed in the way of sophisticated search techniques. Other times, you'll have to rely on your searching skills—your heuristics.

The point of describing these different search strategies—techniques that are often used unconsciously and without much need for articulation—is not to instruct the reader in the ABCs of Web searching. Any competent high school student has already mastered some or all of the techniques we have described, or developed his or her own individual heuristics to speed the research process along. Instead, our point is to emphasize how the information landscape has changed with the onset of the online universe, and how our information-foraging strategies have changed as a consequence. We hope we haven't given the impression that there is no longer a need for personal information-foraging heuristics, and that the Internet knows and sees all. Far from it. We still have to be expert information foragers to navigate the world, whether our goal is shopping for groceries, writing a term paper, or simply driving across town.

But it is abundantly clear that our searching strategies are changing. We are less likely to consult a paper map or to stop at a gas station and ask directions, and more likely to ask Siri or some other "intelligent personal assistant" (as Apple puts it) for a suggestion. We may not be far from the day when taking a road trip involves little more than telling our car our destination (e.g., "Drive to Uncle Mike's house") and letting the onboard computer identify Uncle Mike's address, plot a route to his house (taking account of traffic patterns, recent accidents, and road work), and even help park the car. This type of technology is, at its core, information-based, as the car's microchips use linguistic datasets to decipher our spoken words, review personal directories to glean the identity of Uncle Mike and the location of his house, link up to GPS systems to map out a route, and check enhanced information feeds to make sure the route isn't obstructed by road work, by an accident, or by a tide of pink-clad people marching in support of breast-cancer research. The aforementioned capabilities are already available and some are routine, but next in line are decision-making systems that will "see" cars, pedestrians, and other objects with front-facing and rear-facing cameras and electromagnetic or sonar detection equipment, will interact with sensors built into the roadways, and will drive the car for us, all the while assessing performance and safety information on engine status, inertial forces, internal and external temperatures, weather conditions, road slipperiness, and many other things.

Watson

Will we come to a point where human information-foraging skills are less necessary? Might the Information Age take us to a *Star Trek*-like future in which a computer unambiguously understands our requests, has access to a universe's worth of information, and can even make many of the critical decisions now left to human beings? In small-scale circumstances, that future has already arrived. When an airline captain puts a jetliner on autopilot, the human captain's role becomes one primarily of oversight to ensure that our reliance on the machine-based heuristics isn't misplaced. The autopilot can handle almost all flying tasks (takeoff, ascent, cruising, descent, and even landing), but not the surprisingly complex task of taxiing on the runway. The decision-making expertise of a human captain now includes recognizing situations in which continued reliance on an autopilot is inappropriate because flying conditions are unusual and outside the bounds of what the machine's programming can handle.

IBM's Jeopardy-playing computer Watson is an attempt to take machine assistance in human decision making in a different direction. Watson makes use of deep and varied sources of data and of sophisticated programming that can "understand" conversational English. Watson responds to Jeopardy clues more reliably than even the best human players of the game can manage. Its facility with language can be highly nuanced, handling metaphors, imprecision, veiled references, popular culture, puns, and other tricks of language with apparent ease and arriving at answers faster than the most experienced Jeopardy champions. Watson correctly parsed the clue "William Wilkenson's 'An Account of the Principalities of Wallachia and Moldavia' inspired this author's most famous novel" and correctly responded, Jeopardy-style, with the question "Who was Bram Stoker?" Despite flubbing some seemingly more straightforward questions, Watson easily won the match.

The technology underlying Watson's question-and-answer skills, which IBM has dubbed DeepQA, is a novel and complex combination of natural-language-processing programs, routines for generating and testing hypotheses, and confidence-scoring algorithms, all overlaid on a carefully selected database of relevant information sources.

Watson's Jeopardy-playing skills were a catchy demonstration of the system's capabilities, but IBM didn't design the system for the sole purpose of playing a game. The computer is now moving into the medical arena with the aim of minimizing the information-foraging activities of human doctors. Watson can do something that humans simply cannot: keep track of the ever-expanding volume of medical documentation (published research,

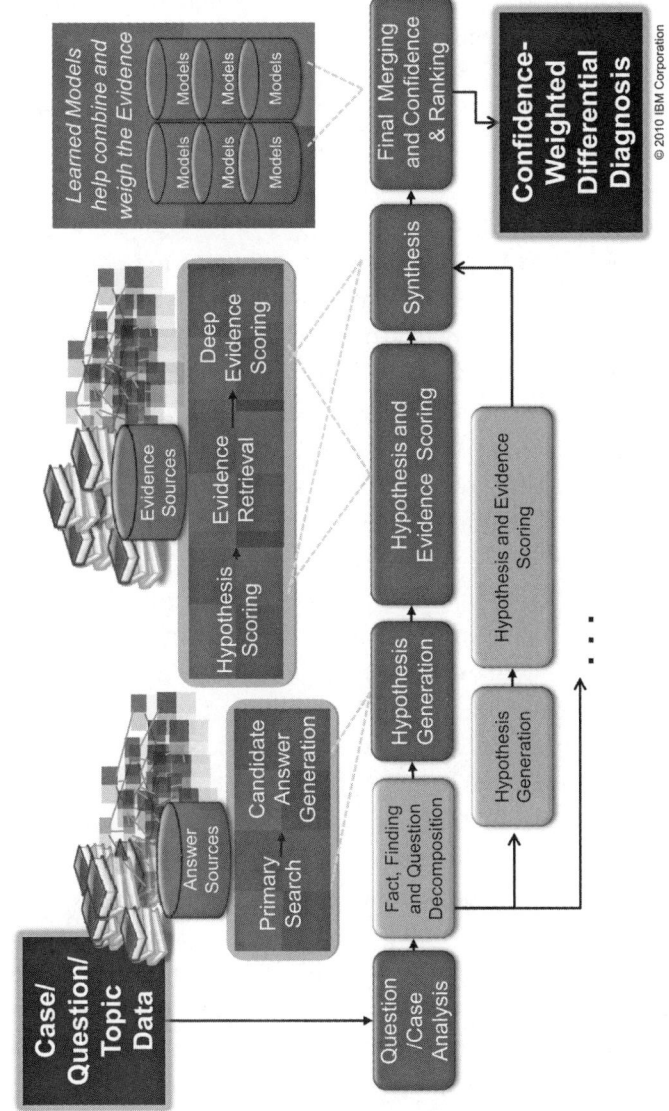

Figure 7.2
IBM's illustration of the Deep QA configuration for Jeopardy (courtesy of IBM, © 2011 International Business Machines Corporation).

case studies, patient records, pharmaceutical literature, continuing education, association guidelines) and of other information sources that may be relevant to diagnosing and treating patients. The system is programmed to understand natural-language queries from members of a medical staff, to sift through millions of pages of medical information in seconds, and to display a set of potential answers to any questions asked, along with a "confidence ranking" about the answer and the underlying documents on which Watson's suggestions are based. Watson not only answers questions but asks them; the system may prompt members of a medical staff for additional information about symptoms, patient history, or previous treatments. In other words, Watson is there to assist in decisions and tasks that are conventionally considered the sole purview of human experts.

Watson is in use on a trial basis at the Memorial Sloan Kettering Cancer Center in New York. After an initial phase in which Watson "learns" from the medical staff at Sloan Kettering by absorbing information from hundreds of thousands of case histories, the system is expected to provide valuable assistance to the staff at Sloan Kettering and ultimately to other medical staffs in other institutions that wouldn't otherwise have access to Sloan Kettering's deep expertise in diagnosing and treating cancers. As the head of Sloan Kettering put it, "Watson's capability to analyze huge volumes of data and reduce it down to critical decision points is absolutely essential to improve our ability to deliver effective therapies and disseminate them to the world."

Watson isn't meant to replace doctors, to second-guess them, to diagnose patients, or to recommend treatments. Instead, it serves as an expert advisor that can draw on a deep database of materials relevant to a particular patient and can help to steer the doctors and nurses toward recognizing symptoms and considering treatment options that they may have had difficulty discovering on their own.

The key phrase in the quotation above is "critical decision points." Not only is Watson compiling information; it is making decisions about what information is most relevant and what information can be set aside. The DeepQA methodology creates several hypotheses from the available information about a patient's condition, then "tests" each hypothesis by looking for information in its databases that either supports or weakens the hypothesis. Beyond simply presenting the results of the system's decision making in the form of summaries of and links to relevant material, Watson is also evaluating the information it has and the additional information it needs to identify the "critical decision points" that should be brought to the attention of the medical community.

One of Watson's anticipated benefits to health-care decision making will be to minimize premature closure, a problem that contributes substantially to medical misdiagnoses. Premature closure is the human tendency to halt an investigation once an apparent solution has been found. In medicine, the identification of a disease that matches the symptoms reported by a patient can lead members of a medical staff to stop seeking alterative conditions that also can produce the reported symptoms. In more common vernacular, it is a case of jumping to a conclusion. Watson, with its capacity to troll millions of documents in fractions of a second, should be able to identify multiple diagnostic possibilities if, in fact, more than one disease can lead to the reported symptoms.

Watson's only real track record, thus far, is the cleverness it has displayed during its Jeopardy matches. There hasn't yet been a concrete demonstration of its utility in the medical arena; the Watson website (as of late 2015) is full of phrases such as "expected benefits." It seems clear, though, that before too long Watson, or systems like it from other companies, will become standard adjuncts to expert decision making in the health-care community. What will this mean for the information-foraging responsibilities of medical professionals?

If tools like Watson live up to their expectations, the information-foraging task for health-care professionals will become simultaneously easier and more successful. Doctors, nurses, students, administrators, and insurers will be able to access, compare, summarize, and synthesize information sources with a depth and a speed not attainable without computerized assistance. Relevant information will be pulled in from sources that may not seem relevant at first blush. A doctor, by necessity, must adopt a fairly narrow focus when reviewing medical advances; a specialist in bone cancer keeps up with papers in the *Journal of Bone Oncology* but would be hard pressed to justify the time and energy needed to stay current with papers in *Cell and Tissue Research*. Computers have no need to restrict their input so narrowly, and can absorb content from millions of articles in hundreds of journals, along with case histories, images, and datasets from a huge volume of sources, without the necessity of "specializing" in a narrow area. A paper in *Experimental Hematology*, a genetic sequence in the Human Genome Project, and a case history from a patient not suffering from bone cancer can all become relevant if their content suggests a connection to the current case at hand.

Perhaps the outcome is less of a change in information skills than might be supposed—for example, perhaps a doctor continues to focus on keeping current in a narrowly proscribed medical specialty and relies on Watson to cast about more broadly, pulling relevant information from otherwise obscure sources. But it's also possible that Watson or a similar tool could result in a change in how members of a medical staff allocate their attention so as to spend more time with patients and less time keeping abreast of the medical literature. Doctors already must make the difficult but humanly necessary decision to learn only so much in the face of a nearly endless flow of new information; a tool such as Watson may encourage them to reduce their reading of the literature further and allow the machine to compensate. It is difficult to imagine in advance how this will play out.

What will happen when Watson—or a similar but even more sophisticated information tool—becomes available to the general public? People already routinely turn to the Internet to explore diagnoses and treatments for symptoms they may be experiencing; the results of their searching are sometimes of significant value, are sometimes misleading, and may even be downright harmful. A more sophisticated self-diagnosis system, with a natural-language capability, would have enormous appeal to the general public, especially if it were to be widely regarded as credible and if its output were to be accompanied by well-caveated expressions of confidence in the results. Systems similar to Watson probably will integrate with insurance companies so that both insurers and (ultimately) patients will be able to use them to compare treatment options and determine the likelihood that specific treatments are covered by a patient's insurance plan.

The combined effects of these varied information tools—search engines such as Google, voice-recognition software such as Siri, and artificially intelligent decision assistants such as Watson—make enormous quantities of information quickly available. They are becoming increasingly sophisticated in their ability to prioritize information so that information foragers can nearly instantly, and with remarkably little effort, find not only relevant information but the best information available.

Fragments: The Invisible Web and the Splinternet

Emerging tools such as Watson magnify a sense that many online users already possess. The Internet sometimes seems to be a vast repository of all human knowledge—a collection of information from the most trivial to the deeply profound, all of it quickly available.

It isn't. Two terms have arisen in recent years to describe some of the fragmented properties of the Internet that interfere with global access to universal human knowledge.

The first of these terms is 'Splinternet', a play on words referring to what is also sometimes known as the Balkanization of the Internet: the splintering of the whole into discrete, smaller pieces that are, to varying degrees, isolated from one another. The other term is 'the Invisible Web', also known as 'the Dark Web', 'the Deep Internet', 'the Hidden Web', and a host of other descriptors that all carry the same meaning: online information that isn't readily available or easily accessed.

The terms 'Splinternet' and 'the Invisible Web' overlap, but they refer to different things. There is nothing particularly invisible about the Splinternet as long as a user is in the right place and is searching in the "right" way. Technology is a dividing force that contributes to fragmentation of the Internet. Some content is designed for particular platforms (combinations of hardware and software) and is difficult or impossible to access with other platforms. Users of laptop computers may have difficulty accessing content designed for viewing on mobile phones, and vice versa. Users of iPads and iPhones search with Siri or access Apple Maps, but those features are inaccessible to users of Android phones. In addition, many devices come with default settings that shut users off from particular content, such as the safesearch filters on most search engines that screen out pornography from search results.

Geography too leads to fragmentation, largely because of laws or government policies pertaining to information access in certain jurisdictions. Users in Canada can access documents denying the Holocaust; users in Germany cannot, as such content is illegal under German law. China has constructed a formidable firewall around the Internet, greatly restricting what its citizens can access. Surfing the Web in China for information on Falun Gong or Tiananmen Square is a very different experience from surfing for information on those topics in the United States.

Even in the most open societies, copyright concerns can splinter content and commercial considerations add an additional layer of restrictions. For example, in the United Kingdom one can access BBC programming that isn't available to viewers outside the UK. Viewers of the content in Google Books will find a relatively small number of books fully available for viewing online, but most of the content is restricted to previews, annoyingly tiny snippet views, or no inside-the-book view at all, because copyright considerations or simply the absence of an electronic file renders the content inaccessible. Napster, once a source of what may have been the most robust music library ever to exist, has been litigated down to ghostly shell of its former self. In each case, walls are built around content as a result of geography, technology, law, or commerce, fragmenting the Internet's information so that pieces of it are difficult for some people and impossible for other people to access.

A significant recent factor in the potential splintering of Internet content is a European Union legal decision regarding the right to be forgotten. A Spanish citizen sued Google, complaining that his rights were being violated because Google had unearthed some embarrassing old information about the repossession of his home—information that, were it not for the power of search engines, would have long since been forgotten by everyone decades after the original event. The Court of Justice of the European Union agreed, ruling that Europeans have a right to be forgotten, and that search engines (Google in particular) have a responsibility to give a user a straightforward way to request that specific information be removed from search results and to make a timely decision as to whether to remove the information or to defend its continued presence. It is too soon after the decision to gauge its long-term effect on Internet searching, but it certainly is possible that future searches on an individual's name will turn up greatly different results in Europe—and in other jurisdictions that are on the verge of adopting the right to be forgotten, including Japan—than it will in parts of the world where the right to be forgotten isn't an established legal principle.

'The Invisible Web', on the other hand, refers to content that may be broadly and universally available, in principle—regardless of geography, legal restrictions, or technology platform—but that is nevertheless terribly hard to find (and once found, often hard to utilize). The invisible content of the Internet doesn't show up in the results of an ordinary Google search. You more or less have to know what you're looking for and where to find

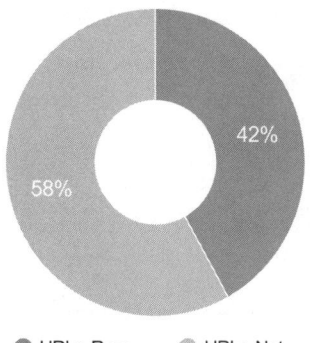

Total URLs that Google has evaluated for removal: 1,214,061 URLs

Total requests Google has received: 342,378 requests

The graph reflects URLs that have been fully processed, while the figures above reflect the total evaluated. URLs that require more information or are pending review are not included in the graph.

● URLs Rem…   ● URLs Not…

Figure 7.3
Google evaluated more than a million URLs under Europe's right-to-be-forgotten rules. (Google and the Google logo are registered trademarks of Google Inc. and are used with permission.)

it—or be lucky enough to stumble across it—in order to gain access. Some have speculated that the Invisible Web dwarfs its visible cousin in size and scope, but no one really knows how much content resides in either the visible or the invisible portion of the Internet.

Perhaps the darkest corner of the Invisible Web holds illegal content deliberately designed to be hard to find. The infamous Silk Road site was a trading post for all kinds of licit and illicit goods and services, including drugs, prostitutes, banned merchandise, and even, if the stories are to be believed, hit men. Created in 2011, Silk Road was accessible only to users who had installed special software and who used an Internet addressing system (originally developed to safeguard military communications) known as the Tor network. The US government closed down the Silk Road site in October of 2013 and arrested its creator. A month later, a revised version was up and running.

Most of the Invisible Web probably serves less nefarious purposes than Silk Road. The US government's intellectual-property databases illustrate the differences between the visible and invisible portions of the Internet. The official copyright database, maintained by the Library of Congress, isn't accessible through a general Internet search with any of the major search engines. For example, a search on the book title *Boris Borborygmus* will return several descriptions of the book, but not its actual copyright registration record. A search for the same title at the US Copyright Office,

Figure 7.4
The FBI shut down Silk Road in 2013, posting this message in its place.

though, returns the full record, detailing that the book was officially registered on January 28, 1987 and was assigned copyright registration number TX0002004158. The copyright record is part of the Invisible Web; a searcher must be aware of the specialized copyright database in order to find the record.

American *patents*, on the other hand, are fully searchable via ordinary Web searching. Although one can certainly use the search tool at the website of the US Patent and Trademark Office (USPTO), knowledge of that special tool isn't a necessary prerequisite to searching for patents (thanks, in large measure, to Google's 2006 creation of a tool for searching the Web for patents). Try searching for the first patent issued in the United States (signed by President Washington) and you're likely to find it without much problem, regardless of your choice of a search tool.

The trademark records held by USPTO may be the most interesting illustration of the distinction between the visible and invisible components of the Internet. The trademark database is a large and significant collection of information about the history of commercial products in the United States, but accessing it with an ordinary Internet search tool is difficult. In other words, the trademarks database is a sizable Internet fragment, and most of its content is beyond the reach of ordinary search tools.

One can search for trademark records at the website of the US Patent and Trademark Office by using the online search tool TESS (Trademark Electronic Search System). TESS is an obscure search tool, one that few people would know to turn to if they were foraging for information on trademarks. And once it has been found, TESS is difficult to master. Designed for people who are already experts in trademark arcana, it offers "Help" tools that provide little useful guidance to newcomers. TESS isn't indexed by Google, Bing, or other search engines, so the trademark information it contains isn't turned up by an ordinary Web search. And because TESS doesn't produce permanent links to its database materials, there is no fixed Web address for an individual trademark record.

Several commercial sites, such as trademarkia.com, have downloaded some of the TESS data and made it available via ordinary search engines. These services deliver metadata—descriptions of the records in TESS—but not the actual documents linked to by the TESS records. As a result, small bits of the trademark files that USPTO has to offer do show up in routine Web search activities, but the vast bulk of the system remains hidden, part of the Invisible Web.

A search in TESS leads users to another Trademark Office database: the Trademark Status and Document Retrieval (TSDR) system. TSDR includes text and image files of the actual documents submitted to register a trademark, along with any subsequent correspondence needed to complete or revise a submission or resolve any disputes. A TSDR record for an individual trademark may contain hundreds of pages of information or may contain nothing. When files exist, they may be little more than legal boilerplate or may include a rich tapestry of a product's brand name and history, including photographs, webpages, newspaper clippings, product packaging, and other bits and pieces of commercial history. There is no way to know what they include without accessing the full TSDR record and having a look.

The image of a Jell-O package shown here as figure 7.6 is a good example of the largely invisible nature of trademark files. It is accessible, in a manner of speaking, to those who make the considerable effort to become familiar with the file content and search tools available at the USPTO website. It isn't available to the vast majority of Internet searchers relying on

25	75204153	2159700	THE CHAMPAGNE OF JELL-O	TSDR	DEAD
26	75202786	2217699	A SLIGHTLY MORE INDULGENT SIDE OF JELL-O	TSDR	DEAD
27	75194276	2140363	JELL-O	TSDR	LIVE
28	75159809	2140238	JELL-O	TSDR	LIVE
29	75133207	2093731	JELL-O	TSDR	LIVE
30	75043171		JELL-O	TSDR	DEAD
31	74720931	2091900	JELL-O REFRESHERS	TSDR	DEAD
32	74720930		JELL-O SPARKLERS	TSDR	DEAD
33	74662335	2091763	JELL-O PUT THE WIGGLE IN A CUP	TSDR	DEAD
34	74617986		JELL-O	TSDR	DEAD
35	74574844	2006811	JELL-O	TSDR	DEAD
36	74351860		JELL-O PUT THE WIGGLE IN A CUP	TSDR	DEAD
37	74237862	1722257	JELL-O	TSDR	DEAD
38	74135560		THERE'S ALWAYS ROOM FOR JELL-O	TSDR	DEAD
39	74050746	1660989	JELL-O LIGHT	TSDR	DEAD
40	74038778	1663545	JELL-O LIGHT	TSDR	DEAD
41	74004262	1653623	THE JELL-O READING ROCKET	TSDR	DEAD
42	73822609	1661646	JELL-O	TSDR	DEAD
43	73677584	1511846	JELL-O	TSDR	DEAD
44	72394483	0936195	JELL-O	TSDR	LIVE
45	71266480	0250035	JELL-O	TSDR	LIVE
46	71034875	0070690	JELL-O.	TSDR	DEAD

Figure 7.5
Some of the TESS and TSDR records for the Jell-O trademark.

Google-type search engines to handle the bulk of their search needs. Of course, the vast majority of Internet searchers have no plausible interest in finding this particular image. The small number of searchers who would be interested aren't likely to find it unless they have specialized knowledge of the Trademark Office's search tools.

The near-invisibility of the 1908 Jell-O packaging file, along with all the rest of the numerous Jell-O TSDR records, is attributable to several factors. First and foremost is the decision of the Trademark Office to not allow its database to be "spidered" by the many search engines that scour the Internet for content. This probably is an unintended result of the fact that the database wasn't designed to produce output with a fixed URL. That is, an individual TSDR records doesn't have a unique, permanent address on the Internet—something that is generally necessary in order for search engines to find and subsequently index a site. Without a permanent URL, there is no "address" a search engine can use to send searchers to a live copy of a webpage. Whether this aspect of the trademark database is a result of security concerns or of some other consideration is difficult to say. It may well be that the designers of the TESS and TSDR systems—systems that probably

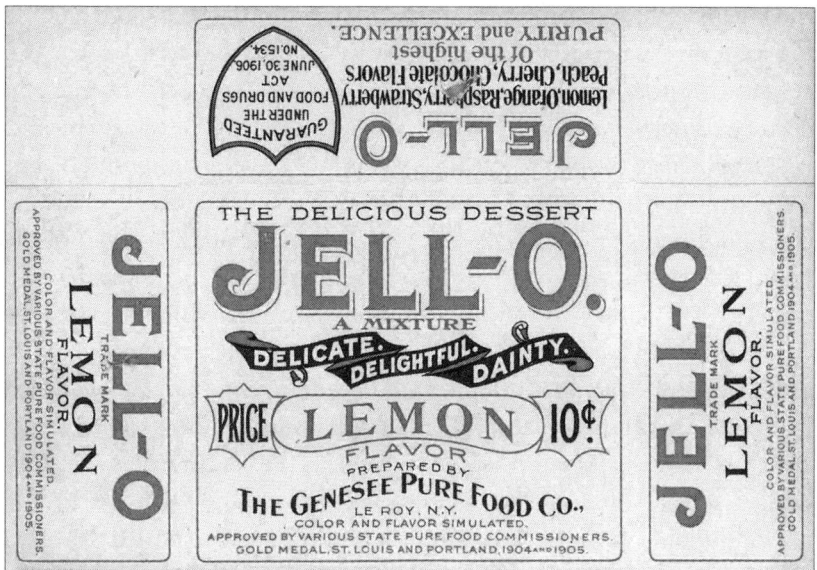

Figure 7.6
An image from TSDR file 71034875.

predate the Internet—simply never gave thought to a means of accessing the content other than directly visiting the Trademark Office website and using the tools provided there. The Trademark Office's search tools were clearly designed to serve a very limited purpose: to allow potential registrants to determine quickly whether a certain phrase is already trademarked. The content was never meant to serve the purpose of broader searching (e.g., by a researcher examining the history of a particular product or company).

Even if the TSDR files were made visible to search engines, the content would still remain largely invisible to would-be searchers. Search engines glean information by reading text. The text associated with the file for the Jell-O package image shown in figure 7.6 (as opposed to the text in the image itself, which is generally not readable by search engines) is bureaucratic, vague, and repetitive. Files are labeled with terms such as 'Specimen', 'Paper Correspondence', 'Unclassified', and 'File Jacket', but there is no text describing a file's content. Similar designations are used for all the millions of files in TSDR. These terms may have been helpful in organizing the original filing of materials, but they render the text fairly useless for distinguishing the content of any file from that of any other file.

Other immense government databases suffer from similar shortcomings, at least from the perspective of ready access by casual viewers. The content is walled off from search engines and is couched in bureaucratese that renders the content much more mysterious than it has to be, even after access is secured. For example, the federal government's effort to ensure Public Access to Court Electronic Records (PACER) has the noble aim of making court documents publicly accessible. But in practice, PACER is part of the Invisible Web: cut off from major search engines, difficult to use, bureaucratically opaque, and potentially expensive to access (as there is a per-page charge for retrieving content). Similarly, the many databases housed at fcc.gov, the website of the Federal Communications Commission, are a rich repository of millions of records pertaining to communications companies and technologies, but are at least as isolated as the court records at PACER or the trademark files at USPTO.

Nor is it only government records that contribute to a more fragmented Internet. Access to newspapers has fluctuated as the Internet has adjusted to various legal and commercial forces. The online history of the *New York Times* is a good example of both the impressive expansion of Internet content and the fragmentation that can render much of that content difficult to access. The *Times* has had an online presence since 1996 (and email news-delivery options even longer). Until 2005, access to the day's news was freely available. In 2005, the paper introduced TimesSelect, which walled off premium content from casual visitors to the website and made it available only to subscribers. That early experiment in paid online news content was abandoned two years later, when the *Times* reopened all its current content to all visitors. The *Times* also made available the vast and wonderful collection in its archives to online searchers, some of it free and some of it for a fee. In 2011, the *Times'* model for access changed again. Visitors to the website could now view twenty articles per month at no charge, but after that would have to pay to see additional content. The threshold was lowered to ten articles a month in 2012.

The paywall imposed by the *Times* illustrates something interesting about the economics of information access: Even with the vast repositories of free information accessible by means of the Internet, the *New York Times*, the *Wall Street Journal*, and other newspapers are banking on the prospects of being able to charge users for access to a premium form of information. Many other services—Lexis-Nexis, Proquest, JSTOR—do the same, charging users for access to information, some of which is available at no charge from other sources. Professional journals charge surprisingly steep fees for individual articles—*Science* articles are $20 each, and the *Cambridge Journal of Economics* charges $38 per article. In this, the Internet is reminiscent of commercial television, which evolved from a system of free access for over-the-air broadcasting to a mixed market of free stations, paid content, and premium services available via cable or satellite. From all appearances, the model of a part-free, part-fee access to online information is here to stay.

Content from the *New York Times* is not part of the Invisible Web; articles from both current and archived news stories appear regularly in the search results of all major search engines. But the *Times* has made decisions that have contributed to the fragmentation of the Internet by making some content that once was freely available harder to access. At the same time, the paper's decision to move its archives online added an important historical resource to the Web that is fully searchable back to the *Times'* first issue in 1851. (The *Wall Street Journal*, in contrast, has been published since 1889, but its online archives viewable through a Google search extend back only to 2010. Earlier issues can be viewed online only through institutional subscriptions to services such as Proquest and Factiva.)

As a final example, consider the Internet Archive's Wayback Machine, available at https://archive.org/web/. Mostly wonderful but often infuriating, it houses hundreds of billions of old webpages many of which would have long since disappeared from view if not for the Archive's efforts to preserve the Internet's history. But the Archive's content can't be viewed by means of an ordinary Google-style search. Nor is the Archive searchable; there is no way to search for, say, websites from 1998 that contain the phrase "digital camera." A user who doesn't know the URL of the site he is looking for is out of luck. This enormous and valuable library of the Internet's history is fragmented both by its isolation from search engines and by the impossibility of accessing content by any means other than using a known URL.

The examples cited above illustrate an interesting phenomenon: More and more information is being added to the Internet that is becoming harder and harder to find. The Internet is expanding at a rapid pace, but the typical Web searcher is being excluded from access to a great deal of the content that would otherwise be available. For services providing information, this aspect of the Internet's growth poses an enormous challenge.

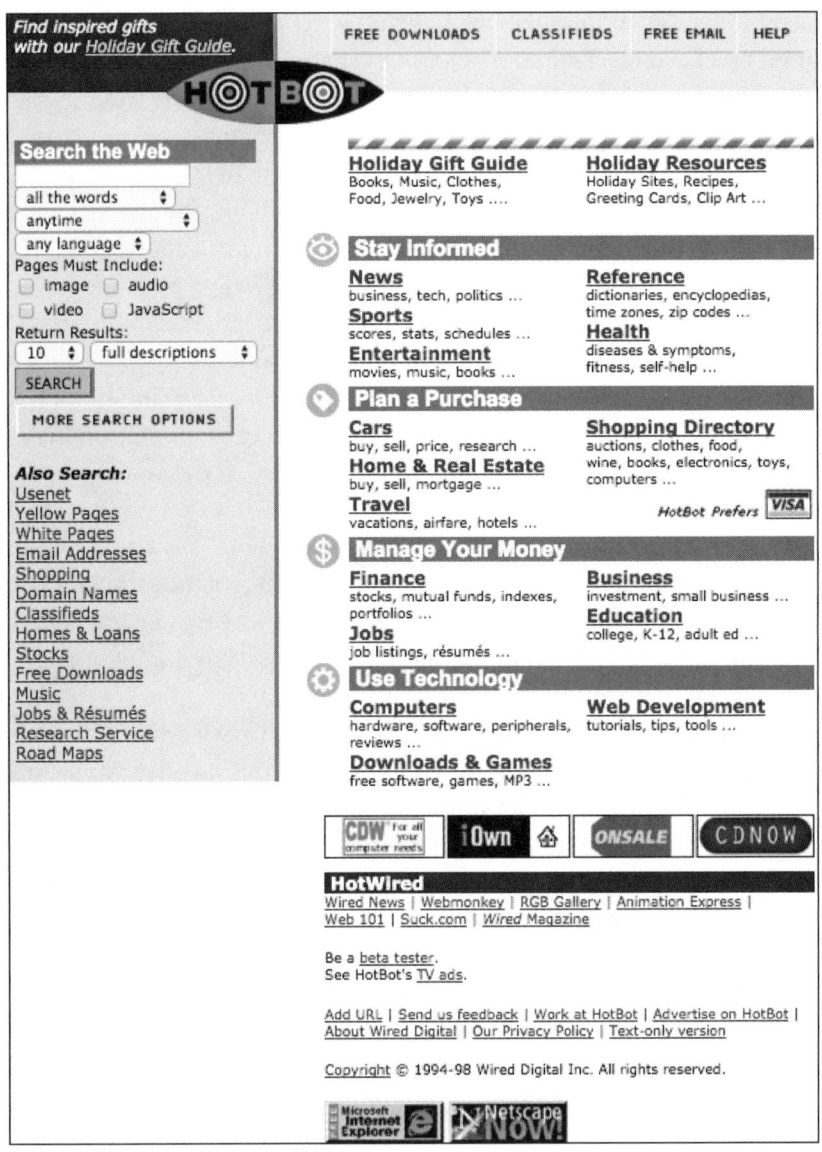

Figure 7.7

A screen shot of the HotBot search engine website as it appeared in December 1998, as stored in the Internet Archive.

Google's stated corporate mission is "to organize the world's information and make it universally accessible and useful." That's a breathtaking objective, reminiscent of Diderot's eighteenth-century *Encyclopédie*, of which he wrote "The goal of an encyclopedia is to assemble all the knowledge scattered on the surface of the earth." Yet as Google has been adding content and consolidating access to information, the Internet has been growing and fragmenting at least as rapidly, and thus a routine Google search misses an enormous amount of potentially accessible information. The Internet Archive has a similarly ambitious goal—"Universal access to all knowledge"—but the shortcomings of that important but relatively small operation are even more glaring.

For Google or for the Internet Archive, fragmentation poses many challenges. There are probably few legal constraints on making the US trademark databases broadly available as part of Google search results; the files, like those of the Patent Office (to which Google now offers access), are already publicly available through TESS and TSDR. The technological hurdles are more significant but not overwhelming. The files, many of which are in image rather than text format, would have to be scanned and put through an optical character-recognition process in order to extract recognizable text content—a process similar to what Google already does to add content to its Google Books collection. The real challenge to Google, or to any other search engine intent on providing near-universal access, is one of prioritization and resources. With so much information hidden from the automated process of crawling the Internet and indexing existing content (in other words, with so many large, important fragments), it becomes enormously difficult to keep up. Keeping up involves finding not only technological solutions but also legal, political, societal, financial, manpower, and institutional solutions.

For the average Web surfer, the presence of the Splinternet and the Invisible Web is generally not very problematic most of the time. The unsplintered and visible part of the Internet that Google and other search engines make available is almost unimaginably vast, and is likely to include pertinent information on almost any search topic. (In 2016, Google reported that it was crawling more than 60 trillion webpages and building an index more than 100 million gigabytes in size!)

The challenge for a general Internet searcher lies not so much in selecting the right fragment in which to search as in constructing a search strategy

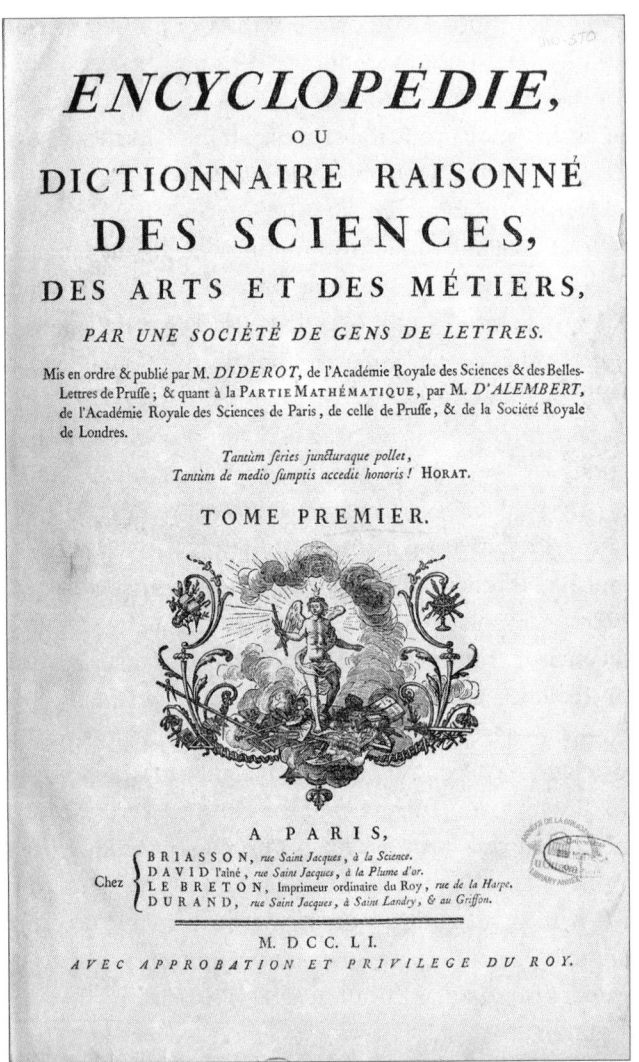

Figure 7.8
The title page of Diderot's *Encyclopédie,* first published in 1751.

that produces the desired content. Even within the context of everyday searches, users learn to adopt specialized strategies to optimize their foraging activities. Someone searching for driving directions might head directly to his or her favorite mapping app rather than rely on a general search. A student writing a homework essay on the life and work of Isaac Newton might go right to Wikipedia to search for information; another student constructing a poster on Jupiter might go directly to NASA.gov for images and information. A person seeking advice on dating might ask Facebook friends for suggestions or might sign on to Match.com rather than Google for generic guidance. As we noted earlier, searching for primary documents from the 1800s on Lincoln's assassination requires some well-honed search strategies to separate out the small number of original documents found online from the vast collections of information written about the assassination in more recent times.

Occasionally, however, users must step outside the bounds of conventional search engines to find some of the Internet's less visible, more fragmented materials. A homeowner or a potential home buyer in the United States who wants to see the tax records on a piece of property has to first find the website of the local (probably county) Real Property office, then navigate the site to locate the online lookup service for tax records (a feature that many, but not all, local governments provide). Similarly, finding a map with the exact boundaries of one's census district entails first locating the Census Bureau's mapping website and then using the site's search tools to locate the correct map for one's needs. In each of these cases, the first task can be handled through Google or another search engine, but the second task leads one into the invisible realm of the Internet. Why don't search engines provide this information directly? Why can't someone looking up a property's tax history simply type his address into a Bing or Google search box, add terms such as 'tax records', and be taken directly to the records he is seeking? After all, typing only an address typically yields not only a map of the house but also street-level and aerial photographs of the property, its sale history, and detailed estimates of its current market value. Why not include tax records too?

Part of the reason is simple market economics. There are more than 3,000 counties in the United States, and there are numerous other jurisdictions that manage local records of real property. A company that wanted to compile this information would have to negotiate arrangements with each individual government in order to fully access, download, and massage the information so that it could subsequently be made available in a routine Internet search. Although Google and some other firms have found it worthwhile to make this sort of effort in compiling other types of data--such as driving car-mounted cameras through almost every street in every city in America (and much of the rest of the world) to take street-view photographs--no search engine has yet deemed it cost-effective enough to compile data on tax records.

Another concern is privacy. Not all counties may be willing to provide their real-property databases for mass consumption. That the information is already available online through a county's own website doesn't mean that the county would permit broader release and easier access through commercial search engines. If counties are willing to make their databases available, Google and similar companies may be hesitant to weave it into their search results, in view of some of the privacy-related issues and complaints that have arisen with other provisions of large amounts of essentially personal information. Google is banned from or severely restricted in taking street-view images in several countries and has paid substantial fines and legal damages in the United States and elsewhere for operations related to such images that were deemed invasions of privacy. It simply may not strike a firm as worth the risk and effort to incorporate real-property databases into its system, despite a stated objective of making all information available to everyone.

8 Openness and Secrecy: The Essential Tension of Government-Held Information

Governments have a fundamental role in simultaneously encouraging, providing, and restricting access to information. In a very real sense, choices made about availability of information define the basic character of nations. Does anyone doubt that information flows less freely in North Korea or Iran than in Japan or Canada? Although explicit "information policies" aren't common, information underlies numerous rights, freedoms, programs, and constraints that governments create for the people of various countries.

The Constitution of the United States, for example, uses the word 'information' only once, requiring the president to "from time to time give to the Congress Information of the State of the Union." Yet several other provisions of the Constitution (including the Bill of Rights and subsequent amendments) are directly related to matters of federal information policy. Freedom of speech and freedom of the press are two critical rights providing for relatively unrestricted dissemination of information. The deliberations and actions of Congress are to be made matters of public record: "Each House shall keep a Journal of its Proceedings, and from time to time publish the same ... ." Information is a central right in criminal cases: "the accused shall enjoy the right ... to be informed of the nature and cause of the accusation." One explicit authority of the federal government, to establish post offices, is also an information-related provision of the Constitution. In the eighteenth century, mail service, after all, was the main communications network, a means of moving information from place to place quickly, affordably, and reliably.

The Constitution also presaged the US government's need for keeping secrets. The Congressional record was to be a public document, "excepting such Parts as may in their Judgment require Secrecy." There is no constitutional guidance as to the manner in which Congress should make its judgments about what information should be collected and what should be kept secret. But this very question, when applied to the government as a whole, is a matter of considerable urgency in current policy debates.

One function absent from the Constitution, but requiring mention, is the central role of government in establishing and maintaining a school system. Publicly funded education is deeply ingrained in the United States and in all other modern political systems. Schooling is a centralized process for disseminating information, and the nature of the information provided has important consequences for students and for the society in which they will participate. Education imparts information selectively. The teaching of history or current events—topics that strongly influence a student's world view—differs greatly from country to country.

The central role of information in government policy followed much the same path as did the concept of information in the broader society: from a self-evident concept at the fringes of national dialogue, requiring little explication, definition, or discussion, to a concept that is central not only to an age of human experience but also to political functioning and freedom. Today's vibrant and passionate dialogues concerning what information government should collect and what information government should keep secret are testimony to the emergence of information as a political topic of central importance.

Involuntary Transparency

An article in *Forbes* referred to the times we live in as the age of involuntary transparency, referring to the work of corporate whistleblowers who reveal business secrets from the inside, groups such as Wikileaks that make hijacked information widely available, leakers of state secrets, and others intent on bringing hidden government and corporate information into the light of day. There have always been organizational attempts at secrecy, of course, and there have always been spilled secrets. But our current era is different.

Part of the difference stems from information technology, which has simultaneously multiplied the power of tools for collecting and screening vast volumes of information, reduced the level of effort needed to penetrate secret systems and walk off with huge troves of secret data, and simplified the pathways for revealing (anonymously, if one so chooses) information not meant to be revealed. At the same time that the National Security Agency can envision global technology-based oversight—allowing the agency to collect information on "anyone, anywhere, anytime"—mid-level security personnel can use off-the-shelf software to copy files and abscond with truckloads of secret information on tiny memory devices, as Edward Snowden and Bradley Manning did.

But a large part of the difference is independent of technological innovations, and revolves around changing human perceptions and values. We are at a moment in history when the scope of government intrusiveness and the degree of public mistrust are unparalleled. Bureaucratic sentiment leans heavily toward the need for ever more sophisticated and powerful information-collection activities—a broad dragnet encompassing not only terrorists and criminals but all people, domestic and foreign, and operating in profound secrecy. The general population is inclined to have less and less faith in government, and is less willing to see it as a benign and functional entity that has its citizens' best interests at heart. People aren't opposed to spying on terrorists and criminals, but are far less sanguine about having their own calls and correspondence trawled in the process. Add to that a general queasiness about corporate data collection—concerns about overreaching, intrusiveness, and lack of security—and, justifiably or not, the loss of faith in once-trustworthy institutions is compounded.

Two court decrees from the federal judiciary, handed down less than two weeks apart as 2013 drew to a close, serve as an effective illustration of the tensions inherent in the sort of large-scale government data collection that we have been describing.

In one decision, US District Court Judge Richard Leon found the NSA's activities to be a vast overreach of government authority creating an "almost Orwellian" system of data gathering that threatens individual freedom and privacy and opens the door to considerable potential for abuse, all without convincing evidence of effectiveness:

[G]iven the limited record before me at this point in the litigation—most notably the utter lack of evidence that a terrorist attack has ever been prevented because searching the NSA database was faster than other investigative tactics—I have serious doubts about the efficacy of the metadata collection program as a means of conducting time-sensitive investigations in cases involving imminent threats of terrorism.

Judge Leon also took issue with the government's unwillingness to provide coherent information in the case, citing a lack of government candor that "defies common sense and does not exactly inspire confidence."

Shortly thereafter, a federal decision by US District Judge William Pauley gave the NSA's information-collection activities a robust judicial thumbs-up, referring to electronic snooping as the government's "counterpunch" to threats to national security and finding that the government had acted reasonably in extending the scope of its electronic dragnet while conscientiously avoiding the kind of overreaching that would incline the courts to rein it in. Judge Pauley was much more accepting of the efficacy of the NSA's efforts, writing in his decision that the collection of phone metadata cast "a wide net that could find and isolate gossamer contacts among suspected terrorists in an ocean of seemingly disconnected data."

Other pronouncements reflect similar uncertainty about the efficacy of mass surveillance systems. President Barack Obama has said plainly that the programs save lives: "We know of at least 50 threats that have been averted because of this information," the president stated, a claim that has been repeated by the NSA in Congressional testimony. Yet his administration has been silent on the details of cases where the information has supposedly proved its effectiveness. Independent studies—for example, a report titled "Do NSA's Bulk Surveillance Programs Stop Terrorists?" that reviewed hundreds of terrorism-linked court cases—have found little evidence of the utility of mass collection of phone metadata.

The contrasting legal decisions, statements, and studies nicely capture the dichotomy in our societal attitudes toward big data as a tool of government oversight. NSA-style information collection may well be everything that people say (or fear) it is: an effective counterpunch to terrorism and crime *and* a menacing invitation to *1984*-style abuse. Oddly, though, there is little concrete evidence with which to make either case. The lack of large-scale terrorist attacks on US soil since September 11, 2001 testifies to the overall effectiveness of our counter-terrorism tools, but not to the specific contributions of "big data" information dragnets. Similarly, the absence of any revelations of large-scale abuses of secret data-collection systems does little to quell concerns that such abuses may have occurred already and are likely to occur at some time in the future, especially in a system that is almost entirely free of public scrutiny. The uncertainties regarding both effectiveness and abuses led Congress, as of 2015, to scale back the program somewhat and impose additional safeguards.

It becomes a matter of deciding who you believe in a situation in which opinions are necessarily formed without the benefit of detailed information. In the end, the availability of concrete evidence of a program's effectiveness or of its abuse may not be particularly relevant. A large segment of the population believes in the program's effectiveness and in the need to deal with new threats. Another large segment of the population is concerned that such activities step over the line, impinge on basic freedoms, and have only limited utility. (No doubt a significant number of people hold both views simultaneously.) Society needs to come to terms with this inherent tension, regardless of the degree to which either set of beliefs is supported by hard evidence.

Whatever facts are available about governments' data-collection programs, the information is screened through each individual's sensibilities. Thus, what to believe comes down to a matter of trust. Am I inclined to believe that my government will almost always act in my best interests, collecting information selectively and judiciously? Or am I inclined to believe that, however good its intentions, a government that has the means to overstep its bounds will inevitably do so? These contrasting sensibilities remind us of Benjamin Franklin's well-known statement that "they who would give up essential Liberty, to purchase a little temporary Safety, deserve neither Liberty nor Safety." But the simple truth is that we, as a society, craft a balance between freedom and security that continually calls for one to be sacrificed for the other, and that continually shifts as we collectively respond to the world around us.

That governments collect data on just about everyone doesn't really come as a surprise, as viewers of *The Simpsons Movie* (2007) are well aware: "Hey, everybody, I found one! The government actually found someone we're looking for!" But the scope, the sophistication, and the intrusiveness of the data collection raise significant concerns, as does the apparent open-endedness of the collection efforts. There is no obvious ending date and no inclination to scale back; the trajectory is one of devising ever-more-powerful means of amassing and analyzing as much information as is technologically feasible, with the hope that the spotlight will eventually dim and the activities will once again take place in society's darkest shadows.

To Americans, Franklin's aphorism is also a reminder of their country's roots. It is a deeply ingrained part of the national culture to mistrust authority in the best of times and to openly resist it when the situation warrants. We grant governments exclusive powers—to police, to regulate, to legislate, to tax, to imprison, to wage war, to spy—but cast a constant and wary eye on how governments exercise those powers. From all appearances, the present level of public mistrust in governments is fairly high, perhaps more so than at most times in American history. Is it really any surprise that the unprecedented scope and scale of government information collection is cause for concern among a sizable fraction of the population of the United States and among sizable fractions of many other populations around the world?

Does Mass Surveillance Equal Big Brother?

If you make a phone call, send an email message, text a friend, or post a letter, your action has a good likelihood of making its way into government databases. Take a commercial airplane flight or visit a foreign country and your travel will be logged. Walk through a city and you will be watched by a plethora of government security cameras (and many private-sector ones). Drive your car more than a few miles and there is a good chance that your vehicle's license plate will be photographed and recorded in an anti-crime database, along with the date, the time, and the location. The US government's Nationwide Suspicious Activity Reporting Initiative has collected Suspicious Activity Reports on untold numbers of individuals, some of whom have done nothing more "suspect" than leaving a cell phone in a public space. Details on international financial transactions (and, we suppose, many domestic transactions) are routinely recorded in government databases.

With every new revelation, the response of the Department of Homeland Security and of various law-enforcement agencies has been a consistent defense of the information-collection activity in question. Although details differ from program to program, the justifications offered can be paraphrased in three ways:

It's absolutely necessary for security.

It's not as bad as it seems.

It's nothing new.

The most compelling defense of the information-collection programs is the first one. Amassing details of people's phone calls, correspondence, finances, and movements is a powerful tool for preventing some crimes from taking place and for tracking the whereabouts of individuals after a crime has occurred. There is no real doubt that the information-collection activities of national, state, and local law-enforcement agencies have been instrumental in preventing some crimes and solving others, including crimes that would threaten homeland security and more pedestrian criminal activities such as robbing banks. Even if the details of such tracking are rarely revealed, it seems obvious that fast access to details of cell-phone use, travel habits, financial transactions, and all the rest would make for a powerful crime-fighting tool.

Of course, with the current generation of monitoring activities, it isn't only criminals who are monitored. The approach of the National Security Agency was quite deliberate. Rather than attempt to isolate individual criminal "needles in the haystack," the NSA opted to gather the entire haystack—or, as one intelligence officer put it, "Collect it all, tag it, store it. … And whatever it is you want, you go searching for it." This broad-brush approach to information gathering has given rise to a generalized concern about government snooping and to more specific concerns about routine approval of secret activities, lack of effective oversight, operating outside the bounds of the law, alienating our overseas allies, and intruding into details of people's personal lives.

These concerns are met with the "It's not as bad as it seems" argument, which generally entails an explanation—reluctantly offered—of the details of how individual programs work: what they do and, as important, what they don't do. Although "monitoring" of phone calls brings to mind images of government agents with earphones listening in on each and every conversation, the NSA phone-monitoring programs do nothing of the kind, but instead keep records of each call's metadata: phone numbers, dates, and times. The programs track who calls who, and when the calls are made, but not the actual conversations taking place. As far as we know, many of the "big data" programs work this way, focusing on the metadata of each message (whether it is a phone call, an email message, or snail mail) rather than the message's content. The fact that the government has a record that you phoned your sister-in-law at 4:27 p.m. on June 7 is intrusive, of course, but "not as bad" as it would be had the government listened in on the conversation.

The "It's nothing new" justification adds to the defense of the program and typically breaks down into two pieces:

We've been doing this for a long time.

It's not only us; other countries, agencies, and even corporations are doing pretty much the same thing.

In other words, collecting and amassing secret data is business as usual, so there is no need to get flustered about it as if it were something new.

Although a case can be made, in rather forced fashion, that the gathering of data by governments truly is business as usual, it's the "nothing new" argument that gives us the greatest pause. Although governments have always done a bit of snooping on citizens' personal lives, only recently (thanks to advancements in information technology) has the sheer scope of the current efforts become possible. To argue that the current programs are "nothing new" is akin to saying that the Internet is nothing new—after all, we have always had access to information sources, and we have long had ways to communicate with one another over vast distances. The statement would be true, in the narrowest possible construction of its meaning, but it is a statement that can be made only by someone deliberately wearing blinders to mask the full situation. At its core, it is so patently false as to be ridiculous. What the Internet makes possible is very new indeed. Claiming that the current degree of government scrutiny is nothing new is ludicrous.

The manner in which technology has changed law-enforcement agencies' use of license-plate numbers is a good example of how a practice that is in one sense "business as usual" is really quite new and categorically different from anything that preceded it.

For as long as license plates have been in use, they have been readily observable. Anyone walking down a street—a policeman, an FBI agent, an ordinary pedestrian—can make note of a particular plate on a specific vehicle at a certain place and time. This is very much business as usual, and it isn't likely that anyone would give a second thought to someone's making such a routine observation. A camera allows an observer to take a quick snapshot of a car's license plate. Most modern digital cameras not only store the picture, but can also record the time and date the picture was taken. A slightly more sophisticated camera, with GPS capabilities, will also record the precise location. We have just described a very ordinary situation—a person standing on the sidewalk and taking a photograph with a camera or a cell phone. But the power of technology is such that this simple act is creating a complex electronic record of exactly when and where a particular car, bearing a particular plate number, was photographed. And optical character-recognition software can "read" the plate and store the number. Internet-enabled cameras can beam the record directly to an online database.

Law-enforcement agencies now have combined several technologies and taken the once rather ordinary act of observing a vehicle's license plate several steps further. Cameras in fixed locations throughout a city automatically snap thousands of photos a day, every time a car passes, record the date, the time, the location, and the plate number, and upload the information. Other cameras, mounted on police cars and other official vehicles, roam the city, creating similar records of thousands upon thousands of license plates.

The information is amassed in a central database. There are now millions of records, some of them spanning years, documenting the details of vehicles' movements. The database becomes part of law enforcement's arsenal. When the police want to know the whereabouts or the habitual haunts of a particular person, they can match that person to a particular license plate and then "mine" the database for relevant information, along the lines of "Aha! Every Wednesday at around 3 a.m., this car passes the camera at 34th and Vine. We'll be there to intercept him on his next trip."

The database is very useful for law-enforcement purposes, as it provides exactly the type of information one would want the police to have when they are looking for a bank robber's getaway car or conducting an Amber Alert search for a missing child. When Vester Lee Flanagan shot and killed two journalists on live television in August of 2015, the car he fled in was quickly tracked in exactly this manner.

But it can be more than a bit disconcerting to realize that one's own driving habits could be just as easily mined from the data, should someone with access to the data want to do so.[1]

The point here is one of emphasis. The "business as usual" act of observing or even photographing a license plate is magnified enormously by technology that can record, extract, store, and retrieve information on a large scale and at high speed. Pretending that such technologically powerful data collection is "nothing new" is duplicitous. It is *prima facie* very new, and very different from what preceded it, in much the same way that a computer is a very different device than an adding machine.

Big Brother may not be here yet, but continual advances in the capture, storage, and retrieval of information are certainly providing the technical tools that a government would need to make Big Brother a reality.

Oddly enough, the multi-faceted tension between surveillance and privacy, security and freedom, secrecy and transparency, leaks and legitimacy, and trust and mistrust comes at a time when both government and corporations probably practice—in the United States, at least—a greater degree of openness than ever before.

Table 8.1
Examples of mass surveillance by government agencies in the United States.

Overall focus	Key agency	Name of program	Scope	Description
Telephones and Internet				
Call metadata	NSA		Tens of millions of Verizon customers; probably billions of calls	Verizon was required to pass along information on originating and destination phone numbers, time and date of call, length of call, and other information independent of the actual call content. This was one of the earliest Snowden revelations.
Cell-phone location	NSA		Five billion records per day from hundreds of millions of individual phones	Location data from cell-phone transmissions are logged daily; focus is on non-US phones, but many US customers included incidentally.
Tower dumps	Numerous law-enforcement agencies		Thousands of requests annually, involving millions of phone records	Law-enforcement agencies request cell-phone tower metadata records to identify geographically specific usage, pinpointing all cell phones in use in a certain area during a certain time period.
Varied	NSA	StellarWind		Broad but undefined access to email communications, phone conversations, financial transactions, and Internet activity. Program may have been discontinued.

Table 8.1 (continued)

Overall focus	Key agency	Name of program	Scope	Description
Telephones and Internet				
Varied	NSA	Prism		Broad but undefined access to Internet communications, including audio and video chats, photographs, email messages, documents, and connection logs, through taps on servers at companies like Microsoft, Yahoo, Google, Facebook, PalTalk, AOL, Skype, YouTube, Apple, and perhaps Dropbox.
Email address books	NSA		About 250 million contact lists annually	A typical day's access included 444,743 address books from Yahoo Mail, 105,068 from Hotmail, 82,857 from Facebook, 33,697 from Gmail, and 22,881 from other providers. Collection occurs at overseas locations, but includes many US contacts.
International data centers	NSA, British intelligence	Muscular	181 million records in a month	Apparently based in the UK, this program intercepts traffic to the Internet "cloud" from Google, Yahoo, and other services. Content includes text, audio, video, and communications metadata.
Webcam images	British intelligence	Optic Nerve	1.8 million users of Yahoo webcam chat service	Millions of still images were collected from webcams; roughly 10% of these contained nudity or pornographic content. It is not known if US agencies conducted similar surveillance.

Table 8.1 (continued)

Overall focus	Key agency	Name of program	Scope	Description
Mail and packages				
US Mail	US Post Office	Mail Isolation Control and Tracking	160 billion pieces of correspondence annually	The Post Office photographs each piece of mail and extracts the address, return address, date and possibly other information to store in a database for an indefinite period of time. The data are routinely used by various law-enforcement programs.
US Mail	US Post Office	Mail Covers	49,000 "mail cover" actions in 2013	Individual mail recipients or addresses are targeted for detailed scrutiny. The Criminal Investigative Service Center of the Post Office copies all envelopes and packages and forwards the copies to the requesting law-enforcement agency.
Post Office customers	US Post Office	Automated Postal Centers		Self-service postage machines photograph each user and retain the photo for 30 days.
Vehicle tracking				
License-plate scanning	Local law-enforcement agencies			Automated photos of plates from fixed and mobile cameras create a database of which vehicles travel where, and when.

Table 8.1 (continued)

Overall focus	Key agency	Name of program	Scope	Description
Financial transactions				
Credit cards, banking	NSA	Follow the Money	180 million records in TRACFIN database	Agency keeps records of credit-card transactions and other financial data for unspecified targets.
Activity-based				
Suspicious activities	FBI, Department of Homeland Security	Nationwide Suspicious Activity Reporting Initiative	Several billion records	FBI collates data, including non-criminal but suspect activities, from thousands of law-enforcement agencies and campus security services.

Secrecy and the Moynihan Commission

This perplexing state of affairs largely reflects the simple truism that information is power. American society experiences the same dichotomy in regard to the sharing of information as it does in regard to other aspects of social power (money, fame, influence), on the one hand concentrating it and on the other striving to distribute it widely. In principle, we put power in the hands of individual citizens. In practice, power is often highly concentrated in a few select institutions and individuals, who guard it carefully and hope to retain it as their own. Information follows a similar pattern. Our traditions require, or at least encourage, broad and unfettered access to information, through principles with such labels as "freedom of information," "community right to know," "freedom of the press," "open government," and "institutional transparency." In practice, information is often held "close to the chest" by those who want to keep the power that information provides available only to a chosen few.

Secrecy is the most restrictive way of limiting access to information held by the government. A "Top Secret" stamp on a document or a data source not only keeps the information away from the general public but also severely limits access to the information within the government. A secrecy classification also has a temporal influence, removing information from scrutiny for indeterminate periods of time—perhaps years or even decades.

A look back at some of the recent history of government secrecy sheds some light on how the challenges of past decades compare with those that American society faces today.

In 1997, the Commission on Protecting and Reducing Government Secrecy, authorized by Congress two years earlier and headed by Senator Daniel Patrick Moynihan, released its findings. The commission's final report began boldly—"It is time for a new way of thinking about secrecy." Its primary message, which it took pains to put in common-sense terms, was this:

> The best way to ensure that secrecy is respected, and that the most important secrets remain secret, is for secrecy to be returned to its limited but necessary role. Secrets can be protected more effectively if secrecy is reduced overall … .

The Moynihan Commission essentially began with the premise (a premise which it convincingly demonstrated to be the case) that the US government kept far more information secret than was genuinely necessary for protecting national interests. Information was classified as secret to avoid embarrassment, to consolidate authority, as a habitual reaction, or for no apparent reason at all. Once information had been made secret, undoing that decision and making the information public was difficult. What's more, the very nature of secrecy keeps not only documents and files but the entire system of secrecy out of view of the public. The consequences of creating excessive secrets, maintaining them almost indefinitely, and avoiding public scrutiny were serious and fundamentally detrimental to democracy, the Moynihan Commission found, for three principal reasons: "policymakers are not fully informed, government is not held accountable for its actions, and the public cannot engage in informed debate."

The need to convene a formal commission on the perils of excessive secrecy runs counter to the impression of American society as open, perhaps the most open and transparent society in existence. After all, the United States has always been committed to a free flow of information. It enshrined a free press in its constitution. It embraced public education as a means of building an informed citizenry. It passed laws requiring open access to government meetings, public review of regulations, freedom of information, and a community right to know. Government publications are in the public domain, are free of copyright, and are available for anyone

Figure 8.1
Daniel Patrick Moynihan (1927–2003), diplomat, senator, and scholar.

to use, whereas in many Commonwealth countries government publications—even published laws—are covered by Crown Copyright and may not
be freely copied without consent of the Crown. In the US, court records
are publicly accessible, as are police reports, campaign contributions, professional license records, and a great deal of other federal, state, and local
government information.

The American commitment to openness, transparency, and the active
provision of information is very real. But so is the American penchant for
secrecy. The Moynihan Commission recognized this, referring to the long-
standing conflict between secrecy and an open society:

From the beginning of the American republic, and especially over the past half century, a tension has existed between the legitimate interest of the public in being
kept informed about the activities of its Government and the legitimate interest
of the Government in certain circumstances in withholding information; in short,
between openness and secrecy … .

The commission was referring here—and its report was largely focused
on—*formal* secrecy, recognized by three "pillars" of secrecy: classification
of something as a secret, identification of those who are privy to the secret
information, and sanctions for leaking secret information to parties outside

of the small circle of those allowed to share in it. This is secrecy in an almost cinematic sense, with certain information stamped, in large, bold letters, "Top Secret," "Eyes Only," "Confidential," or any of numerous other categories meant to keep the information away from public view. The report didn't call the legitimacy of such classifications into question: secrecy serves a valid function in the protection of national security and the maintenance of privacy for records about individuals. But the commission recognized the compelling desire to treat many information resources as secret ("the rule is stamp, stamp, stamp") even when secrecy does little or nothing to protect national interests or individual privacy. "Information is power," the commission wrote, "and it is no mystery to government officials that power can be increased through controls on the flow of information."

The Moynihan Commission's report also acknowledges, even if only in passing, the great bulk of other types of information the government produces (and often withholds). This is the information in federal files that isn't stamped "Secret," but is nonetheless deliberately kept from public view. In fact, the commission identified "52 different protective markings being used on unclassified information … . Included among these are widely used markings such as "Sensitive But Unclassified," "Limited Official Use," "Official Use Only," and "For Official Use Only." It is information that isn't secret, per se, but that is withheld anyway. The report refers to this as "marked" information.

The Moynihan Commission's report is relatively silent, however, on government information that is neither "classified" nor "marked." That includes the vast bulk of the information the US government produces—memos, email messages, talking points, draft reports, discussion papers, policy pieces, backgrounders, spreadsheets, meeting minutes, sign-in sheets, phone logs, whitepapers, photographs, recordings, and innumerable other types of documents, databases, and files that exist in a no-man's land of accessibility: not secret, and not marked, but not readily available to the public either.

The spectrum of government information that is withheld from public view now runs from Secret through Marked to Uncategorized. All these types of information can be requested by the public under the guidelines of the Freedom of Information Act. But not until a FOIA request has been received does an agency begin evaluating the requested material to determine whether it should be released to the public.

A considerable amount of information *does* get released—often visibly and with attention to ease of access—for consumption by the public. Some information is public as a result of a FOIA request, but most is available as a routine matter of bureaucratic policy. At the website of any federal agency you can find an impressive volume of reports, images, and data on the topics the agency covers. The federal government has gone a step further, amassing information from various agencies at sites such as regulations. gov, USAjobs.gov, data.gov, investor.gov, and grants.gov to facilitate the dissemination of information and public access to it.

The active provision of information from the government to citizens is one of the hallmarks of the American system. The government of the United States may well be the most information-rich institution in existence. Its commitment to *information* as an essential component of public policy, citizen participation, economic management, political representation, regulatory oversight, warfare, espionage, and national security helps us to understand why American society is simultaneously the most open and the most secret society. We have so much information at our disposal, as a nation, that we can make more information publicly available than any other country does and simultaneously withhold far more information than is possible anywhere else.

With that secrecy-openness spectrum in mind, we can return to the main recommendation of the Moynihan Commission about the desirability of reducing government secrecy and ask "How are we doing?"

The commission released its report in March 1997, four and a half years before the terrorist attacks of September 11, 2001. Where is the US in the post-9/11 era in terms of its balance between openness and secrecy? Secrecy, by its very nature, doesn't lend itself to straightforward measurement, but common sense suggests that the US is much more vested in secrecy now than it was at the time of the Moynihan Commission's report. The size and the scope of America's anti-terrorism apparatus were hinted at by the Snowden leaks, but its true scale is unknown because the entire system operates in almost complete secrecy.

Government openness too has been affected by terrorism. Information that once was publicly available thanks to the nation's commitment to open government has now been withdrawn from view because officials had second thoughts about the wisdom of making so much information available to those who might potentially use it against us. For example, detailed reports on toxic chemicals handled at the nation's chemical plants once were publicly available but now are available only to emergency response personnel. A schedule for declassifying government secrets introduced by President Bill Clinton (Executive Order 12958) was rescinded by President George W. Bush (Executive Order 13292). As secrecy has been expanding and openness (of some materials at least) has been shrinking, the phenomenal growth of the Internet has provided government agencies with a tool for delivering information to the public in unprecedented quantity with unprecedented ease of access.

To simplify the picture, let us separate information from government sources into three pools: a secret pool (in which information is tightly and deliberately withheld), a public pool (containing just the reverse, information deliberately made available for public consumption), and an everything-else pool (in which the information is kept out of view of the public, either because its status regarding public availability is undecided or because there is no simple mechanism for making the information publicly accessible). We are still faced with the inability to quantify the size of any of these three pools, but again common sense makes it inarguably clear that each of the pools has grown substantially in size since the 1997 release of the Moynihan Commission's report, if for no other reason than that the sheer quantity of information in the world has multiplied many times over these past few decades, as have the ease and the speed with which new information can be created and stored.

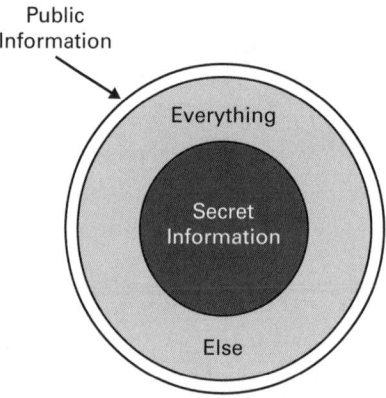

Figure 8.2

We have been making the case (a compelling one, we hope) that freeing up the flow of information in the economic sphere makes for more robust, responsive, and sustainable economic activity. Might the same be true in national and international policy? Can better access to information, more or less on its own, promote the objectives of global-scale peace and security? Put another way, is it to our benefit to move as much information as is possible out of the secret pool, where access is denied, and out of the everything-else pool, where access is limited, into the public pool, where the information can be readily accessed and reviewed?

The answer would seem to be Yes. Severely restraining the flow of information is the hallmark of tyranny. The world knows almost nothing of substance about North Korea. That country operates in profound secrecy, both internally (relative to its own people), relative to its neighbors in Asia, and relative to the rest of the world. In the absence of disclosure about almost anything, it isn't possible to build up relationships of mutual trust.

'Trust' is also the operative word underlying the Snowden revelations. Awareness of the scope of government secrecy and meta-secrecy (that is, keeping even the existence of secrets a secret) has eroded the diminishing sense of trust that ordinary US citizens already had for their government even further. Add to that the damage to trust among allies and the expanding distrust of those already inclined to not give the US government the benefit of the doubt and the cost of collecting and keeping secrets begins to seem a Faustian bargain at best. Apple and Google are making their operating systems harder to de-encrypt, chiefly in response to users' concerns that the government was illicitly snooping into communications and activities that should remain private. But the FBI has warned that stronger encryption will protect criminals if law-enforcement agencies can't access information even on the cell phones and computers confiscated during criminal investigations.

There is no doubt that some secrecy is warranted. As individuals, we make such decisions routinely in our personal lives, keeping some information about ourselves secret even from those we are closest to. As consumers, we expect stores, schools, hospitals, churches, and governments to keep our private information secure and out of the hands of those who don't have permission to access it. As citizens, we accept the government's need to maintain secret information and probe the secrets that others keep—up to a point. But we remain skeptical, reasonably so, of a government that keeps too many secrets of its own and probes too deeply into the secrets of others. This strikes us, collectively, as a government trying to excessively concentrate the power of information among too few individuals.

Expanding the Pool of Public Information

Government can and should be much more open with the information it generates. There is no reason it should not. The information that the government generates is created at public expense for the public good and should be, for the most part, publicly available. This holds for both secrets by fiat and secrets by happenstance; the more accessibility to information, the better.

For information made explicitly secret, we think the recommendations of the Moynihan Commission still make sense: set a time limit on secrecy, routinely apply it to all records, then make the information public once the time limit has been passed. There would be exceptions, of course, but the secrecy of most secrets would have an expiration date. The Moynihan Commission recommended a limit of 10 years for government secrets, after which either the information would be made public or the secrecy classification would have to be recertified by senior managers. Few secrets would be retained beyond 30 years, and only in cases in which an individual's life or the nation's security was clearly in jeopardy. The commission's recommendations offer sensible guidelines for recrafting the nation's framework for secrecy—guidelines that are still valid today.

There is considerable merit in having most of the information in the everything-else pool made publicly available more or less in real time. It seems to us that if government employees knew with certainty that every one of their memos, email messages, policy papers, reports, and databases would soon be in the public domain, most of them would pay considerable attention to how those materials might look to an outside observer. The content of the materials probably would change, and so might the content of government actions. Sunshine is the best disinfectant.

The notion of operating in a fishbowl, so that the world at large can view our phone records, email messages, and so on, runs counter to our habits and our culture. After all, the controversy over NSA-style mass surveillance stems from the sense that it is an inappropriate intrusion into private communications. Aren't government employees entitled to that same privacy in the course of their communications? The Freedom of Information Act and other open-government statutes largely answer that question in the negative, suggesting that works produced by government bureaucrats should be in the public domain. There is a large gap, though, between principle and practice, as we have tried to make clear. Most government records remain out of sight of the public.

Some of the most famous bits of privileged (i.e., not-for-public-consumption) government information to unexpectedly see the light of day were the materials that spilled out of the Watergate scandal, particularly the secret tape recordings of White House conversations. Suppose the recordings hadn't been secret. Suppose the tape recorder had sat right on the president's desk, so that all present understood that their conversation was taped for posterity. Suppose, too, that everyone understood that the materials would sooner or later be made publicly available. Would the conversations that took place have been the same? More to the point, would the subsequent actions on the part of the Nixon Administration been the same if the participants had been aware that their schemes would one day be public? There is no way of knowing the answers to these questions, of course, and we do not suggest that the president of the United States and members of his staff aren't entitled to keep some secrets. But there is certainly a strong suspicion that limiting secrets makes a difference, and that people in a glass house behave very differently than people hidden behind opaque walls.

Consider the email traffic from a more recent scandal. A monstrous traffic jam in Fort Lee, New Jersey, was caused by lane closures on the George Washington Bridge. The traffic jam was deliberate, an act of political retribution. Apparently, the mayor of Fort Lee hadn't been sufficiently supportive of the governor's re-election bid. Much has been written about the political "culture" in the governor's office, a culture presumed (by some, at least) to have inclined staffers to believe that such retribution was acceptable. But there is also an informational culture—a culture that allows staffers to believe that their communications (such as the email message "Time for some traffic problems in Fort Lee") are privileged and will never see the light of day. If the office culture had been more along the lines of "If I write this down, someone in the press, or in the opposition, or among the public is going to see it," it seems much less likely that the Fort Lee email message would ever have been sent. Of course, staffers would still have been free to message one another in code, arrange to meet at a park bench to hatch their schemes, or communicate in other ways that would leave no permanent record. Political conspiracies and simple bad behavior might still be the order of the day. But open access to government communications makes it more difficult to coordinate everyone involved and to arrange for bad behavior. Conspiring is considerably harder when government operates in a much more transparent fashion.

We will offer one more example to drive home the point. In the summer of 2013, news sources began reporting on a nearly buried Department of Defense report on the US military's decades-long efforts to identify the fate and, if possible, retrieve the remains of the tens of thousands of missing-in-action soldiers from World War II, the Korean War, and the war in Vietnam. An Associated Press article on the report began as follows:

The Pentagon's effort to account for tens of thousands of Americans missing in action from foreign wars is so inept, mismanaged and wasteful that it risks descending from "dysfunction to total failure," according to an internal study suppressed by military officials ... .

The General in charge of the MIA operations ordered that the report not be circulated and prohibited anyone from making copies of it. According to the aforementioned AP article, "the Associated Press obtained a copy of the internal study after Freedom of Information Act requests for it by others were denied." In response to the reports in the press, the Department of Defense quickly announced that it was undertaking a determined and thorough review of the situation. "Sometimes media reports raise attention in ... a department of 3 million people," the DoD's spokesperson, George Little, added. "It certainly sometimes helps to have press stories shed light on issues that are out there."

The incident puts government secrecy in an interesting and fairly unflattering light. A report that was scathingly critical of a military program was kept secret, not for reasons of national security or individual privacy, but for no apparent reason other than to avoid embarrassment. Researchers relying on the Freedom of Information Act to request a copy of a report were turned down, despite the fundamental intent of the law to make government information available unless there is a compelling reason for nondisclosure. The AP obtained a copy of the report, presumably through an unnamed insider who leaked the report to the press, perhaps breaking the law in the process. News of the report's findings caused outrage among the public and in Congress. The Department of Defense acted quickly to quell public concern, even offering some mild praise for the importance of press stories that "shed light" on important policy issues that are otherwise easy to overlook.

Imagine that scenario unfolding in a different context: that of the monthly release of unemployment data. The Department of Commerce, embarrassed by the most recent set of data—information that shows the administration's policies have been unsuccessful in reducing unemployment—decides to keep the data secret. The decision would be ludicrous.

A more open government could go well beyond access to email messages, documents, and data. Congressional debate is televised, as are many courtroom proceedings. It is certainly possible, technologically, to expand that sort of access and provide live webcam feeds from the meeting rooms of all Senate and House offices and from the conference rooms of all federal and state agencies and departments. Anyone with an interest could be the proverbial fly on the wall at any of the meetings held in the wired conference rooms. All this would be technologically possible. But would it be wise?

Governments around the world are asking for more and more information from their citizens and are relying on ever more intrusive tools to collect this information, including phone records, email data, Web searches, license plates, and even the comings and goings of "snail mail." The government compiles lists of email address books, cell-phone contacts, social-media friends, and even apps downloaded. The push for more information, almost always made in the course of the valid drive for greater security, has been technologically and politically aggressive, expansive, and intrusive.

Is it unreasonable to ask for the reverse—that is, to ask for much greater openness on the part of governments that are imposing so much more involuntary openness on the populations they serve? One consequence of governments' push for greater information about the citizenry—efforts carried out, more often than not, in great secrecy—has been an undermining of public trust. This may be the right moment in history to revisit the social contract between people and government, retune the balance of who provides information to whom, and begin to restore the public's trust in the government(s) that exist to serve the public interest.

As we described above, one category of data that the government collects in huge volumes is communications metadata. If you make a phone call, send an email message, or post a letter, the government doesn't (necessarily) know the content of your communication, but it does store—and can access at will—the fact that the communication took place, who sent it, who received it, and when it occurred.

In a simple tit-for-tat world, ordinary citizens would have access to the same type of who-calls-who metadata about their governments. With a few clicks of a mouse, a citizen could see who spoke to the president by phone this week, what agencies contacted the Speaker of the House, what email messages were exchanged by climate-change scientists at the National Oceanic and Atmospheric Administration, or who the governor's deputy chief of staff has been texting.

Revealing government metadata appeals to a fundamental sense of fair play: If you can see our data, we should be able to see yours. But metadata alone doesn't strike the right balance as an information-access strategy. Citizens are entitled to privacy and have no obligation to make their communications publicly available. Government, on the other hand, has exactly that obligation; government information is supposed to be public, barring an explicit finding that it should be withheld. Government metadata should be publicly available, but only as a first step for citizens to access government data.

In other words, now that we know who emailed who, do we have the right to see the messages? In many cases, the answer is Yes. Official email messages are part of the records that government creates that are publicly releasable under the Freedom of Information Act,[2] unless a message falls under one of the exemptions allowed under that act. Email communications are routinely included in responses to FOIA requests, as can be seen by reviewing materials in any of the "Electronic Reading Rooms" that numerous government agencies make available.

The US government has a genuine commitment to the principle of information access, but struggles with the practice. The creation of a well-meaning federal website, data.gov, embodies both sides of this phenomenon. The goal is laudable, but the data are often obscure, especially to potential

OPEN GOVERNMENT

Since his first full day in office, President Obama has prioritized making government more open and accountable and has taken substantial steps to increase citizen participation, collaboration, and transparency in government.

Data.gov, the central site for U.S. Government data, is an important part of the Administration's overall effort to open government.

Figure 8.3

White House Visitor Records Requests
A list of White House Visitor Record requests

	NAMELAST	NAMEFIRST	NAMEMID	UIN	BDGNBR	Type of Access
1	MATTHEWS	GARY		STARMX		AL
2	DOYLE	PATRICIA		STARMX		AL
3	MATTHEWS	SANDY		STARMX		AL
4	MALONE	SHARON		STARMX		AL
5	WILSON	WELLINGTON		STARMX		AL

Figure 8.4

users not already familiar with their source. For example, with some fanfare, the site made available a database labeled White House Visitor Records Requests. Nowhere, however, does the site offer an explanation of what this database actually is. Is it a list of visitors to the White House? Is it a list of people requesting visits to the White House? Is it a list of those who have requested the White House visitors list? Although it probably is the first, the list's bureaucratically cryptic title offers only hints. Other features go unexplained. What are "STARMX" and "UIN"? What is "AL" access? Are there other forms of access? Will everyone viewing this list decode BDGNBR as Badge Number?

We don't mean this as an exercise in nitpicking, but merely to emphasize the gulf that too often exists between intent and actuality when it comes to making government data publicly available.

The government's commitment to freedom of information notwithstanding, the bar is set very high for individuals actually wanting to obtain internal information from government agencies. A FOIA request is time consuming and resource intensive and requires "going to school" to understand the nuances of the FOIA process. Once a request has been made, the requester can easily wait six months, a year, or longer before receiving the requested information (if, in fact, any information is forthcoming—agencies often assert exemptions and deny FOIA requests). Agencies respond to FOIA requests by searching through their files—paper and electronic—for materials that may be responsive to the request. Each piece of information is reviewed by the agency, and a decision is made as to whether the material is releasable. The released materials are first thoroughly reviewed and edited to remove details considered private or sensitive. The person or entity requesting the information can be assessed a substantial fee for the agency's time and effort in responding to the FOIA request. The results can be quite erratic. Different agencies asked for the same piece of information can make different decisions regarding releasing all, some, or none of the requested information.

Freeing Up Freedom of Information

In some respects, the barriers posed by the FOIA process are akin to the barriers a government agency may have to overcome in some of its own information-collection activities, such as crafting a subpoena, convincing a judge to approve it, setting up a wiretap, and adhering to stringent rules and restrictions on what can be collected and how it can be obtained. But, of course, for the government much of that difficulty has been removed in the era of large-scale automated collection of personal information.

The barriers to access of government information should be similarly lowered. At present, each unclassified information item the government creates occupies an uncertain status until the item is "FOIA'd." Only at that point does the relevant bureaucracy review the item and decide to publicly release all, some, or none of it. But the process can be changed so that an item would be presumed to be fully releasable as it was created unless a concrete step were taken to assign an item some other status.

In essence, we are suggesting a reversal of the policy on transparency of government-created information. As the system is currently constructed, information is largely withheld as a matter of course. Only after an agency

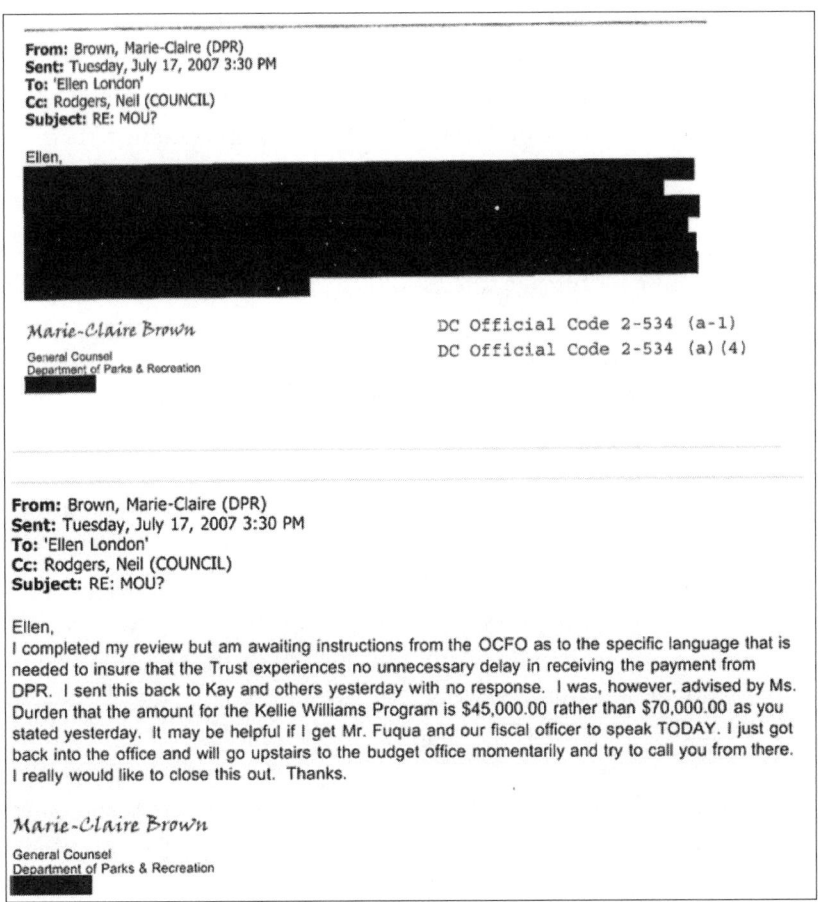

Figure 8.5
Freedom of Information Act requests for email records resulted in the same email released from different sources redacted in different ways.

has received a public request for some information does the agency review the information and makes a judgment as to its releasability. In the reverse scenario, information would automatically be made publicly available unless, by some well-defined bureaucratic process, a decision were made that the information should be withheld.

In principle, a shift toward what might be called hypertransparency regarding government information makes sense. Government would become more accountable, agencies would become more efficient and effective (really!), and individual bureaucrats would be less likely to keep things out of public view merely out of habit. (Recall the Moynihan Commission's characterization of the inherent tension between "the legitimate interest of the public in being kept informed about the activities of its Government and the legitimate interest of the Government in certain circumstances in withholding information; in short, between openness and secrecy.")

The legitimate interest of the government has grown enormously. As a consequence, the legitimate interest of the public to stay informed about the activities of its government has grown just as precipitously. These convergent interests have created not only a need for government transparency but also a need for a hypertransparent system of public access to government information.

Hypertransparency poses substantial but not insurmountable challenges.

Making government-generated email messages more accessible is certainly possible but not necessarily simple. An email system could readily be tweaked so that each email message sent or read would be flagged with a status symbol to indicate that the message was "fully releasable" or that it had some more restrictive status, such as "releasable after removing personal information," "releasable after redaction," or "not releasable." (Bureaucracies would certainly want other categories too; these are merely mentioned as illustrations.) A member of the public viewing email metadata (a list of who sent what to whom, with subject headings and dates) could click on a "fully releasable" email message and instantly see it, or could click on a partly releasable document to initiate a request for an appropriately redacted version.

An important feature of such a system would be the main default option—email messages would be treated as "fully releasable" unless an action were taken to keep them withheld. This reverses the current situation, in which email messages (and most other materials) are withheld unless an explicit decision is made to release them. The default isn't necessarily overridden message by message. The Office of Criminal Investigation in the Internal Revenue Service, for instance, might decide that all its email messages should be treated initially as "not releasable," since many of them include private details about individual taxpayers. In this case, only the office's metadata would be made public, but the content of the email messages would be handled just as is done after a routine

FOIA request, and would be made available only upon request and after an internal review.

On the other hand, the Office of Legislative Affairs of the IRS would be less likely to override the "fully releasable" default option, since it doesn't handle much confidential taxpayer information. Email messages from that office would follow the default scenario: All metadata would be provided, and the content would be available unless the author of an email message overrode the default and put the message into a more restrictive category.

Additional complexities are involved. Many people receive the same email message, and in turn may forward it to others with additional information added; even if the original email message is "fully releasable" the added information may not be. A fairly sophisticated search tool would be needed to enable people to mine the information on millions of email messages in order to find content relevant to their interests. For the sake of discussion, let us imagine that the difficulties have been worked out, and that government email messages become vastly more accessible to anyone wishing to view them. Metadata records on all email messages are available, many of the actual messages are accessible, and a simple Google-type interface allows ready access to both. How does that change the situation?

For one thing, a government agency's degree of openness to public scrutiny becomes immediately quantifiable: Agency A tags 90 percent of its email messages as "fully releasable" while Agency B tags only 3 percent. If Agency B is the CIA, then the lack of openness may be defensible. If, on the other hand, Agency B is the Army Corps of Engineers or the Fish and Wildlife Service, the lack of transparency raises challenging questions. For example, is it really necessary to keep 97 percent of Fish and Wildlife email messages out of view of public scrutiny?

For the public, a system that would reverse the barriers to access by creating a presumption of availability would mean that government information would be accessible quickly, inexpensively, and much more comprehensively than is currently the case. Information formerly relegated to FOIA requests generated by professional seekers of information—public-interest groups, investigative journalists, lawyers—would now be easily available to high school students learning about government, individuals seeking to know more about the agencies they interact with, and pretty much anyone who feels a need to "peek under the hood" of how the government works.

For agencies, the cost of responding to FOIA requests would be minimized, since all documents would be clearly categorized as they were created, and FOIA requesters would be able to scrutinize much of the material directly without the need for an agency to intervene in a cumbersome and resource-intensive compilation-and-review procedure.

Can Hypertransparency Really Work?

The benefits of hypertransparency notwithstanding, we are certainly not naive enough to suppose that such an information milieu would be warmly welcomed by agency bureaucracies. On a conceptual level, public employees would object to losing the capacity to confer with one another—and with outside parties—in a private manner, without the risk of others' having access to their email conversations. On a practical level, public employees probably would recoil at the thought of having to "classify" each communication as either available or not available.

But a hypertransparent system could be structured in a way that would be responsive to concerns and would minimize objections. "Private" communications would still be available—indeed, would comprise the great majority of communications for many offices. There is little doubt that a division within the Department of Justice investigating organized crime would want to keep—and would be able to keep—most of its communications private. Nor would employees in this division be required to tag each and every email message with a "not releasable" indicator, as the division's default setting would keep email messages private.

For employees whose email messages would be publicly available (and let's not forget that most messages are already available through the FOIA process), some employees might still be deeply reluctant to operate in such a publicly viewable fashion; others might not. Over time, we imagine, organizational cultures would change so that hypertransparency would become the norm and would cease to be a matter of concern.

The main point of this chapter is not so much the mechanism for hypertransparency in government. Our email example is exactly that: an example or illustration of what hypertransparency might look like in operation. Our primary message, though, is that some sort of improved access to

government information can go a long way toward restoring the balance—
and some of the trust—between government agencies and the public they
serve. To be meaningful, though, the improvements have to be of a size
and stature to rival the enormous scale of mass surveillance operations now
under way at all levels of government. A commitment to the principle of
hypertransparency is a first important step. Once that step has been taken,
we believe, the mechanisms will follow.

9 Information as a Policy Tool: The Toxics Release Inventory

On December 2, 1984, late at night, a runaway chemical reaction at a Union Carbide pesticide-manufacturing plant caused a tank to rupture, releasing a cloud of toxic gases and aerosols into the air around Bhopal, India. The poisonous cloud spread through the area, quickly killing several thousand people who lived in the shantytowns surrounding the plant. Thousands more died of exposure-related injuries in the weeks, months, and years that followed. All told, more than 500,000 people were exposed to the poisonous vapors. The Bhopal incident was one of the worst industrial disasters in history.

The storage tank in Bhopal held more than 40 tons of methyl isocyanate, a highly toxic chemical in its own right and capable of readily forming other acutely toxic chemicals—phosgene and hydrogen cyanide, for example—under the conditions of its release. The heavier-than-air vapors hugged the ground, killing people, livestock, pets, wild animals, and plants and poisoning local food and water supplies.

In the immediate aftermath of the Bhopal disaster, safety officials around the world scrambled for an important yet scarce commodity: information. Where else was methyl isocyanate in use? In what quantities? Were other pesticide plants running similar processes? Were manufacturers of products other than pesticides using methyl isocyanate? Were other communities in danger?

The short answer to these questions was that no one knew. No one person or organization had information on the big picture of methyl isocyanate use. In the United States, Union Carbide officials knew where the chemical was in use at other Union Carbide plants, but could only speculate on what equally dangerous materials were being used by Dow or DuPont. Environmental and safety inspectors in West Virginia were familiar, to a point, with chemical plants in that state, but not with those in New Jersey, California, or Louisiana. The federal Environmental Protection Agency (responsible for chemical safety) and the federal Occupational and Safety Health Administration (responsible for worker protection) had smatterings of details about which chemicals were used where, but their information was far from complete.

While government and industry experts had scattershot information on where methyl isocyanate was in use, communities surrounding chemical plants in the United States were entirely in the dark. The public had almost no access to information on what chemicals were present at a facility, how toxic those chemicals might be, or whether a plant had a history of leaks or accidents. The lack of information extended beyond a community's residents. Firefighters and other emergency responders also had little information about the dangerous substances that might be present at an industrial plant. On February 2, 1985, the *Los Angeles Times* ran a post-Bhopal story, headlined "Trade Secrets Hold Chemical Industry in Toxic Shroud," that highlighted some of the difficulties of getting access to information about toxic chemicals. But trade secrets were only part of the story. Plenty of information about chemical plants and other industrial operations was, in principle, available. But the information was so inaccessible and (when accessed) so obscure that it provided very little in the way of answers to the concerns of communities and local governments asking "Could an accident like the one in Bhopal happen here?"

In the aftermath of the Bhopal disaster, the safety of chemical processes was scrutinized and enhanced around the world through a variety of mechanisms—some mandatory and others voluntary, some initiated by the chemical industry and others by governments. The US Congress passed the Emergency Planning and Community Right-to-Know Act, which was signed into law by President Ronald Reagan on October 17, 1986. The emergency planning component of the law created a network of state and local entities tasked with evaluating chemical risks and planning for emergency response in the event of a dangerous release. The right-to-know component created information mechanisms to better inform both the emergency planners and the community at large. One of the most important of the new information tools was the Toxics Release Inventory, a sort of standardized accounting system for tracking the presence of toxic chemicals in industry and releases of chemicals into the environment. TRI had several novel features (little recognized at the time) and ushered in a new era of environmentalism by using information as a primary instrument of public policy.

Several things distinguished TRI from anything that had come before.

It was program independent. The Environmental Protection Agency, the agency charged with implementing TRI, already had pollutant databases galore, each database tied to a specific program. Programs for controlling air pollution maintained several large databases detailing locations of smokestacks, vents, open tanks, and other sources of air pollution, along with some details about how much pollution each source might emit. Programs for controlling water pollution kept records on the pipelines emptying wastes into rivers, lakes, and oceans. Hazardous-waste programs tracked shipments of solid materials trucked off-site to landfills and incinerators. The databases were all designed and managed for one primary purpose: to help EPA program managers (and their counterparts in the states) keep tabs on their respective programs, and to document what was working well and what needed additional administrative attention. TRI was different. There was no underlying pollution-control program that provided a basis for the chemical inventory, and there were no permits, standards, or requirements for the management of chemicals. TRI didn't prohibit companies from handling certain chemicals, nor did it restrict them from releasing chemicals into the environment. It required only one thing: regular provision of information. And under the rubric of the right to know, the information was meant for public consumption. EPA staffers were, of course, welcome to make use of the data in TRI, but that wasn't the program's primary reason for being. TRI existed to inform the public. No previous environmental program had made the public's right to know its primary purpose.

A database was mandated. The law establishing the Toxics Release Inventory had a seemingly simple mandate built into its language: "The Administrator shall establish and maintain in a computer data base a national toxic chemical inventory [and] shall make these data accessible by computer telecommunication and other means to any person on a cost reimbursable basis ... ." As far as we know, this was the first time that a computerized information system was mandated by US law. Of course, agencies had been building data systems for decades before this mandate (including many that were already in use at the EPA). But the Emergency Planning and Community Right-to-Know Act marks a turning point: Now the advantages of electronic data management were recognized as fundamentally important to realizing the intent of the law. Even though widespread access to the Internet was still ten years in the future, the crafters of the TRI legislation recognized the importance of compiling the data and mandating its electronic availability to the public.

It was national and consistent. The Toxics Release Inventory is managed as a national data system, and the importance of that is hard to overstate. Before TRI, many environmental databases were hybrid systems that had some components designed by the EPA, some designed and maintained by individual states to serve their own programs, and some designed and maintained by local entities with substantial environmental programs of their own. The result was a data mish-mash, with national systems that provided few data on their own but simply offered pointers to other databases in other jurisdictions. Even if one were to make the effort to track down the available data systems (no small feat), the lack of consistency between systems designed by different entities for different purposes made meaningful analysis of the information almost impossible. Even worse, each environmental program had developed its own language for referring to pollution. Chemicals that a program dealing with air pollution recorded as volatile organic compounds were called by different names in other programs: "chemical oxygen demand" in a database of water permits, for example, and "mixed solvents" in a hazardous-waste program. Informationally, the programs were a Tower of Babel, each talking a language the others couldn't comprehend.

TRI brought consistency across all environmental media. It adopted the straightforward language of chemistry, reporting not on imprecise substances such as "solvents" or "still bottoms" but on the actual chemical components of a waste stream: benzene, mercury, trichloroethylene, formaldehyde. The use of this common, widely recognizable, clearly understood nomenclature made consistency possible. TRI also adopted consistent and simple units of measure: pounds per year of pollutant release. This stood in sharp contrast to a bewildering set of specialized reporting requirements and units used in other programs, such as the Air Program's requirement to document the 99th percentile of one-hour daily maximum concentrations, averaged over three years.

The innovations built into TRI, though interesting, probably don't warrant being labeled "revolutionary" on their own. But the effect of bringing forward all this information on toxic chemicals in an easy-to-access and easy-to-understand manner—in short, in a much more transparent fashion—transformed the management of toxic chemicals (in the United States and around the world—more on that later) and, in an important way, shifted the balance of power among government, industry, and the public when it came to making decisions about what is and what isn't environmentally acceptable industrial pollution.

TRI instantly became a kind of environmental report card for manufacturing plants in the United States. Reporting was mandatory, and for the first time the US had a fairly comprehensive and accessible set of data on the sources of hundreds of individual chemical at thousands of facilities. The data could be (and were) "sliced and diced" in various ways—for example, into toxic chemical air emissions, toxic chemical water discharges, and toxic shipments to landfills. Some analyses totaled up releases of all TRI chemicals; others displayed data more selectively (e.g., releases of carcinogens, or heavy metals, or chlorinated organics). The TRI data were compiled to create national maps, Top Ten Polluter lists in various states, and countywide lists of TRI reporting facilities arranged by parent company, by industry sector, and number of chemicals reported.

Companies were required to report, and nothing more. There was no legal mandate in the TRI program to do anything about the pollutants that were reported, other than to file an annual TRI report. In general, the releases being reported were entirely legal, allowed by the various air, water and hazardous-waste permits that any large manufacturing plant is likely to have. TRI's chief role was to collect and provide information on the reported releases; members of the public could freely access the data and do with them what they would.

That companies were required only to report, and nothing more, was a particularly unusual aspect of an environmental regulatory program. Other regulatory programs—for example, clean-air and clean-water programs—mandated levels of permissible environmental releases; reporting requirements were useful for documenting that release restrictions were being met. TRI imposed no such release restrictions, but merely required that environmental releases be reported in a transparent and easily accessible manner.

Put yourself in the position of a plant manager who opens the newspaper one morning to find his facility listed as the largest polluter in the city, or the county, or the state, or the country. Imagine the conversations that take place when you bring your children to a school soccer game or when you bump into a neighbor in the supermarket. For that matter, put yourself in the shoes of the CEO in the company's headquarters. Although you may be hundreds or thousands of miles from the facility, you may have to field questions—from reporters, stockholders, analysts, environmental groups—about your company's being listed as the worst toxic polluter in a particular region. The simple provision of information not only shines a spotlight on chemical releases but creates a powerful psychological dynamic for eliminating, or at least reducing, the amounts reported. As TRI amassed data year after year, the element of time became significant. A plant either increased its level of emissions and was faced with explaining the increases to the public, or decreased its emissions and had something of a "good news story" to tell.

The result of the public scrutiny brought about by TRI—a scrutiny made possible by using information as a conscious policy tool—was a very rapid reduction in toxic chemical releases. In 1988, early in the TRI program, total releases (to air, water, and land) and transfers (to incinerators and other

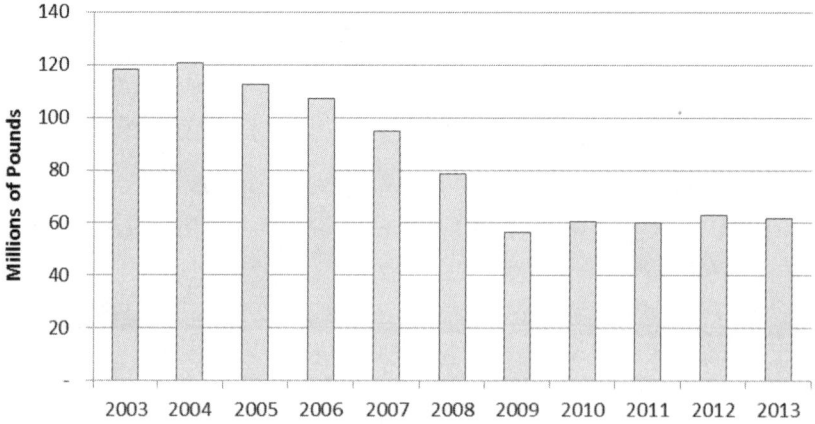

Figure 9.1
Air releases of carcinogens, 2003–2013.

treatment facilities) of toxic wastes amounted to 3 billion pounds. Within ten years, the total was reduced to 1.7 billion, and ten years later, in 2008, to 1.1 billion pounds. Totals from 2009 on have all been less than a billion pounds a year. (These quantities are based on the original TRI chemicals and the original reporting industries to allow for "apples-to-apples" comparison.) The total reductions are the cumulative result of many factors, both legal (regulatory requirements) and economic (improved efficiency of operations). TRI can't take all the credit for the downward trends, but in comparison with other types of environmental wastes for which a right-to-know system isn't in place (e.g., agricultural pesticides, municipal wastes, and construction debris) the overall reduction in toxic industrial wastes is remarkable.

TRI demonstrates the old adage—a theme of this book—that information is power. It gives members of the public, who historically have been isolated from environmental decision making, a tool with which to more capably understand pollutant discharges in local communities and a means by which to become active participants in the decision-making process. But several decades after its first dramatic revelations, TRI's power seems somewhat muted. The annual release of TRI data, though still newsworthy, rarely makes the front pages. A community's shock at learning of previously unknown releases of toxic chemicals has given way to a certain familiarity, almost an acceptance, of base-line conditions regarding the presence and emission of chemicals. But that, too, is a change worth noting: Now information has the power to make the unfamiliar familiar, and to leave people with a sense that they now better understand the manufacturing operations in their communities.

In several ways, the power of the right-to-know program to effect change continues to increase. TRI looms large when companies make decisions to use or not use a particular chemical, or to increase or decrease the amount of a chemical already in use. Company managers are hesitant to increase the use of chemicals that will show up in TRI reports as toxic releases, and plant personnel are routinely asked to indicate whether a new material being considered for purchase contains any TRI-listed chemicals.

TRI reporting—or something very similar—has expanded well beyond the United States, even though the law creating the inventory applies only to companies operating in the US. On the one hand, multinational companies tend to adopt uniform reporting measures for their facilities around the world, to the extent that doing so is feasible. Many companies use TRI reporting as a basis for reporting chemical emissions in their worldwide operations. The impact of TRI has not gone unnoticed in other countries, and several have adopted TRI-like national reporting. Canada has a Pollutant Release and Transfer Register, and Mexico has a similar instrument. Canada, Mexico, and the United States produce a joint report on North American chemical releases each year.

TRI exemplifies the use of information as a tool of public policy. It achieved policy goals of more fully engaging the public in environmental decision making, and in driving down releases of toxic chemicals. But there is no reason to suppose that the effectiveness of the right to know has to be restricted to TRI (in particular) or to the environmental field (in general). Information, in any context, provides an opportunity for a person to react to the information; information made widely and readily available allows a broad swath of the public to react to the information or choose to ignore it.

In his book *Steps to an Ecology of Mind*, Gregory Bateson refers to a unit of information as "a difference which makes a difference." Telling the public that one plus one equals two is not an information-rich communication, as the fact is almost universally known already; the information makes little difference to its recipients. Making it known that last year a furniture-manufacturing plant 1.4 miles from your house released into the air 24,000 pounds of methylene chloride, a carcinogenic chemical, is more robust from an information standpoint. It is a difference (in knowledge) that makes a difference (in awareness) and that may well lead to a difference in behavior (minimizing releases from the factory).

The broadcasting of information in a right-to-know manner—readily available information in an easily understood format—makes a difference in a self-adjusting, automatic, partly unconscious fashion. In this sense, it is much like the operation of Adam Smith's invisible hand bringing about a difference in the price and availability of goods in the marketplace. If members of a community respond with broad outrage when informed about chemical releases by a firm's plant, their expressions of anger and concern create pressure on the firm to reduce the plant's overall releases. The firm then chooses a course of action. Perhaps it opts to ignore the response, or to explain the plant's releases in a press release. Perhaps it opts to host a community meeting with concerned citizens. Perhaps it decides that its best course of action is to reduce the releases, or even to eliminate its use of a toxic chemical and replace it with a non-toxic chemical that doesn't have to be reported to TRI. Whatever the firm's choice, it is acting in response to the community's expression of concern The process bears at least some resemblance to corporate decisions to decrease production of one shoe style, and increase another, in response to consumers' demand.

We can see information making a difference in this manner in all arenas of human activity. A news story about a fire in an overseas sweatshop has stimulated corporations around the world to assure customers that their products aren't made in such facilities, or, if they were, that they are now disassociating themselves from doing business with any supplier whose facilities lack adequate safeguards for workers. Photos of prisoner abuse at Abu Ghraib have influenced national policy on the handling of prisoners of war. Annual scorecards of school performance have brought about changes in the numbers of parents who register their children at a certain school. Information is ubiquitous and has always been a ubiquitous influence on all types of human activity.

We mentioned earlier that TRI quickly became a report card of sorts for the facilities covered by the right-to-know program. The analogy between TRI and a student's report card is revealing, as both mechanisms invoke the power of information to, at the very least, focus people to pay attention and, in the best of outcomes, bring about positive change. The actuality that a student's parents, friends, or neighbors see the student's report card isn't the only thing that creates pressure on the student to improve his or her performance. The mere possibility that the report card will be seen by others is, itself, a significant source of pressure. Whether a student's parents actually see the report card, the likelihood that they will creates a motivation for better performance. Similarly, no one in the community in which a manufacturing plant is situated may ever access the plant's TRI report, but the possibility that someone will, one day, access it creates a motivation for the plant to be able to report smaller quantities of pollution with each passing year.

The point is that nothing in particular has to happen in order for an information tool to have a substantial influence on human decisions. The human mind has the ability to play "What if," as in "What if dad compares my report card to my brother's?" or "What if a reporter runs a story on my TRI releases?" This alone is enough to bring about change, even if dad and the reporter are fully occupied on other tasks. In a similar vein, if the Internal Revenue Service never audited anyone's tax returns, there would be far less of an incentive to honestly report income and taxes owed. The possibility of being audited—even if such an audit never occurs—creates a considerable incentive for honest reporting.

10 Tools, Power, and Participation: Information in the Decades Ahead

Throughout this book we have focused on the role of information in human activities, from shopping to governing, arguing for the importance of high-quality information and open access to information when there is no compelling reason for secrecy. We have described tools for improving the quality and the completeness of information in the overall market and particularly in health care, government agencies, and annual reports.

We have also emphasized the recurring theme "information is power," but of course that isn't necessarily true. Information can confer tremendous authority at times, and can result in greater awareness and participation. But it can also be trivial, overwhelming, misleading, or incomprehensible. It can be feckless, which is why the better-informed of two political candidates has no guarantee of winning an election; other factors, such as an especially engaging smile, can prove more influential than access to all types of information. And yet the winning candidate will almost certainly make use of potent informational tools—for example, lists of donors, demographic data on voters, social media, opinion polls, and phone banks.

"Information is power" is really our shorthand for something more elaborate and more elusive than the simple phrase suggests. Information is no guarantee of power, just as owning a bicycle is no guarantee that you will use it to speed across town. But the bicycle gives you the potential to move faster and further than you could on foot. Information does the same thing; it makes certain types of power possible. To stretch the analogy even further, a small bike with training wheels can empower a small child in certain ways, but less fully than a mountain bike empowers an adult-sized rider. Information comes in different varieties and flavors, and creates different potential utilities for its end users.

We also have made use of the old engineering adage "garbage in, garbage out." We find, looking back over what we have written, that "GIGO" is a more universal phenomenon than one might first suppose. Bad input not only confounds computer models; it affects all the systems we have looked at in this book: the health-care system, the Soviet Union, environmental management systems, financial reporting, government bureaucracies, and the economic system as a whole. When information inputs are severely limited—because the information is false (Enron), missing (Starbucks), unnecessarily confusing (hospital bills), too restrictive (environmental regulation), outdated (Soviet Five-Year Plans), confidential (business), or top secret (government)—the outputs from the systems are suboptimal.

By necessity, the decisions based on those outputs are suboptimal as well, creating widespread inefficiencies in how the systems perform. The inefficiencies are ultimately correctable and, in the happiest of situations, can even lend themselves to self-correction. We saw this in the Dupreshi example: The sustainability-reporting mechanism created what can be thought of as a mini-marketplace for information. Everyone "consuming" information from the Dupreshi website had the option of commenting on what information was valuable, what information was credible, and what information was suspect. The dynamics of the site created an incentive for providing additional details and establishing what actually was occurring at the Dupreshi facility. Bit by bit, the process, at its best, separates the wheat from the chaff.

However one chooses to interpret the phrases we have used, the links between high-quality information and the capabilities of institutions and individuals will strengthen in the decades ahead. As ordinary objects become ever more sophisticated conduits for information, society will continue to grapple with the tensions between the empowerment these objects confer and the threats of an expanding information milieu.

Telephones are already sophisticated devices for receiving and transmitting information. Soon other items—refrigerators, televisions, cars—will be hooked in to the information cloud that the Internet is becoming. A nascent technology dubbed Li-Fi even envisions Internet-enabled light bulbs that will not only illuminate our homes and workplaces but also allow high-speed data transmission, even when the lights are turned off. Tiny pill-shaped health-monitoring devices that patients swallow will temporarily transmit medical information, as will smart contact lenses that monitor blood sugar. Wireless implants offer more permanent capabilities.

The innovations on the horizon are wildly interesting and touch upon almost all areas of human activity. Google's Flu Tracker is an early-warning system for flu outbreaks that takes note of increased activity in Web searches for "flu shots" and similar terms. A site called HealthMap.org takes a more comprehensive approach, consolidating information from searches, news items, official reports, medical forums, and diverse other sources to identify outbreaks of infectious diseases around the world; the site claims to have spotted the 2014 Ebola outbreak in West Africa more than a week ahead of the World Health Organization's first announcement of it. Information-exchange applications, such as Uber and Lyft, have disrupted industries. Companies are exploring the prospects of using real-time data gleaned from consumers' photos, sales transactions, and direct data inputs from shoppers to generate instantaneous financial statistics; that, in turn, promises a fuller, faster, more finely detailed picture of inflation data, employment levels, and other changes in the economy well before the Federal Reserve and the Department of Commerce publish their assorted statistical updates.

Of course, changes and innovations that are positive for some industries and some fields may carry significant negatives for others. The taxi industry certainly isn't enamored with peer-to-peer ride-sharing services, and physicians profess little affection for the complex electronic health-records systems that are coming to dominate the health-care industry. The types of tensions that emerge with new technologies are illustrated, in a small way, by the commercialization of Internet-enabled eyeglasses. Google Glass was the first widely publicized wearable fashion accessory with full Internet capabilities. The somewhat awkward looking but not totally unattractive eyewear offers high-speed wireless Internet access, responds to users' voice commands, and displays results on one lens. The display is visually equivalent to viewing a 25-inch screen. This compact technological marvel weighs no more than an ordinary pair of glasses.

Functionally, Google Glass isn't very different from a typical smartphone in its informational capabilities. Both devices can help users find the nearest Chinese restaurant, navigate to grandma's house, keep abreast of breaking news stories, and take photos and videos at a moment's notice. It's that last function that has generated controversy.

Figure 10.1
An early adopter of Google Glass (source: Wikipedia).

A user of Google Glass can take a photograph or begin recording a video with a subtle, almost undetectable command. People generally rely on some visual cues that they are being recorded, such as a camera or a cell phone held in a characteristic I'm-taking-a-photo position. Google Glass offers no such obvious cues. A Google Glass wearer could be recording video images in a locker room, at a confidential business conference, on a beach, or during a casual but presumably private conversation. The technology strikes some as an overly intrusive invasion of privacy. Some restaurants and other businesses have banned the wearing of Google Glass devices on their premises out of concern for privacy, and a few casinos have prohibited it out of a fear of card counting.

The resistance to Google Glass surprises some adherents of the device, since the capability to record almost any situation has existed for years in cell phones and in even smaller devices (such as hidden "nanny-cams "and "spy pen" video cameras). Google Glass, they argue, is no different. But like the automated license-plate-reading cameras we discussed in chapter 8, Google Glass takes capabilities for monitoring to a higher level, even though it merely consolidates several existing technologies rather than creating a fundamentally new form of electronic record keeping. The fate of

Google Glass is uncertain, as Google has withdrawn the device from the market, at least temporarily. But the technology will continue to mature, and as devices become lighter, more powerful, and less obvious, and as battery life improves, the appeal of wearable computing is likely to increase and concerns about it are likely to multiply.

Web-enabled eyeglasses aren't the only things that are going to give us pause. We are comfortable with the notion that Santa Claus knows when we are sleeping and when we are awake, but will we be so sanguine about the Internet having that information? A day after a strong late-night earthquake rattled northern California, a company called Jawbone published a graph of how the quake disrupted sleep patterns in the area. In Napa Valley, close to the epicenter, 74 percent of people were shaken out of bed; in San Francisco (45 miles away) about 55 percent were awakened; further still, in San Jose, only 25 percent. Jawbone gleaned the data from users of one of its products: a personal activity tracker, worn as a bracelet, that tracks eating habits, exercise levels, and body motions. Although the data Jawbone reported were consolidated and anonymous, they represent a growing phenomenon of people who are always online, even in their sleep.

The emerging era of ubiquitous online connections from a wide variety of devices, dubbed the Internet of Things, will be a substantial factor in the magnification and reshuffling of social power related to information tools.

Consider what an Internet-enabled refrigerator will bring to a household. Efforts to create smart refrigerators have relied on bar-code readers and

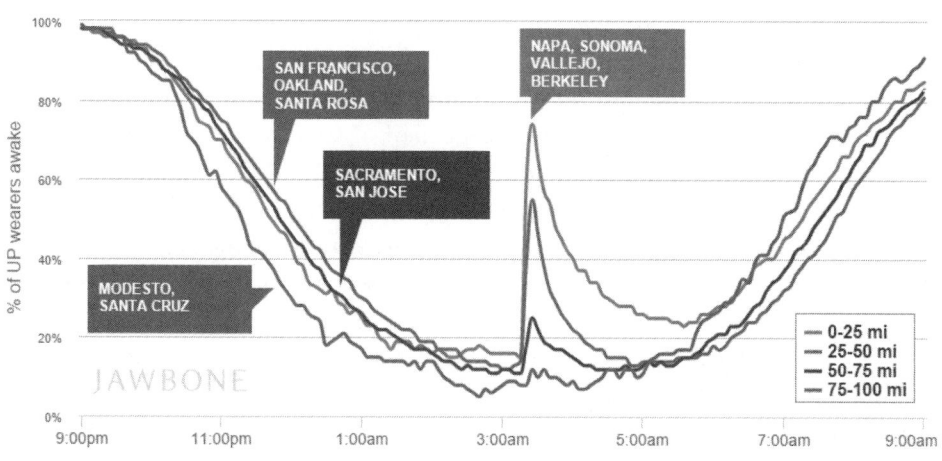

Figure 10.2

other identification technologies to keep track of what is stored in them. So far such devices have been clunky, expensive, and unimpressive, but so were the early wearable computers. In the years to come, smart refrigerators will grow more sophisticated, more versatile and cheaper. The technology, if it catches on, will probably track contents in something akin to the way human beings do—for example, by visually "recognizing" a green pepper or a container of orange juice and using available cues to gauge quantity and freshness. These smarter refrigerators will be able to notify owners when it is time to go food shopping, to prepare a shopping list, and perhaps even to do the shopping itself by messaging an order to a supermarket. The system will be able to suggest meals on the basis of the items on hand, and to issue a warning when a certain food or beverage is approaching the end of its shelf life. Chemical sensors could even be on the alert for telltale odors of putrefaction.

A smart refrigerator is more than simply a convenience. The capabilities to track food items, monitor freshness, and make better use of the items on hand make individual consumers more efficient. This is no small achievement. Like the innumerable tweaks we discussed earlier—countless small changes that can lead to a more sustainable marketplace—smart refrigerators could conceivably bring about significant positive changes to our overall food system.

But smart appliances, with always-on connections to the World Wide Web, open doors to other scenarios as well. A refrigerator will become a two-way communication device, not simply delivering information to "you" but sending information to "them." A refrigerator will come with an end-user licensing agreement, terms of service, and a privacy statement, just as Web browsers, video games, and smartphone service packages currently do. Your food items may become part of your overall demographic profile—for example, if the sensors detect a birthday cake, you may start seeing ads for birthday presents. Certain refrigerated medicines may trigger "helpful" communications from pharmaceutical companies, nursing facilities, or even funeral homes. These advertisements may be displayed on your refrigerator's built-in screen, may show up in your email inbox, may appear on your smart television, or may be transmitted to any of dozens of other devices.

And darker intrusions will be possible. A smart refrigerator, like any online device, can be "hacked" (although what hackers would do with such access is a bit harder to imagine). Law-enforcement agencies may desire to "search" refrigerators remotely, much as they would do at an in-person search of a home, looking for cash, body parts, or drugs. Spy agencies may search for certain ethnic or foreign-sourced food items as clues to the identity of those using the refrigerator. Landlords may try to track quantities of food consumed as an indication of the number of people living in a household.

There is no way of knowing precisely how any new smart technologies will play out, but it is safe to say that any new technology has ramifications that go well beyond the individual user. Each new information tool plugs its users into a cyber-ecosystem in which no one is quite independent of anyone else. The primary user of the technology—the owner of a smart refrigerator, say—puts its information capabilities to use, thereby enhancing, in a small way, his or her own informational status in the world. But these same capabilities also restructure society in a modest but significant way.

Ideally, smart refrigerators can mean a more effective food system overall, with lower food costs, less food waste, and more efficient use of the energy needed to deliver, store, and dispose of food. Those are good outcomes that benefit society as a whole. In a less-than-ideal situation, however, tensions may arise—between private, commercial, police, and government concerns—that may require public discourse to find the appropriate balance between competing priorities, or (to put it another way) the appropriate balance of power.

As we were drafting this chapter, the shooting of a teenager by a policeman inflamed tensions in the Missouri community of Ferguson and ignited national debates about several matters. One of these matters is purely informational: Should more police be required to wear body cameras so as to record their interactions with civilians? Body cameras are regarded as presenting a much more complete and unassailable accounting of such interactions than witnesses' personal recollections, with their seemingly inevitable he-said-she-said, yes-he-did-no-he-didn't quality. The cameras are presumed to have a moderating influence on the behavior of both the police wearing them and the public on the opposite end of the camera lens. When inappropriate behaviors would be unambiguously recorded and deniability would be less available, the inappropriate behaviors of all parties would be minimized—or so it is hoped.

We are intrigued, though, with another tool capable of providing information on interactions between police and civilians: Five-0, a cell-phone app created by a group of teenage programmers. Five-0 is essentially a form that one fills out to rate an interaction with the police. At a minimum, it is a convenient, always-at-hand tool for keeping a methodical record of one's interactions with the police. It can easily be used immediately after a traffic stop, a stop-and-frisk action, or a response to a 911 plea for assistance. But the potential power of an app like Five-0 lies not in the individual ratings of police activities, but in the consolidation of thousands or millions of such records on the Internet. Five-0 information is designed to provide anonymity to the individuals creating the report, but to be accessible to anyone using the app. Users can view individual reports on individual police officers or can consolidate rankings for entire communities. The app creates "a dynamic grade for courtesy and professionalism" both for individual police officers and for communities. The police force in one town may receive an overall grade of A from citizens pleased with their interactions, while a neighboring town might receive a C and the next town over an F. One wonders what rating the police in Ferguson would have received before the shooting death that triggered months of unrest in that community.

Figure 10.3
A screen shot of the Five-0 app for rating interactions with police.

At the time of this writing, Five-0 has just been released and doesn't have any track record to speak of. We can only wait and see how widely it will turn out to be used and what effects its use will have. As is true of any online service, Five-0 might well be supplanted by some other tool that grabs users' attention. But it isn't difficult to envision that a tool of this sort might enable communities to provide important feedback to their local police about the collective level of satisfaction with police services. Nor is it difficult to imagine websites and news articles along the lines of "The 10 Worst Police Forces in the US" or "The Top Five Police Forces in Texas" that will be based on fine-grained information from Five-0-style feedback.

It seems likely that, at some point, the capabilities of tools such as Google Glass, body cameras, sleep-monitoring bracelets, and Five-0 will merge. When almost everyone is connected to the Internet full time and is able to record interactions, to create reports, and to upload geocoded, anonymous information for the rest of the world to access, it is possible to imagine that everything from police to pedicures to pediatricians will receiving crowdsourced ratings from the masses.

Five-0 and related services are, in essence, people-powered report cards similar to those offered by most shopping websites—for example, Amazon's five-star rating system, which lets shoppers quickly gauge users' satisfaction with a product, and which itself served as a starting point for our suggestion of a sustainability rating system based on inputs from users. A patient-based rating system for doctors, clinics, and hospitals could provide information that at present is missing from our health-care system—information that would lead to invisible-hand-style improvements in the market for medical services.

Many factors come into play that might make rating tools useful or render them quite useless. Five-0 could be used to unfairly malign a particular officer or police force if one person were to take it upon himself to file a series of negative reports and organize his friends and acquaintances to do likewise. A police officer might have a grudge against another officer and use the app to file invented complaints. One doesn't have to read many user-provided comments at Amazon or at other shopping sites to recognize that some of the laudatory comments seem generic, uninformed, and excessive, and to surmise that they probably were posted because a business offered a small benefit to anyone who posted a positive review of the product.

Figure 10.4
Genuine, or fake?

In our imaginary example of the Dupreshi product-sustainability web-page, the users' comments included information that was directly contradictory to statements from the company, leaving visitors to the site uncertain as to which statements best reflected the true state of affairs. Yet the Dupreshi webpage, taken as a whole, provided useful information. The presence of ambiguous and unverifiable information created a dynamic for self-improvement in the system. A similar dynamic is in play in sustainability ratings, in shopping sites' product ratings, in sites for rating physicians, and in apps such as Five-0. Amazon would have a hard time staying in business if the information at its shopping site were not reliable. As merchants and users moved to "game" the product-rating system, Amazon took steps to improve its reliability. For Five-0 to be a viable tool in the long term, it would have to do likewise. The same holds true for any other rating scheme.

The examples we have discussed throughout this book have the potential to rebalance societal relationships between individuals and institutions, as do the suggestions we have made for revising information systems in commerce, health care, government bureaucracies, and financial reporting. We would like to close this chapter by stating, as clearly as we can, why such rebalancing is called for.

First, very large institutions are collecting very large banks of data on ever-increasing numbers of people in ever-finer detail. National-security organizations compile data the government deems necessary to protect society from threats of terrorism. Police departments collect data deemed necessary to maintain social order. Government agencies require information needed to collect taxes, to issue drivers' licenses, and to do various other things that government agencies do. Businesses have been equally productive in finding ways to identify, collect, collate, and analyze huge banks of information on individuals' creditworthiness, Web and email habits, online and offline spending, educational records, geolocation information, criminal history, property ownership, phone use, legal entanglements, and debt obligations, and are probably collecting equally large amounts of information in categories we aren't even aware of.

This trend toward amassing large data files in increasingly fine detail for more and more individuals throughout their lives is going to continue, grow more pronounced, and become even more routine as the Internet of Things makes possible the tracking of our individual lives down to daily eating, exercise and sleeping habits. This tracking will take place with very little notice, and will unfold for decent, even noble reasons—the information can be used to provide substantial benefits for everybody, ranging from increased national security to free access to Google Maps, online translations, and other wonderful tools of the Information Age.

But when governments and businesses have a vast, almost endless set of information on each individual, it seems fundamentally necessary that each individual have better information tools with which to understand and interact with governments and businesses. It doesn't seem likely to us that the informational tools of government agencies and commercial enterprises will be weakened or curtailed in any significant way, so it becomes necessary to strengthen the informational tools available to anyone who wishes to make use of them. If we may belabor our catchphrase one last time, information is power. And power belongs to the people.

Second, we are, admittedly, enamored with the prospects of using information, in a more or less pure form, to bring about positive change. By "pure form" we mean using information itself as the agent of change. This is easily clarified by reference to the Toxic Release Inventory, which we described in chapter 9. Before TRI, agencies created permit programs requiring companies to reduce pollution, and collected information as a means of making sure the requirements were being followed. The environmental permit was the agent of change—the thing intended to modify institutional behavior regarding pollution—and the information was a compliance tool to make sure the intended changes were occurring. TRI achieves much the same end—substantial reductions in toxic chemical releases—not because such reductions were mandated but because the public provision of information (the report-card effect) created a powerful incentive for the reporting companies to reduce the quantities of pollution they released to the environment.

TRI wasn't the first program that made environmental data available to the public, but it differed from all previous environmental data systems in several important ways. It provided consistent information across all sources, and the data were easily available, with much "friendlier" access tools than older systems offered. TRI also answered questions that were important to the general public, rather than to environmental specialists. Permit writers who collected data wanted answers to questions along the lines of "Is this particular piece of equipment operating within specified parameters before discharging materials into the air or water?" Communities downwind or downstream from a facility were more likely to be interested in questions such as "What is emitted from the plant?" "How much?" and "Are emissions getting larger or smaller with time?"

The ability of information to answer general, obvious questions as well as specialized, arcane questions deserves elaboration because its importance is easily overlooked. We saw this earlier in the Securities and Exchange Commission's "Show me the money" explanation of financial reports. However, the report from Starbucks didn't really show the money (not very clearly, anyway), although it displayed a host of fairly minor details about the company's operations that addressed specialist interests. Shoppers have no way to answer straightforward questions such as "Was this shirt made in a sweatshop?" or "Is this food genetically engineered?" Patients can't answer very basic questions about health care—"How good is my doctor?" "How much will my treatment cost?"—because the current marketplace simply doesn't provide information pertaining to those particular questions.

Though we may now be in the Information Age, we haven't yet learned to give information very much attention. It is still something we get on other topics, but rarely is it the main topic itself. Today's pre-eminent information managers, librarians, often get requests along the lines of "I'd like some information on China" or "I need information on Ebola," but we are fairly confident that few librarians have had to field the request "I'd like some information on information, please." The glare of a very strong spotlight on the technology of information management—storing, moving, securing, and manipulating data—hid in the shadows a weak focus on the information itself—weak enough so that economists could hypothesize about perfect information without ever coming to grips with what even pretty good information looked like in real-world transactions. The American Medical Association can offer the "perfect" DoctorFinder service seemingly without considering what sort of information patients would like to have about the doctors they are about to visit. The Securities and Exchange Commission insists that the rules for financial reporting require companies to "show the money" even while the companies' reports omit big chunks of the picture of where the money comes from, where it goes, and how it is being used. Government agencies are bound by freedom of information as a means of engaging the public, yet manage to withhold the bulk of the information generated and, in the name of transparency, often provide information that is nearly impossible for the public to make sense of.

Throughout this book, we have made reference to looking at our societal systems through a lens of information. Let's apply that lens to one final example of a discrete system that serves a valuable function and appears to work reasonably well, but that could be much more valuable and work much better after several improvements.

Consumer Sentinel is a large database maintained by the Federal Trade Commission, the agency that has, in its own words, "championed the interests of the American consumer." Consumer Sentinel houses the records of millions of consumers' complaints, detailing allegations of identity theft, telemarketing scams, phony sweepstakes, bogus health products, misleading money-making opportunities, and many other activities. The information is used by law-enforcement agencies throughout the United States and around the world to identify victims of scams and to compile evidence on the nature of various fraudulent activities and the financial losses they cause.

The complaint records contained in Consumer Sentinel originate from a variety of sources. Roughly one-third of the information in the database comes from complaints filed directly with the FTC by means of telephone hotlines, online complaint forms, and other methods. About 5 percent of the complaint information comes from businesses in the private sector, particularly Western Union, Moneygram, and Publishers Clearing House. Almost all of the remaining information fed into Consumer Sentinel comes

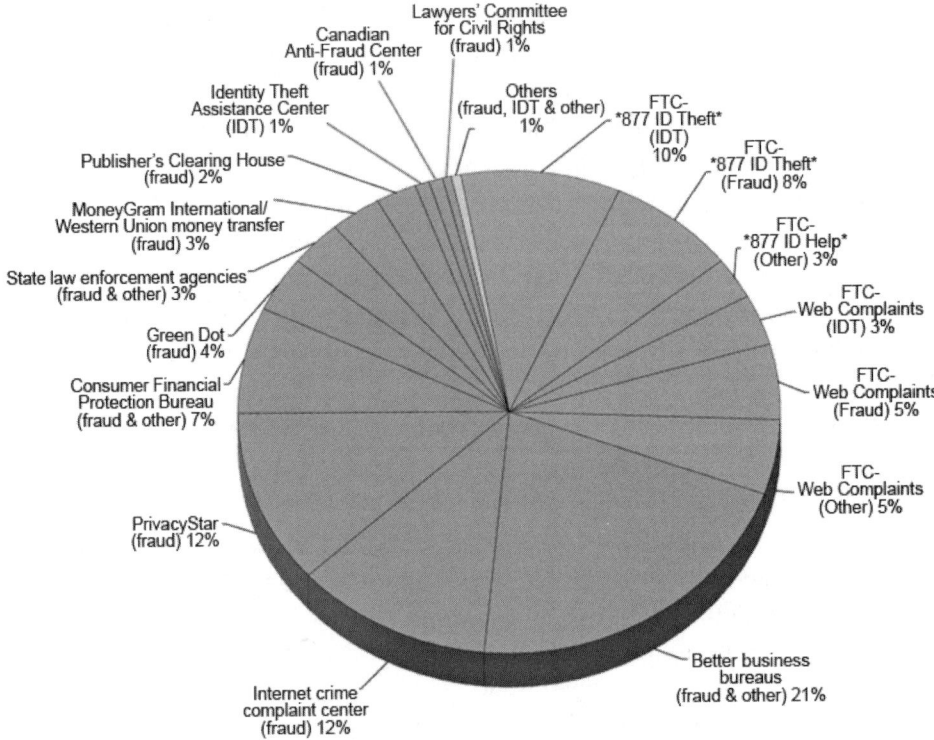

Figure 10.5
Sources of 2.1 million complaints received in 2013 by the Federal Trade Commissions' Consumer Sentinel.

from governmental and non-profit programs aimed at assisting consumers with fraud complaints.

From an administrative perspective, the collection of information sources—illustrated in more detail on the pie chart from the FTC in figure 10.5—makes good sense. The information providers are largely governmental or quasi-governmental organizations charged with protecting consumers from fraudulent activities and inclined, by their very mission, to share data with one another.

When we look at this at through an information lens, the perspective changes. Yes, these information providers are valuable sources of information. But are there other potential sources of data that have even better information available? Sources with more records, finer-grained detail, quicker access to complaints data? Sources that can serve as early-warning systems when new scams arise, or when older ones resurface? Think of the experience you may have had when filing a complaint. Was the Federal Trade Commission or your state attorney general's office your first point of contact, or more a last resort? If you are like most consumers, your initial complaint regarding a disputed charge, if the merchant can't provide satisfaction, is made to the company that transmitted the billing charge to you—perhaps American Express, Visa, or MasterCard; perhaps PayPal; perhaps a phone company that bills not only for telephone services directly provided but also for third-party services such as apps and games. These firms, by necessity, become referees of sorts between consumers and merchants when charges are in dispute.

Credit-card companies generally keep records of disputes, defer collecting payments on disputed charges, and act as a communications conduit between customers and merchants trying to get disputes resolved. A credit-card company may also act as final arbiter of the dispute, charging the amount back to the merchant so that the customer doesn't have to pay or determining that a product or a service was appropriately delivered, that the merchant responded to any complaints, and that the customer is responsible for the charge originally billed.

The record keeping involved in tracking and managing disputes is a potential treasure trove of information for the FTC or a similar organization. Any sizable merchant relying on credit cards and online payment services for handling transactions will undoubtedly have a small but steady trickle of transactions that end up being disputed by customers. The presence of outstanding disputes, by themselves, are no reason to suspect a company of wrongdoing; even a million outstanding disputes may not be much of a red flag for a company involved in billions of transactions.

But it would require only a little number crunching of the raw data to see that certain merchants stand out: merchants with an unusually high percentage of disputed transactions, for example, or those with a sudden spike in disputes. A merchant that has, say, 0.1 percent of its charges in dispute may well be statistically typical, whereas 10 percent of charges in dispute is a clear sign that something is terribly amiss—exactly the type of thing that consumers should be alert to, and that the FTC should be looking into. Yet Consumer Sentinel doesn't take advantage of the rich sources of data that credit-card companies and similar payment processors could provide.

The literature on Consumer Sentinel's database offers no discussion of why some sources of data are included while others are not. Data from government sources (including the FTC) dominate the system and were perhaps the easiest sources to obtain and integrate into a central database. A smattering of data from Western Union and Publishers Clearinghouse are included, but for the most part data from private firms—including those with the most obvious capabilities for providing dispute-related insights—are missing from the overall picture.

It is easy to imagine obstacles to incorporating private-sector data into a public-sector database: the FTC may not have the authority to compel data submission; consumers' privacy concerns may stand in the way of data transfer, and costs to both government and industry may pose an obstacle to gathering data and painting a fuller picture of consumer disputes. But it is also possible to imagine solutions to any or all of these concerns that would allow the FTC to overcome obstacles, build a more robust system, and better target merchants for review when their dispute records signal practices causing widespread problems for consumers.

It may also simply be the case that the FTC never thought to include data from credit-card companies and similar commercial sources. Consumer Sentinel has the feel of a government-built system focused on government data sources—a system that expanded to include several non-governmental sources as something of an afterthought. Overlooking what is probably the best source of data on consumer disputes, if that is what occurred, would be a prime example of neglecting to view possibilities through the lens of information.

Consumer Sentinel has another built-in constraint that is worth examining through an information lens: The data in the system are available only to law-enforcement agencies. The FBI, state attorney generals' offices, local police departments, and computer-crime task forces can access the information. But despite the word 'consumer' in the title, an actual consumer wishing to know if a certain business has a large portion of outstanding disputes can't use Consumer Sentinel to find out.

From an informational point of view, denying access to those who could most make use of the information that Consumer Sentinel provides imposes an unnecessarily severe restriction on the overall flow of information. For example, the FTC relied on internal data when bringing an enforcement case against a company named Your Yellow Pages. The FTC claimed that YYP was engaged in a broad scam to fool businesses, churches and even local governments into thinking a solicitation from YYP was actually an overdue bill for advertising in the Yellow Pages. The YYP solicitation even included Yellow Pages' well-known "walking fingers" symbol. The FTC shut down YYP's operations and froze its assets in 2014.

The data in Consumer Sentinel formed part of the basis for the case against Your Yellow Pages. The frequency, nature, and consistency of complaints alerted enforcement officials to potential abuses through misleading solicitations for payment. However, the individuals and small businesses who were solicited by YYP had no way of seeing the red flags, at least not in Consumer Sentinel's database, since the system is totally closed to public view. Imagine the power of providing consumers with a quick online lookup service so that anyone could check a company's record.

Through an administrative lens, the self-imposed limitations of Consumer Sentinel's database make perfect sense. Relying almost exclusively on government sources of data sidesteps the sticky issues of either commanding or cajoling data from the private sector. Restricting data access to law enforcement avoids many of the privacy concerns that would arise from allowing full public access to a database that included private information, such as the names and addresses of the individuals involved in disputes.

But the administrative picture should be seen side by side with the perspectives gained through the lens of information, and some obvious and straightforward questions should be asked: What are the best sources of information on disputes involving consumers? How can the data be put to best use in meeting the interests of the consumers that FTC seeks to serve? Who should have access to the database? Such questions argue for an expanded conception of the Consumer Sentinel effort that would make use of additional sources of information and would allow public access to select portions of the data.

Looking back, we can understand the administrative point of view that created the Consumer Sentinel information system with a strict law-enforcement focus, a highly selective set of information sources, and careful prescriptions as to who can and who can't access the system's information.

Looking forward, we can foresee the evolution of a system, with a broader informational focus, in which the most robust information sources are included in the dataset and the information is managed so that a much wider range of users have access to the value—perhaps we should say the power—that the information provides.

Epilogue

We don't really believe everything we have written in this book. However, we have done our best to make our case—more precisely, to make several cases:

• Information should emerge from the shadows as a crucial topic in its own right.
• Information alone can be a powerful agent of change in the world.
• Specific mechanisms we suggest—in health care, government, financial reporting, and the global marketplace—can bring about substantial positive changes.

In the course of presenting our ideas, we have made a number of assertions:

• Walmart could change the world by requesting sustainability information from its suppliers.
• The American Medical Association could improve health care by making information on doctors more transparent and more meaningful.
• Companies could create a more efficient investment climate by providing better financial data.
• Government should become hypertransparent as an important step toward restoring public confidence.

We recognize the inchoate nature of the above recommendations. We have presented them in this book not with an expectation that our ideas are so cogent, so clear, and so compelling that they all will be quickly accepted and implemented. Rather, our hope is that our presentation is cogent enough, clear enough, and compelling enough to encourage conversations about these concepts—conversations that can raise issues we missed, expand and refine the mechanisms we have outlined only briefly, and identify opportunities, problems, and solutions that have yet to be articulated, and can provide momentum for turning concepts into real-world practices.

A conversation about information itself, the cornerstone of our Information Age, is certainly in order. We have written a book on information without ever actually defining what the term means. Information has joined the pantheon of concepts (including justice, love, and pornography) that are readily recognizable and undeniably real yet difficult to pin down. There is a dual nature to how society uses the term. There is a recent technological meaning that treats information as a physical quantity measured in gigabytes and independent of the person sending or receiving the information, and there is an older, more human conception that treats information as a meaningful communication between individuals. People tend to use both meanings, casually and without much conscious thought, depending on the context of the exchange. But as information emerges as a more central focus of our human-made systems (as we strongly suspect it shall), more precise meanings may be in order.

A similar conundrum exists for the notion of information quality, a term with a chicken-and-egg paradox. Information is of high quality when it can successfully and reliably answer the questions we pose to our human-created systems. We can't always articulate the right questions, however, until we have high-quality information to inform our thinking. High-quality information often has a less-is-more aspect: Transparently making available the right information, even in limited amounts, can be more fruitful than a huge and clumsy "data dump" that few can put to use.

Part of the conversation has to be about courage and confidence. Bringing forth better information in an atmosphere of broad accessibility will mean exposing blemishes. The US Army will have to be confident enough to make public an embarrassing report on operations to locate those missing in action. Medical professionals will have to be courageous enough to advocate the availability of health-care data now kept largely out of sight. Manufacturers will have to assess their own willingness to document what they do. Bureaucrats will have to decide whether their day-to-day email messages and phone records are subject to public access. These things can all happen by mandate, much as the Freedom of Information Act imposes requirements for a certain amount of transparency in government and the Securities and Exchange Commission does for business. But mandates are only one option. A culture of openness, underlain by an institutional confidence, can also go a long way toward making more and better information more freely available.

Another part of the conversation will concern what secrets are worth keeping and what information should we routinely reveal. As individuals, we grapple with such questions in our personal lives, making some things known to the world and other things to only a select few and keeping other things entirely to ourselves (or at least try to do so). Our institutions must address the same questions, and must find answers appropriate to the information milieu of the present and the future, even though our habits of secrecy were established in decades past.

The new habits of openness and secrecy will emerge in response to rapid changes in information technology. We have witnessed this already with the creation of secret systems to store and analyze billions of phone records, email messages, and other electronic records. We have seen it with the secret intrusion into Sony's private computer systems to disrupt the company's operations and with the US government use of secret tools to conclude that North Korea was behind the incursion. In an age of diffuse terrorism in which ISIS and Al Qaeda can freely spread a message of destruction through the versatility of the Internet, we will have to confront questions about the price society pays for maintaining a free and open system.

The effectiveness of information as a tool to influence decisions—of institutions as well as individuals—also warrants a good deal of additional attention and discussion. We believe that disclosure of some products' links to practices such as child labor can bring about substantial changes in those practices. But the record on the ability of disclosures to influence personal choices is actually somewhat mixed, and greatly influenced by the vagaries of human psychology. Disclosures about the health impacts of tobacco appear to have been quite influential. Providing nutrition and calorie information for menu items at fast-food restaurants, on the other hand, may not make much difference in the decisions of most of the consumers of such items or of the restaurant chains. As George Lowenstein at Carnegie Mellon University has noted, there is a requirement in California to label caskets with a warning that sealed caskets are no better than unsealed caskets at preserving human remains; one wonders if such information makes a meaningful difference in the choice of caskets. A better understanding of the parameters that make disclosure an effective instrument of behavior change in some situations but not in others will help us to target the best uses of information as a policy tool.

We will also have to confront the reality of our collective human values. The commercial marketplace parses the diversity of human desires with remarkable ease. If digital photography is widely preferred over film photography, the market shifts quickly and effectively to provide consumers with digital cameras. As marketplace information expands—as we argue it must—to include social and environmental concerns, there is no advance assurance of what products and issues will thrive in the new market and what products and issues will wither and vanish.

We used bovine growth hormone as an example in chapter 5, and a point we made there is worth repeating. Consumers may or may not respond to the presence of BGH information. The responses may be fairly uniform, so that one product or another disappears. Much as in the case of the favorable response to digital cameras, BGH labels may mean that use of BGH vanishes as the market rejects it; however, it may mean that BGH-free products may vanish if it becomes clear that consumers don't much care one way or the other. In all likelihood, though, markets won't head to either extreme, but will develop as a geographic patchwork in which some communities favor BGH-free products and others do not.

BGH is something of a fringe issue, but how would consumer markets respond if information on greenhouse gases, child labor, chemical pollution, or worker safety were to become a universal facet of commercial transactions? Everyone in the world shops, but who can know how the world's shoppers would react to such information? Would climate change become the Polaroid of the sustainability marketplace, unable to sustain itself as consumers around the world rejected products associated with emissions of greenhouse gases? Or might the reverse happen? Might a market with sustainability information demonstrate that a large chunk of global consumers really don't give any weight to climate-change considerations in making their product purchases?

The idea behind introducing better information into the market—for example, better information on doctors and hospitals to the health-care market and better financial reporting in the investment community—is to give the market an opportunity to react to the information. Whether there actually is a reaction is up to the billions of individual consumers making trillions of discrete choices.

We hope to see a focus on information quality that advances as meaningfully and impressively as the current emphasis on advancing information technology. Until that happens—and certainly, even after it happens—we will have to forage in an imprecise world, seeking out the information that we need in order to make informed choices in our lives. The forager of old who came across an unfamiliar berry wondered "Will this make me sick if I eat it?" The information we would like to have at hand isn't always available.

But unlike our ancestors, we now have the means at our disposal to fully re-craft our information resources. Financial reporting may be stubbornly locked in by traditional accounting norms and regulatory requirements going back decades, but those are human-created constraints that can change and improve through further human activity. Data on the costs of medical procedures, on outcomes, and on sanctions are locked away and inaccessible because of decisions made when one set of circumstances prevailed; we can opt to make them public and accessible as we find ourselves facing a new set of circumstances. We can let the market conveniently lose all information on sweatshops or toxic chemicals, or we can decide that that is precisely the information that we want to have, and should have, in order to make better shopping choices.

Low-quality information contributed greatly to the demise of the Soviet Union. Better information in the capitalist marketplace, though no assurance of paradise on Earth, can go a long way toward more fully reflecting our collective values as human beings—values that, we believe, could help make the world more sustainable, more prosperous, and, quite simply, kinder.

Notes

Chapter 3

1. In comparison, consumers spend about $320 billion a year in out-of-pocket health-care expenses, according to estimates from the Centers for Medicare and Medicaid Services.

2. Occasionally, a single Yes/No piece of information may be all that is needed. As Adam Smith noted, "for some time after the discovery of America the first inquiry of the Spaniards, when they arrived upon an unknown coast, was whether there was any gold or silver to be found nearby. By the answer they received, they judged whether it was worthwhile to make a settlement there or whether the country was worth conquering."

3. "What patients say about their doctors online: A qualitative content analysis," *Journal of General Internal Medicine* 27 (6), 2012: 685–692.

4. Although the cost data are available at the Hospital Compare website, they were, at the time of this writing in early 2014, difficult to access. A non-government site, KaiserHealthNews.org (operated by the Kaiser Family Foundation), makes the Medicare cost data available in a much more user-friendly form, as can be seen in the version archived at https://archive.today/j1OtY.

Chapter 4

1. The 2012 Global Responsibility Report includes these details on coffee buying: "Starbucks sourced 545 million pounds of premium quality green (unroasted) coffee from 29 countries in 2012, and paid an average price of $2.56 per pound." Simple math reveals they spent $1.4 billion on coffee. We knew they weren't deliberately hiding this information, even though details this clear didn't make it into the company's financial reporting.

2. Oddly, the tools of the Information Age have rendered supermarket price information less clear. The plethora of coupons, shoppers' clubs, loyalty programs, card

rebates, sale events, and other special offers—many of which are themselves designed to collect information about consumers—often mean that supermarket product prices can be just as confusing as airlines' ticket prices.

Chapter 5

1. Presumably, five-star shoes.

2. The abbreviation rBST (for recombinant bovine somatotropin), or simply BST, is sometimes used instead.

Chapter 6

1. For the sake of simplicity, we will refer to Walmart in the example, though any of the large entities mentioned could take the initial step we are describing.

2. Not all journalists are equally adept at recognizing suspect posts on the Internet. When the farcical newspaper *The Onion* named North Korea's dictator Kim Jong Un "the sexiest man alive," the news was duly reported by the official Chinese newspaper, *People's Daily* (http://www.npr.org/2012/12/01/166293306/the-onion-so-funny-it-makes-us-cry).

Chapter 8

1. In 2011, Florida Highway Patrol Officer Donna Watts ticketed a driver for speeding at 120 miles per hour. The driver was a Miami policeman. Officer Watts' DMV records were subsequently accessed more than 200 times by 88 officers from 25 law-enforcement agencies. Watts is suing for invasion of privacy, claiming she was repeatedly harassed at home and over the phone by people making use of her private driving records.

2. We are referring to the Freedom of Information Act, a federal law, as convenient shorthand to encompass not only federal FOIA requirements but also the many state and local open-access laws and other federal access laws, such as the Electronic Freedom of Information Act Amendments of 1996.

References, Resources, and Additional Reading

Here we list some documents that are mentioned in the text or that expand on some of the notions we have discussed there. Readers can make use of their own information-foraging skills to unearth reams of additional resources on every topic we have touched upon.

Chapter 1

Encyclopaedia Britannica, eleventh edition (1911), volume 14, slice 5: Indole to Insanity.
This fascinating example of information consolidation in the early twentieth century is available at http://www.gutenberg.org/files/40009/40009-h/40009-h.htm. The latest version of the *Encyclopaedia Britannica* is available at http://www.britannica.com/.

General Catalogue, University of California, Los Angeles, 1950 (http://www.registrar.ucla.edu/archive/catalog/50-51catalog.pdf)
This course catalog includes an early example of a college course focused entirely on the topic of information.

Ralph Hartley, "Transmission of Information," *Bell System Technical Journal* 7 (1928): 535–564.
A classical paper in information theory, available at http://www.uni-leipzig.de/~biophy09/Biophysik-Vorlesung_2009-2010_DATA/QUELLEN/LIT/A/B/3/Hartley_1928_transmission_of_information.pdf).

Claude Shannon, "A Mathematical Theory of Communication," *Bell System Technical Journal* 27 (1948): 379–423 and 623–656.
Another seminal paper on information theory from Bell Labs, available at http://cm.bell-labs.com/cm/ms/what/shannonday/shannon1948.pdf.

Francis Crick, On the Genetic Code (Nobel Prize lecture, 1962) (http://www.nobelprize.org/nobel_prizes/medicine/laureates/1962/crick-lecture.html)
The recognition of DNA as the central information molecule of life was a turning point in modern biology.

FOIA.gov
A US government website (http://www.foia.gov/) with content pertaining to the history, intent, and application of the Freedom of Information Act.

Barack Obama, Memorandum on Transparency and Open Government, 2009 (http://www.whitehouse.gov/the_press_office/TransparencyandOpenGovernment)
President Obama's statement of principles and direction regarding open government during his administration.

Mindi McDowell and Allen Householder, Why Is Cyber Security a Problem? US Computer Emergency Readiness Team, 2013 (https://www.us-cert.gov/ncas/tips/ST04-001)
The US Computer Emergency Readiness Team is the one of the country's front-line defenses against attacks on its information infrastructure. The team's website includes detailed materials on steps individuals, organizations, and the government can take to secure their cybersystems.

HistoryofInformation.com
A large and growing timeline and encyclopedia-style collection of articles on the emergence of information technologies and the influence of information management during human history (http://www.historyofinformation.com/).

Chapter 2

Naum Jasny, "A Close-Up of the Soviet Fourth Five-Year Plan," *Quarterly Journal of Economics* 66 (1952): 139–171.
A detailed look at the Soviet process for managing (or attempting to manage) its national economic activity. A preview is available at http://www.jstor.org/discover/10.2307/1882940?uid=3739256&uid=2&uid=4&sid=21101722800323.

Foreign Broadcast Information Service, USSR Report: Consumer Goods and Domestic Trade, 1983 (http://www.dtic.mil/dtic/tr/fulltext/u2/a349428.pdf)
A detailed US government account of the Soviet Union's five-year planning process, including development of institutions such as the All-Union Scientific Research Institute of Film Materials and Artificial Leather and the Central Scientific Research Institute of the Leather Footwear Industry.

Herman Daly and John Cobb, *For the Common Good: Redirecting the Economy toward Community, the Environment, and a Sustainable Future.* Boston: Beacon, 1994 (preview available at http://books.google.com/books?id=TZAIU1yqyRkC).

Adam Smith, *An Inquiry into the Nature and Causes of the Wealth of Nations*. London: Methuen (first published 1776; full text available at http://www.econlib.org/library/ Smith/smWN.html).

London Directories
Historical city directories for London dating back to 1638, available at https:// familysearch.org/learn/wiki/en/London_Directories.

Joseph Stiglitz, Information and the Change in the Paradigm in Economics (Nobel Prize Lecture, 2001) (available at http://www.nobelprize.org/nobel_prizes/economic -sciences/laureates/2001/stiglitz-lecture.pdf)

George Akerlof, Behavioral Macroeconomics, and Macroeconomic Behavior (Nobel Prize Lecture, 2001) (available at http://www.nobelprize.org/nobel_prizes/economic -sciences/laureates/2001/akerlof-lecture.pdf)
Stiglitz and Akerlof were pioneers in highlighting the significance of information to the field of economics.

Chapter 3

Centers for Medicare and Medicaid Services, National Health Expenditure Projections 2012–2022. (2012) (available at http://www.cms.gov/Research-Statistics-Data -and-Systems/Statistics-Trends-and-Reports/NationalHealthExpendData/downloads/ proj2012.pdf).
The US government's estimates of health-care costs in the context of the overall economy and projections for future costs, including comparisons of government costs, insurance costs, and out-of-pocket expenses.

John Carreyrou and Tom McGinty, "Taking Double Cut, Surgeons Implant Their Own Devices," *Wall Street Journal*, October 8, 2011 (partly viewable at http://online .wsj.com/news/articles/SB10001424053111904106704576582621677354508).
Physicians—surgeons in particular—may have financial incentives to recommend some treatments and procedures over others, a potential conflict of interest that isn't generally apparent to a patient.

Roni Caryn Rabin, "The Confusion of Hospital Pricing," blog post, April 23, 2012 (http://well.blogs.nytimes.com/2012/04/23/the-confusion-of-hospital-pricing/).
The title pretty much captures it!

Roni Caryn Rabin, "Wide Variation in Hospital Charges for Blood Tests Called 'Irrational,'" *Kaiser Health News*, August 15, 2014 (http://kaiserhealthnews.org/news/ wide-variation-in-hospital-charges-for-blood-tests-called-irrational/).
Hospital charges varied by a factor of 1,000 in one extreme case, but order-of-magnitude differences are routine.

Everything Is Transparent When the Choice Is Clear (https://healthcarebluebook .com/)
An interesting experiment in providing easy online access to information on price comparisons for health-care services.

DoctorFinder (https://apps.ama-assn.org/doctorfinder/home.jsp)
A physician look-up service, provided by the American Medical Association, that could readily be expanded with additional information on costs, care, history, ratings, and outcomes.

RateMDs.com (https://www.ratemds.com)
An online rating service, based on feedback from patients, that provides information on satisfaction with medical services that is difficult to come by otherwise.

Peter Eisler and Barbara Hansen, "Thousands of Doctors Practicing Despite Errors, Misconduct," *USA Today*, August 20, 2013 (http://www.usatoday.com/story/news/ nation/2013/08/20/doctors-licenses-medical-boards/2655513).
Although information on misconduct, sanctions, malpractice, and other troubling aspects of physician care exists, it is not routinely available to patients who are choosing a doctor.

Centers for Medicare & Medicaid Services, "Hospital Compare" (http://www .medicare.gov/hospitalcompare)
An online tool for comparing hospitals. It is based on extensive Medicare information concerning procedures, outcomes, and patient satisfaction.

Centers for Medicare & Medicaid Services, "Physician Compare" (http://www .medicare.gov/physiciancompare/)
Although it is similar in principle to Hospital Compare, the utility of Physician Compare is hobbled by a lack of access to the full set of information available in the Medicare system.

Dow Jones & Company, Motion to Intervene, *Florida Medical Association v. Dept. of Health, Education and Welfare* (2011) (http://www.dowjones.com/pressroom/ presskits/secrets/MotiontoIntervene12511.pdf)
A legal filing by the *Wall Street Journal* arguing that the importance of access to statistical information from Medicare files by journalists and by the public outweighs the medical community's claim of privacy. Courts' opinions on releasing the data have fluctuated.

How Much Medicare Pays for Your Doctor's Care (http://www.nytimes.com/ interactive/2014/04/09/health/medicare-doctor-database.html)
An interactive database, created by the *New York Times*, that is based on data released from Medicare on procedures performed by and reimbursements provided to individual medical practices. Users can look up statistics on individual doctors included in the database.

Steven Brill, "Bitter Pill: Why Medical Bills Are Killing Us," *Time*, March 4, 2013. (http://time.com/198/bitter-pill-why-medical-bills-are-killing-us/)
An in-depth look at mechanics of medical bills, and factors contributing to their variability, impenetrability and seemingly exorbitant pricing.

US Department of Health and Human Services, National Practitioner Data Bank (http://www.npdb.hrsa.gov/topNavigation/aboutUs.jsp)
A medical "sanctions" database that includes information on malpractice suits, medical fraud, disciplinary actions by state medical licensing boards, and similar sources regarding professional competency. The data are not publicly available.

Chapter 4

US Securities and Exchange Commission, "Beginner's Guide to Financial Statements" (http://www.sec.gov/investor/pubs/begfinstmtguide.htm)
The SEC explains the purposes of the information content in financial statements, leaving it to individual investors to determine how well the information provided actually meets the intended purposes.

Bethany McLean, "Is Enron Overpriced?" *Fortune*, January 19, 2006 (http://money.cnn.com/2006/01/13/news/companies/enronoriginal_fortune/)
The beginning of the end for Enron. By the close of the year, the company was bankrupt.

Justin Fox, "Why the Government Wouldn't Let AIG Fail," *Time*, September 16, 2008 (http://content.time.com/time/business/article/0,8599,1841699,00.html)
It was not only criminally negligent companies such as Enron that had impenetrable financial reports.

Starbucks Annual Reports (http://investor.starbucks.com/phoenix.zhtml?c=99518&p=irol-reportsAnnual)

Starbucks Global Responsibility Report Goals & Progress (http://www.starbucks.com/responsibility/global-report)

David Lenter, Joel Slemrod, and Douglas A. Shackelford, Public Disclosure of Corporate Tax Return Information: Accounting, Economics, and Legal Perspectives," *National Tax Journal* 56: 803–830 (http://www.ntanet.org/NTJ/56/4/ntj-v56n04p803-30-public-disclosure-corporate-tax.pdf)
The authors advocate for some (but not full) disclosure of tax filings and provide good historical and policy context on the subject.

US General Accounting Office, Comparison of the Reported Tax Liabilities of Foreign and US-Controlled Corporations, 1998–2005 (http://www.gao.gov/new.items/d08957.pdf)
Nominal tax rates notwithstanding, many corporations pay little or no taxes.

Leon Stafford, "Coke Hides Its Secret Formula in Plain Sight in World of Coca-Cola Move," *Atlanta Journal-Constitution*, December 8, 2011 (http://www.ajc.com/news/business/coke-hides-its-secret-formula-in-plain-sight-in-wo/nQPMm/)

US Consumer Product Safety Commission, CPSC Takes Safety to the Front Lines, 2012 (http://www.cpsc.gov/en/Newsroom/News-Releases/2012/Port-Surveillance-News-CPSC-Takes-Safety-to-the-Front-Lines-Prevents-More-Than-360000-Violative-Units-from-Reaching-Consumers-in-2nd-Quarter-of-Fiscal-Year-2012/)
Many products reach the US market without a full accounting of their origin and ingredients or of safety concerns.

Global Reporting Initiative (https://www.globalreporting.org)
The GRI promotes a framework used by organizations around the world to report on institutional sustainability initiatives. The reports provide an overview of the actions taken, but generally do not include details about individual products.

National Organic Program, US Department of Agriculture (http://www.ams.usda.gov/AMSv1.0/NOPFAQsHowCertified)
More than 25,000 farms and businesses in the United States and elsewhere have been certified as complying with organic regulations, allowing both the entities and individual products to be labeled "certified organic."

Chapter 5

Stephanie Mlot, "Infographic: Just How Big Is Amazon.com?" *PC*, December 17, 2012 (http://www.pcmag.com/article2/0,2817,2413305,00.asp)
An interesting overview of the scale of Amazon's sales activities for more than 180 million products.

Staples.com, Identifying Green Products (http://www.staples.com/sbd/cre/marketing/easy-on-the-planet/identifying-green-products.html)
Merchants and shoppers have a number of certifications to choose from. Fair Trade, Green Seal, Rainforest Alliance, and other certifications provide useful information but are generally available on only a small number of products.

Wikipedia, "Bovine somatotropin" (live page: https://en.wikipedia.org/wiki/Bovine_somatotropin; archived retrieved version: https://archive.today/7o4vx)
An excellent (on the date we retrieved it) overview of the uses of BGH, its regulatory status around the world, and the concerns some have about its use.

Chapter 6

Melody M. Bomgardner, "Walmart and Target Take Aim at Hazardous Ingredients," *Chemical and Engineering News*, February 2014: 17 (http://cen.acs.org/articles/92/i7/Walmart-Target-Take-Aim-Hazardous.html)
Major marketers use both a "carrot" approach and a "stick" approach in working with suppliers to limit the presence of high-priority hazardous chemicals in products sold.

Holly Williams, "CBS News Goes Undercover in a Bangladesh Clothing Factory," CBS News, May 22, 2013 (http://www.cbsnews.com/news/cbs-news-goes-undercover-in-a-bangladesh-clothing-factory/)
Despite repeated exposés of this type, the absence of reliable information about where products originate and how they are produced leads to continuing abuses in the global production system.

Joanna Lupo, "A Tale of Two Feedback Systems: eBay vs. Amazon," feedbackfive.com, June 9, 2015 (http://www.feedbackfive.com/blog/amazon-feedback-vs-ebay-feedback/)
Brief explanations of how two major online retailers maintain quality in their crowdsourced feedback systems.

Wikipedia, Video guided tour #2: Why does Wikipedia work even though anyone can edit it? (https://upload.wikimedia.org/wikipedia/commons/transcoded/9/90/Wikipedia_video_tutorial-2-Reliability-en.ogv/Wikipedia_video_tutorial-2-Reliability-en.ogv.360p.webm)

Chapter 7

Pamela Effrein Sandstrom, "An Optimal Foraging Approach to Information Seeking and Use," *Library Quarterly* 64, no. 4: 414–449 (http://www.jstor.org/stable/4308969)
Perspective from an information scientist on how strategies for finding information mirror our most basic, hard-wired foraging strategies for finding food.

Brian Walsh, "Your Ant Farm Is Smarter Than Google," *Time*, May 27 (http://time.com/118633/ant-intelligence-google/)
The helter-skelter patterns of foraging ants leave pheromone trails that, over time, result in self-organization and self-optimization of foraging activity.

"How Much Information Is There in the World?" sciencedaily.com, February 11, 2011 (http://www.sciencedaily.com/releases/2011/02/110210141219.htm)
Periodic attempts to measure the total quantity of information in the world effectively document the rapid growth in information resources from year to year.

Sergey Brin and Lawrence Page, The Anatomy of a Large-Scale Hypertextual Web Search Engine, Computer Science Department, Stanford University, 1998 (http://infolab.stanford.edu/~backrub/google.html)
The classic paper in which the founders of Google lay out a strategy for improving search results by moving beyond keyword recognition and considering "pagerank."

Chapter 8

Ellen Nakashima and Ann Marimow, "Judge: NSA's Collecting of Phone Records Is Probably Unconstitutional," *Washington Post*, December 16, 2013 (http://www.washingtonpost.com/national/judge-nsas-collecting-of-phone-records-is-likely-unconstitutional/2013/12/16/6e098eda-6688-11e3-a0b9-249bbb34602c_story.html)
A news report on a finding by US District Judge Richard J. Leon that eavesdropping by the NSA on a conservative legal activist probably crossed the line into illegal activity. The case opinion in *Klayman v. Obama* can be found at https://ecf.dcd.uscourts.gov/cgi-bin/show_public_doc?2013cv0851-48.

Sari Horwitz, "NSA Collection of Phone Data Is Lawful, Federal Judge Rules," *Washington Post*, December 27, 2013 (http://www.washingtonpost.com/world/national-security/nsa-collection-of-phone-data-is-lawful-federal-judge-rules/2013/12/27/4b99d96a-6f19-11e3-a523-fe73f0ff6b8d_story.html)
A news report on a federal case, *ACLU v. Clapper*, in which a US District judge reached an opinion opposite that reached in *Klayman v. Obama*. (On *ACLU v. Clapper*, see http://apps.washingtonpost.com/g/documents/world/us-district-judge-pauleys-ruling-in-aclu-vs-clapper/723/.)

American Civil Liberties Union, "You Are Being Tracked: How License Plate Readers Are Being Used to Record Americans' Movements" (2013) (https://www.aclu.org/technology-and-liberty/you-are-being-tracked-how-license-plate-readers-are-being-used-record)
A detailed look at the growth of automated plate-recognition technology and its use by law enforcement.

US Senate, Report of the Commission on Protecting and Reducing Government Secrecy (1997) (http://www.gpo.gov/fdsys/pkg/GPO-CDOC-105sdoc2/content-detail.html)
The Moynihan Report on government secrecy advocated a much more nuanced and less permanent approach to creating and maintaining government secrets.

data.gov
A government-created website (http://www.data.gov/) devoted to making the vast collection of federal data resources more readily available to the public.

vault.fbi.gov/
The FBI, like many government agencies, maintains an online "reading room" (http://vault.fbi.gov/) where users can access previously classified documents that have been made publicly accessible.

Claudette Roulo, "Defense Department to Review POW/MIA Command Operations," American Forces Press Service, July 9, 2013 (http://www.defense.gov/news/newsarticle.aspx?id=120427)
A brief but revealing article on the Department of Defense's response to media reports of possible inadequacies in POW/MIA operations.

Elizabeth Cole and Judy Barsalou, Unite or Divide? The Challenges of Teaching History in Societies Emerging from Violent Conflict, Special Report, United States Institute of Peace, June 2006 (http://www.usip.org/sites/default/files/resources/sr163.pdf)
A cogent discussion of how the teaching of history shapes public opinion, concepts of justice, and paths of reconstruction in conflict-ridden areas.

Jackie Calmes, "Obama Says Surveillance Helped in Case in Germany," New York Times, June 20, 2013 (http://www.nytimes.com/2013/06/20/world/europe/obama-in-germany.html)
The president makes the case for the value of secret surveillance activities around the world.

Alan Suderman, "Why Many Reporters Don't Bother with FOIA Requests," Washington City Paper, June 15, 2013 (http://www.washingtoncitypaper.com/blogs/looselips/2012/06/15/why-many-reporters-dont-bother-with-foia-requests/)

Chapter 9

Wikipedia, "Bhopal Disaster" (https://en.wikipedia.org/wiki/Bhopal_disaster)
Background on the horrendous 1984 accident generally regarded as the one of the worst industrial disasters in history.

Wikipedia, "Toxics Release Inventory" (https://en.wikipedia.org/wiki/Toxics_Release_Inventory).
This Wikipedia article provides a good overview of the development of TRI, including the involvement of David Sarokin in developing the original concept of a national toxics inventory.

US Environmental Protection Agency, "The Toxics Release Inventory (TRI) Program," 2016 (http://www2.epa.gov/toxics-release-inventory-tri-program)
The Environmental Protection Agency's main webpage for TRI includes several tools for easily accessing TRI data on local communities.

http://www.rtknet.org
The Right-to-Know Network specializes in consolidating access to numerous sources of environmental information, including TRI data, and providing tools and information for citizens who want to make use of the information.

Chapter 10

Eugene Mandel, "How the Napa Earthquake Affected Bay Area Sleepers," Jawbone.com, August 25, 2014 (https://jawbone.com/blog/napa-earthquake-effect-on-sleep)
Analysis of data from wireless activity monitoring devices worn by users in the San Francisco Bay area revealed how sleep patterns were disturbed by a middle-of-the-night earthquake.

Janna Anderson and Lee Rainie, "The Internet of Things Will Thrive by 2025" (http://www.pewinternet.org/2014/05/14/internet-of-things)
This post from the Pew Research Center consolidates the opinions of technology experts regarding the growth of the Internet of Things in the next decade.

Ryan Grenoble, "Teens Create 'Five-0' App to Help Document Police Brutality," Huffington Post, August 18, 2014 (http://www.huffingtonpost.com/2014/08/18/teens-police-brutality-app_n_5687934.html)

Consumer Sentinel Network, Federal Trade Commission (https://www.ftc.gov/enforcement/consumer-sentinel-network)

Index